MISSION TO TASHKENT

Peter Hopkirk is the author of two books dealing with intelligence work in Central Asia. He has travelled extensively in the region where the events described in this book took place.

Also available from Oxford Paperbacks by Peter Hopkirk:

The Great Game
On Secret Service East of Constantinople
Foreign Devils on the Silk Road
Setting the East Ablaze
Trespassers on the Roof of the World

Mission to
TASHKENT

by

Lt.-Col. F. M. BAILEY

C.I.E.

*Gold Medallist of the Royal Geographical Society,
Livingstone Gold Medallist of the Royal
Scottish Geographical Society*

OXFORD
UNIVERSITY PRESS

OXFORD

UNIVERSITY PRESS

Great Clarendon Street, Oxford ox2 6DP

Oxford University Press is a department of the University of Oxford.
It furthers the University's objective of excellence in research, scholarship,
and education by publishing worldwide in

Oxford New York

Auckland Bangkok Buenos Aires Cape Town Chennai
Dar es Salaam Delhi Hong Kong Istanbul Karachi Kolkata
Kuala Lumpur Madrid Melbourne Mexico City Mumbai Nairobi
São Paulo Shanghai Singapore Taipei Tokyo Toronto

with an associated company in Berlin

Oxford is a registered trade mark of Oxford University Press
in the UK and in certain other countries

Published in the United States
by Oxford University Press Inc., New York

The moral rights of the author have been asserted

Database right Oxford University Press (maker)

First published by Jonathan Cape 1946
First issued as an Oxford University Press paperback 1992
Reissued 2002

British Library Cataloguing in Publication Data

Data available

Library of Congress Cataloging in Publication Data

Bailey, F. M. (Frederick Marshman), 1882–1967.
Mission to Tashkent / by F. M. Bailey.
p. cm.
Originally published: London: J. Cape, 1946.
1. Bailey, F. M. (Frederick Marshman), 1882–1967. 2. Spies—Great
Britain—Biography. 3. Soviet Union—History—Revolution, 1917–1921—Secret service.
4. Uzbeck S. S. R.—History—Revolution,
1917–1921—Secret service. I. Title.
947.084'1'092—dc20 DK265.9.S4B35 1992 92–6839

ISBN-13: 978-0-19-280387-0
ISBN-10: 0-19-280387-5

2

Printed in Great Britain by
Clays Ltd, St Ives plc

CONTENTS

To my wife

INTRODUCTION

by Peter Hopkirk

'AN absolutely first-class man,' noted the Viceroy of India on the personal file of Lieutenant-Colonel Frederick Bailey, the author of this remarkable narrative, before sending him through the passes into Bolshevik Central Asia on the hazardous mission which it describes. Although the modest Bailey would not have dreamed of revealing Lord Chelmsford's glowing commendation, and would not have thanked me for doing so now, few who knew this deceptively mild-looking but formidable officer would have quarrelled with the Viceroy's judgement.

Born in Lahore on 3 February 1882, and educated at Wellington and Sandhurst before joining the Indian Army as a subaltern, he was always known as Eric to avoid confusion with his father, also a soldier and also called Frederick. A fine shot and horseman who thirsted for adventure, he was the very stuff of John Buchan heroes.

By the outbreak of the First World War, Bailey had earned himself considerable distinction as a Central Asian explorer, traveller, intelligence officer and naturalist. In 1904, as a Tibetan-speaking subaltern, he had ridden into the forbidden city of Lhasa as a member of Colonel Francis Younghusband's expedition sent by Lord Curzon, then Viceroy, to investigate alarming reports of a Russian presence there. Later, his solitary travels in unknown and lawless regions of Tibet and China earned him the highly prized gold explorer's medal of the Royal Geographical Society. From these pre-war journeys he brought back many specimens of birds, butterflies and plants, including the tall, handsome Himalayan blue poppy which will for ever be associated with his name.

By this time, because of his exceptional linguistic and other skills, this tough and resourceful young officer had been spotted by his superiors and transferred to the Indian Political Department, the élite body which, during the years of Anglo-Russian rivalry in Central Asia, had produced so many of the British players in the Great Game. Between 1905 and 1909, Bailey served as British Trade Agent—really a cover for political intelligence work—at Gyantse in southern Tibet. In 1911 he accompanied a British punitive expedition into northern Assam as its intelligence officer, while in 1914 he was awarded the coveted MacGregor Medal, named after a former Indian Army head of intelligence, for explorations contributing to the defence of India. Captain Bailey, as he then was, was already shaping up as a Great Game player in the classic mould, and was an obvious choice for the Viceroy to send on a delicate and dangerous mission into a land torn by anarchy and civil war following the Russian Revolution.

The outbreak of the Great War found Bailey on home leave in Scotland. He immediately asked to return to soldiering, and after lecturing to the Royal Geographical Society on his travels and being invested with the CIE by King George V, he was sent to France with the Indian Expeditionary Force. There, some weeks later, he was shot through the arm by a German sniper, but because there was a grave shortage of Urdu-speaking officers he remained at the front for some time. Eventually, however, his condition worsened and he had to be evacuated to hospital in England. On his recovery he was again attached to the Indian Army, but this time sent to Gallipoli with the 1st/5th Gurkhas. There he was twice wounded, the second time being shot through both legs, and shortly afterwards found himself back in hospital in London.

Bailey's superiors in Delhi now decided to claim him back, fearing the loss of one of their finest political officers, not to mention one of their rare Tibetan-speakers. For a time he was posted to the North-West Frontier, where Turkish and other hostile agents were trying to incite the tribes to join in a Holy War against the British. Finally, he was posted as an intelligence officer to the small, isolated town of Shushtar, in supposedly neutral Persia.

Here a very different kind of war was being fought from that of Flanders or Gallipoli. It was an undercover struggle between British and German intelligence officers for the hearts and minds of the Persian government and people. While the British were desperate to keep the Persians neutral, the Germans were doing all in their power to drag them into the war against Britain. Their aim was to persuade them to send their troops, commanded by German officers, across India's thinly guarded frontiers to liberate Muslims there from British rule. Already German agents had tried to coerce the Emir of Afghanistan into doing likewise, unleashing his warlike tribesmen through the passes leading to India. However, the hard-headed Emir had rebuffed them. With the Persians, too, they had been hardly more successful, although they had turned some parts of the country into battlefields between tribes they had won over, and troops sent from India to protect British communities and interests there. A number of British officers and others had been killed, wounded, or kidnapped by pro-German tribesmen, and some small communities forced to flee for their lives.

In March 1918, when he had been in Shushtar for some months, Bailey learned that a three-man murder squad had entered the town, where he was the sole European, intending to kill him. Having already been at the receiving end of three bullets, Bailey was relieved to get orders to leave Shushtar immediately and return to India. There he was to take command of a small secret mission bound for Central Asia to try to discover what was going on there following the Russian Revolution and the Bolshevik seizure of power. To give him the authority this called for, he was to be promoted to the rank of Lieutenant-Colonel.

It is necessary to explain here, in slightly greater detail than Bailey himself does, the political background to his mission, not to mention to his book. When he first wrote it, as long ago as 1924, there was much that he was unable to say, for the British intervention in the Russian civil war was still a highly sensitive issue between the two governments, which had only just established full diplomatic relations. Indeed, not until 1946 was Bailey able to obtain clearance from the Foreign Office to publish it. Even then, nearly thirty years after the events it described, a good deal had to be omitted, and the names of certain individuals disguised to protect them or their descendants from Soviet wrath. Britain and Russia were then still allies from the Second World War, the Cold War not yet having begun, and the British government had no wish to see old antagonisms stirred up needlessly.

Bailey therefore includes nothing in this book from the 17-page top-secret report which he wrote for his chiefs on his return. This revealed the contacts he made with the principal anti-Bolshevik organizations in Russian Turkestan, and his endeavours to obtain funds for them. Today this report can be seen in the India Office Library in London, as well as in the National Archives in Delhi, where Soviet scholars first came upon it in 1970, making full use of it to blacken both Bailey and the British government. However, despite the absence of this material, *Mission to Tashkent* remains one of the best books about secret intelligence work ever written, as well as a great adventure story. In my own book, *Setting the East Ablaze*, which deals with the exploits of Bailey and others at this time, I have tried to include many of those things he was obliged to omit, so I will not repeat them here.

Finally we must look at the reasons for sending Bailey and his companions first to Kashgar in Chinese Turkestan, and then on to Tashkent in the heart of Bolshevik Central Asia. By now, following the Revolution, virtually all Russian resistance to Germany and Turkey had ceased, as the Russians turned to fighting among themselves in a bloody civil war which was to last until 1922. The collapse of the Tsarist armies all along the Eastern Front left a large and alarming gap through which, in theory, a Turco-German army might pour. Already the Turks were threatening to seize the vital oil-city of Baku on the western shore of the Caspian Sea. From there they would be free to cross to Krasnovodsk on the eastern shore, where the Transcaspian railway began its long journey across the desert to Ashkhabad, Bokhara, Samarkand, and Tashkent. Were the enemy to seize this railway, they would be able to move substantial bodies of troops eastwards, and eventually be able to threaten Afghanistan and British India.

Even if they could be prevented from taking Baku and seizing Krasnovodsk and the railway, there was another threat to India looming in Central Asia. During the war, thousands of POWs, mainly Austrians, had been transported by the Tsarist authorities to camps around Tashkent, from where escape was obviously difficult. However, because they felt no ill-will towards them, and were out of the war anyway, the Bolsheviks had freed them, although they had no means of getting them home. Word had reached Delhi that German officers among them were endeavouring to forge them into a fighting force for use against British India. At the same time, the intentions of the Bolsheviks, who were themselves recruiting soldiers among the POWs, towards British India were far from certain. Among Bailey's tasks was to try to discover what both the Germans and the Bolsheviks were up to, and to try to spoil both their games, by whatever means.

Meanwhile, further west, a small British force from Baghdad, commanded by General Lionel Dunsterville, had been landed at Baku, following the overthrow of the Bolshevik government there by their rivals for power. The idea was to train and advise, not to mention encourage, the people of Baku to defend their city against the advancing Turks. In the event they found that the new government, which had invited them in, had expected a far larger British force which they had believed would defend the city for them. However, with only 1,000 British troops at his disposal, Dunsterville could not hope to hold out for very long against the vastly overwhelming Turkish force. After a few weeks he was forced to withdraw in order to avoid being massacred, and leave Baku to its fate.

At the same time a small British military mission under General Wilfrid Malleson was sent to Meshed, an old British listening-post in north-eastern Persia, to try to discover what was happening in Transcaspia, just across the frontier, and also to try to persuade the local people, who had also ousted the Bolsheviks, to resist any Turkish or German attempt to seize the railway. But the Bolsheviks in Tashkent were determined to recover Ashkhabad, the Transcaspian capital, and began advancing towards it from the east. Malleson, who had some 500 British-Indian troops under his command, now found himself fighting the Bolsheviks on behalf of his new allies in Ashkhabad. Several bitter and bloody clashes took place, in which the Bolsheviks came off second best. It was the first time since the Crimean War that British and Russian troops had fired upon one another, and it did little to improve the Bolsheviks' temper in Tashkent, as Bailey was soon to discover.

By this time the war with Germany and Turkey was virtually over, following the collapse of the former on the Western Front and the latter in Palestine and Syria. This removed the threat of an enemy advance eastwards along the Transcaspian railway, or through Persia, towards Afghanistan and India. But there still remained the threat to India posed by the German and Austrian POWs in Turkestan, not to mention the increasingly hostile Bolsheviks in Tashkent.

Such then was the extremely confused situation in Central Asia when Bailey and two fellow-officers, Major Stewart Blacker and Major Percy Etherton, prepared to leave Delhi for the passes of the north. From Hunza they would cross the mountains into Chinese Turkestan and proceed to Kashgar, a one-time British listening-post from the Great Game era, which was to serve as the mission's staging-point for its entry into strife-torn Bolshevik Central Asia. From Kashgar they would ride through the Tien Shan mountains to the Russian frontier, and thence to Tashkent, the Bolsheviks' headquarters, where so much of the action of this book is set. For eventually Bailey was to find himself alone there, playing a deadly game of cat-and-mouse with the Bolshevik secret police which was to last for sixteen months. It is an extraordinary story, as the reader will soon discover, told with almost breathtaking understatement by the nonchalant Bailey, a Great Game player to his very fingertips.

CHAPTER I

PERSIA TO KASHGAR

ONE day in March 1918, when in Shushtar in the province of Arabistan in South Persia, I received a startling telegram: Was I medically fit for a long and arduous journey? I replied that I was. Then, a reply: Would I go to Kashgar in Chinese Turkestan, passing through India to receive orders as to what I was to do?

I was in many ways glad to leave Shushtar. I had taken over a species of blood feud from my predecessor and three murderers had a few days before entered the town with the avowed intention of murdering me. The narrow streets made murder very easy. I was the only European in the place. There were only three other people who spoke English, one, Mr. Moustofi, the Persian Deputy Governor; the second, my Persian clerk; and the third an Armenian telegraphist. I had some sympathy for the last. He and his family had been illtreated by the Turks, and his one desire was to kill Turks. When he escaped and joined our forces he was told that he would assist in the killing of far more Turks by practising his profession of telegraphist. Eventually he found himself in Arabistan miles away from any Turks at all. The Persian governor, Vikar-ul-Mulk, was a charming man; he spoke a little French and we became great friends.

I travelled by car and river to Basra where I handed over my duties to Captain Fraser. Along with other affairs I passed on my blood feud. In the end, the murderers who were tired of being hunted around gave themselves up on a guarantee of their lives and served a term of imprisonment. I picked up a steamer for Karachi whence I travelled to Delhi and Simla and received detailed orders and made preparations for my long journey. I certainly never contemplated that it would take me twenty-one months and lead me from Kashmir through Chinese and

Russian Turkestan into Persia and down to the Baluchistan border before returning to Delhi.

I was to go to Chinese Turkestan in charge of a Mission. This consisted of two officers, Major P. T. Etherton, an officer who had made an adventurous journey some years previously from the Pamirs through to the Siberian railway, and Major Blacker, who in 1914 had travelled from India to Kashgar and thence to the Russian railway and so to England. We had also a small party of men of the Guides under a jemadar and a small civil ministerial staff, headed by Shahzada Abdul Rahim Beg of Kokhand. He was related to one of the rulers of the Central Asian Khanates who had been ousted by the Russians and had settled near Peshawar. I had felt some hesitation in taking the Shahzada as I feared complications might develop owing to his dynastic connections in the province of Ferghana, the name given by the Russians to the former Khanate of Kokhand; but the difficulty of finding a suitable substitute with a knowledge of Turki was insuperable. I impressed on him the importance of keeping quiet as to his origin but to no purpose; it was not long after our arrival in Kashgar that he was generally referred to as 'Shahzada Sahib' (Prince). Eventually, therefore, I did not take him with me into Russia; but replaced him by Khan Sahib Iftekhar Ahmad, the head clerk of the Kashgar Consulate General, whom Sir George Macartney placed at my disposal. The Khan Sabib was an efficient, reliable and useful man, with much local knowledge, who spoke Turki fluently. This last qualification eventually enabled him to escape from Russian Turkestan in disguise without great difficulty.

After receiving my orders in Simla, we travelled to Kashmir. On our way through Rawal Pindi we stayed with the 39th Royal Garhwal Rifles and here I was glad to find an old friend, a Tibetan named Gongkar serving as a lieutenant. I had served and travelled in Tibet and once met Gongkar's father in the south-eastern part of the country and had seen something of the boy himself in England. He had been educated at Rugby. He died shortly after his return to his own country.

April 1918 found our party organizing in Srinagar for the journey over the snows to Gilgit and the Pamirs. Secrecy as to our object was advisable but it was not possible to maintain this in Srinagar, while arranging to take a large party over the passes at a time of the year when even the usual small shooting parties were discouraged. Perhaps I had not then learnt how to parry innocent questions. One resident asked me casually how many coolies I was taking and when I replied 'About one-hundred-and-sixty', he shut up like a clam and years later told me that he at once realized that it must be a 'hush-hush show'.

We left Srinagar in houseboats on April 22nd, 1918 and followed the usual route to Gilgit. To overcome difficulties of accommodation on the road, we travelled in three parties, each under an officer. I put on my skis and practised a little on the snowy slopes of the Tragbal Pass, and the next day travelled for five miles in this way. The Burzil was under deep snow and we were held up a day here by a blizzard. The day I crossed the Pass, May 2nd, we started at one-fifteen a.m. to take advantage of the hard frozen snow. After sunrise when the surface of the snows was softer I put on my skis and had the most delightful run into the Burzil Chowki arriving there five hours ahead of the next man.

There is little to be said about the journey for the next few days. Our march usually started at about five or six. At nine or ten we would halt for breakfast and a rest, usually in some beautiful irrigated oasis under mulberry or other fruit trees with a natural iris garden under foot. We would complete the day's march by one or two p.m. The heat in the narrow rocky Indus Valley with little shade was trying but this made the contrast when we reached lovely green-clad villages the more striking and pleasant. We arrived at Gilgit on May 8th. Here we stayed a day or two with the late Colonel C. A. Smith, the Political Agent. We played the Gilgit form of polo, a thing I was not to do again until fifteen years later when, as Resident in Kashmir, I flew to Gilgit in one-and-three-quarter hours from Risalpur, instead of the seventeen days the journey took in 1918.

One of our anxieties and difficulties was the question of communication. The telegraph ended at Gilgit. There was a telephone line to Hunza between sixty and seventy miles further on, but the repetition of ciphers down this did not have the best results. Between Hunza and Kashgar the only communication was by runner, and messages took ten or twelve days. There was a Chinese telegraph line from Kashgar to China. Telegrams from Simla by this route took eleven days and were undecipherable when received. We therefore took with us a number of carrier pigeons and a motor-cycle. Our idea was to try to run a motor-cycle service on any flat portion of the plains of Turkestan or the Pamirs that was possible and to use pigeons in other places. The experiment did not work. The pigeons mostly served to fatten the beautiful falcons of the Hunza Valley and the cycle also proved impracticable, though Blacker overcame the petrol difficulty by driving it with the vodka made by the Hindus in Kashgar for the Russians to drink. The really useful improvement was the extension of the telegraph line to Misgar, the highest village in the Hunza Valley. This shortened the time to a valuable extent especially when a reply from India was required.

At Minapin we were met by His Highness Sikander Khan, Mir of Nagar, who lunched with us, and the next day we entered the territory of the Mir of Hunza. His late Highness met us with his son, the present Mir, named Ghazan Khan. Our road for the next few days was through the steep lands of Hunza. The whole road from Gilgit to the Chinese frontier is pretty bad and may be considered one of the defences of this part of the Indian frontier. It has often been described and photographs will give a better idea than long descriptions. We had at times to cross glaciers which came right down to the road, but away from these the weather was so warm that we did not trouble to put up our tents but slept in the open. Glaciers are very variable creatures and I believe that the

Pasu Glacier which we had to cross, not without difficulty and danger, has now retired and the road passes below the snout. As we ascended the valley the air became colder. This was reflected on the flora and fauna: I saw several ibex and shot one fair-sized trophy. I also shot some ram chukor (*Tetraogallus himalayanus*). When approaching the Mintaka pass we received news that a German accompanied by a Hindu was only four days' journey away to the west in Afghanistan.

We had brought with us food for the whole of our party but not for the local carriers from Gilgit. They were to make their own arrangements and these coolies had been given money to buy their own rations. When still two or three days' journey from the Chinese frontier the coolies started getting restive. They had not enough food. This was, of course, their own fault and I was a little inclined to break into the separate rations carried for the small party of sepoys and others. However the situation became serious and at Boihil one Zaheria, the ringleader of the trouble, stripped himself naked and lay down and refused to move as a protest. It was impossible to force hungry men to carry loads in this steep, cold country and in the end I had to give them some of our separate rations, a disquieting business; but on crossing the frontier at the pass we were met on the Chinese side by a welcome present of food from the Chinese which eased the situation. On May 22nd we crossed the Mintaka pass at the head of the valley up which we had travelled since leaving Gilgit. The height of the pass is 15,450 feet. On the pass I shot a wheatear (*Oenanthe deserti oreophila*).

After crossing the pass we dismissed our Hunza coolies and used yak transport, but I took Zaheria on with me as a punishment for several days. He became quite reconciled and a willing and useful member of the expedition, and I parted from him with regret later in Kashgar.

On descending on to the Pamirs we were met by guards of honour of Chinese troops and Gilgit scouts. One could not fail to be struck by the slovenly appearance of the Chinese when compared with the smartness of the Gilgit men who were, after all, the most irregular of irregulars and only trained for two months in the year.

What were these Gilgit scouts doing in Chinese territory? When the war broke out there were numbers of Germans, Austrians and Turks in Shanghai and other parts of Eastern China. They were cut off from the land route to Europe by Russia, and the sea route by Japan and ourselves. The only way was the very arduous journey right across Asia to Kashgar and thence via the Wakhjir pass into Afghanistan; this is the only pass leading from China into Afghanistan which does not pass through Russian or Indian territory. In Afghanistan they would find a neutral and they hoped a friendly country.

A glance at the map will show what an enterprise this was and it speaks volumes for the energy and sense of duty of those who tried it.

Early in 1916 small parties, consisting of two or three men each, began to arrive from China at Khotan. They all carried passports issued by a Norwegian consul but no passport bore the visa of any Chinese authority. Their arrival at Khotan was reported to Kashgar by the British *Aksakal* ('White Beard', as the leaders of the small communities of British-Indian traders in Turkestan are designated). Sir George Macartney insisted on their being sent back owing to their lack of proper visas. This was done on one or two occasions, but then the local Chinese officers seemed inclined to allow such parties to proceed.

One day a report was received that two Norwegians, Andersen and Friedriksen, had arrived. They were, they said, returning to Norway and were looking forward to meeting the British consul in Kashgar. It was subsequently learned that they were not following the direct road to Kashgar but had diverged south-westwards. Sir George telegraphed to Peking to check up their Norwegian passports, and when no trace of the issue of these could be found, orders were sent to intercept them with a small party of Hunza scouts. The N.C.O. of our guard was the man who had actually been in charge of the party. He could not, of course, arrest them in neutral Chinese territory. Disguised as a local man he met these supposed Norwegians in Chinese Turkestan many days' journey away from the frontier. He made friends with them and when they said they were making for Afghanistan he said that he was also going there and knew the roads, so he joined their party and was gladly accepted as a useful companion and guide. After a few days they asked him if they were not moving very far southward; he allayed their suspicions; but instead of taking them into Afghanistan he led them to the top of the Mintaka pass where he was met, by arrangement, by more of the Gilgit scouts. The moment the Germans were on the British side of the frontier cairn, the N.C.O. disclosed himself, covered them with his revolver and took them prisoner. They were eventually interned in India until the end of the war. One of these men was named Dunkelmann and was a secretary in the German Legation in Peking. He spoke Chinese well and had one thousand pounds in sovereigns with him.

It had been increasingly difficult to control these small parties of enemy subjects. We had the right to keep some troops on the Chinese Pamir, though we had not so far exercised it. The Russians had, however, exercised their similar rights, and maintained a detachment of Cossacks, whom we met later, at Tashkurgan. Sir George consequently insisted on this small guard of Gilgit scouts being posted just on the Chinese side of the frontier to intercept enemy subjects.

After crossing the pass we saw our first *yurts*, the poleless tents of Central Asia. We slept in these during our journey over the Pamirs. They were more stable, roomier and warmer than our own tents. They were called 'Kirga' by the Persian-speaking inhabitants and 'Ak-oi' by the Kirghiz. The word *kibitka* was, I found, used not only for these tents but also for any small native house. I once travelled for a month in Tibet with the Tashi Lama who had one of these tents entirely covered outside with leopard skins in place of felt. The inside was lined with silk and hung with sacred pictures, while a magnificent circular carpet, made to fit the tent, covered the floor; the whole made the most luxurious tent it is possible to imagine.

We were anxious to see and if possible shoot *Ovis Poli*, Marco Polo's great sheep of the Pamirs. We saw many females but no rams of any warrantable size. There were many pigeons (*Columba rupestris turkestanica*) which supplied our menus, and I shot a Tibetan sand-grouse (*Syrrhaptes tibetanus*), a new locality for this bird. A day or two later I shot a chukor (*Alectoris graeca*), a form of French partridge. I made a small collection of butterflies at the greater heights, the names of which are in the appendix.

On May 27th we reached Tashkurgan. Here was a Chinese officer styled an Amban, a man I thought too young to hold a post with such a title. The only previous Amban I had met was the Chinese Amban at Lhasa in 1904, a man of immeasurably higher rank and importance than the commander of this small frontier post. There was also a detachment of Cossacks under Captain Vilgorski. The detachment was anti-Bolshevik, but the captain was not very sure how long they would remain so. Subsequently poor Vilgorski had a very bad time and, fifteen years later, he arrived as a refugee at Srinagar in Kashmir, where I met him.

Our men gave the Cossacks a dinner and the entertainment was reciprocated, so our time in Tashkurgan, which included a dinner with the Chinese officer, was comparatively lively. At Tashkurgan I took the photo of a little girl, the daughter of a friendly Beg. Some months later I had to send a secret messenger from Tashkent and, as a sign of the genuineness of the messenger, I gave him a copy of this photograph which he showed to the girl's father with the information that he had been sent by the man who took the photo. This convinced the Beg that the message came from me and it was duly forwarded.

The Chinese Amban asked me to wait in Tashkurgan for a few days while he reported my arrival to his superiors! I told him that this was impossible and we parted on friendly terms on the 29th, accompanied by an escort of four Chinese soldiers. I had had Chinese escorts of this kind before and knew how useful they could be, not actually as a protection but as orderlies willing to turn their hands to any useful job. Captain Vilgorski and a dozen Cossacks accompanied us for a couple of miles. I bought a pony and Cossack saddle from them. I found the saddle comfortable after I had got used to the different style of riding.

On the 30th we crossed the Chichiklik pass (about 13,000 feet). We had great difficulty owing to the poor condition of our transport animals. The next day we found ourselves considerably lower, as was witnessed by the birds — golden orioles, dippers, magpies, etc., and the vegetation which included maidenhair ferns. An observation calculated from the boiling point of water showed our camp at Toile Bulung on May 31st to be 9,520 feet above sea level. The people of the Pamirs were Sarikolis, who spoke Persian; on this side of the pass we were among Kirghiz who spoke only Turki. On June 1st we crossed another pass, the Tort Dawan (12,800 feet), where I collected a mountain finch (*Montifringilla brandti brandti*); that night we had a small fall of snow. The next day we crossed the steep Kashka Su pass (12,650 feet). There were numbers of ram chukor, chukor (*Alectoris graeca pallida*), horned larks and finches on the road, and I obtained specimens of another mountain finch (*M. nemoricola altaica*); a rose finch (*Carpodacus rubicilla severtzovi*), a bird common in Tibet where I had often found the nests; a bunting (*Emberiza icterica*); a horned lark (*Otocorys alpestris diluta*); and a magpie (*Pica pica hemileucoptera*), of which I found a nest containing five eggs on June 4th. Marmots were also seen on the road. Among butterflies was a fine swallow-tail like our English one, but much larger. As we got lower the temperature became uncomfortably warm and large flocks of sheep were being driven to the higher grazing grounds.

On June 5th we were due to reach the town of Yangi Hissar

where the Chinese were preparing an official reception. This demanded punctuality, and our watches had not been set since we had obtained the correct time by telephone at Hunza three weeks before. I had an idea: we knew from the map the longitude of Yangi Hissar and from this it was not difficult to calculate from the *Nautical Almanack* the time at which some convenient star would cross the meridian. We therefore hung two strings with weights, one due north of the other, and when our stars crossed the two strings in line we knew they were on the meridian and a simple calculation enabled us to set our watches. Just as we were starting next morning a messenger came in from Sir George Macartney with a watch! This not only proved how accurate our calculations had been, but also how his long experience in this out of the way spot had led him to consider questions of time and space which might escape the foresight of some of us.

We had a great reception at Yangi Hissar, where we were greeted by Chinese soldiers with banners and with trumpeters who played us through the beflagged streets. The whole procession raised a formidable curtain of dust which nearly choked us. Later Chinese officers met us, and the afternoon was spent in receiving and returning visits. From here on for the next two days our way into Kashgar was a succession of such ceremonies including many *chajans*, i.e. tea and refreshments prepared for a short rest. It became embarrassing when we found one of these invitations from the civil, another from the military officer, one from the British subjects, etc., one from the Russian subjects, etc. In these matters the climax was our actual arrival at Kashgar on June 7th, six weeks after our departure from Srinagar. Sir George Macartney met us and we rode through the hot streets of the town which had been beflagged in our honour. We reached the consulate at lunchtime and our long journey was over. We spent the next day or two exchanging visits with the Chinese and Russian officers.

Although the Russian revolution had been in full swing

for some months, the Russians at Kashgar were still adherents of the imperial Russian regime.

In our contacts with the Russians, language was a difficulty. Only the acting Consul-General, Mr. Stephanovitch, spoke English and his charming wife French. At big dinners I usually found someone who spoke Persian. After dinner we would play the gramophone and dance Russian dances or gamble mildly at *Deviatka* in depreciated Russian currency. On these occasions the ladies played *Deviati Val* (Ninth wave), a supposedly quieter and less exciting game.

Once we gave a big dinner to the foreign community. There were over thirty present. The only strong drink available in Kashgar at this time was a spirit distilled from maize by the Hindu traders. This was very strong and raw. The small amount of other wines we had brought from India would have gone nowhere in this party. My neighbour asked a question in Russian which I did not understand. It was interpreted. 'I hear you have a special drink in your country called "whisky"! It has been the ambition of my life to taste this.' I at once sent for a bottle, and told my friend that we mixed it with water. This seemed to horrify him. He never mixed water with his drinks. He took a good stiff glass neat and made what I took to be an appreciative remark. 'What did he say?' I asked. 'He says it is the most delicious thing he has ever tasted.' Conversation became more lively and personal. Were any of the British officers married? No, they were not. 'Then do you think one of them would marry my daughter? That is she at the other end of the table. She is eighteen!'

We also had parties with the Chinese rulers of the country. One day we all drove out to a midday meal with General Ma, the Ti Tai (military commander) of Kashgar. He was a Tungan — a Chinese Mohammedan and a terrible tyrant of obscure origin and quite illiterate.

When the Chinese revolution broke out in 1911, the Ambans and other Chinese officials in Turkestan were murdered. The Governor at Urumchi was in grave danger and was saved by this man who was then head of the Tungans in Urumchi and who organized a defensive body of Tungan troops to protect the Governor. As a reward the Governor made him Ti Tai of Kashgar. Here he indulged in extortions and forced loans from the merchants, coupled with mutilations and atrocities which are too awful to describe. The civil officers were in terror of him and could really do nothing without his permission. General Ma honoured us by dining in full dress uniform and wore a large star on each breast. During the meal he unscrewed the front of one of these and disclosed to me a photograph of Yuan Shi Kai, President of the Chinese Republic. By way of conversation I asked whether the other star also opened. 'Yes,' he said, 'I have put my own photograph in that one.'

In 1924 the Governor of Sinkiang (Chinese Turkestan) dispatched troops to deal with this tyrant. By skilful manœuvring in two columns, the movements of one of which were kept secret, the New City where Ma resided was captured by surprise at daybreak. The General was wounded, taken out the next day and shot publicly; his body was tied to a kind of cross and the delighted populace took vengeance on the corpse.

Sport in Kashgar in winter is quite good, but in July this relaxation was not possible. For exercise and amusement we started a mild kind of polo, and I also made a small collection of butterflies and birds. Once towards the end of June when riding in the country I came on a tall poplar tree in which were the nests of several hobbies. I thought I would train these beautiful little hawks — their long wings almost like those of a swallow, though I knew that they were not considered a satisfactory bird in falconry. I brought four young birds in, one from each nest, and kept them during the weeks I still stayed in Kashgar. When fledged they got very tame and lived in the tall trees of the consulate garden and would come on to my hand to be fed. Later they became more shy and less inclined to be fed, and I found the pellets under the trees where they roosted composed of beetles' wings, and saw the birds hawking insects late in the evening. When I left for Tashkent the birds had settled down and their descendants are, I believe, nesting in the consulate garden to-day.

Other birds collected in Kashgar included two doves, *Streptopelia decacto stoliczkae*, and *S. turtur arenicola*, a form of our turtle dove; a rock-dove (*Colomba livia neglecta*) of which I had obtained a specimen in Hunza; a wagtail (*Motacilla alba personata*); a large lark (*Galerida cristata magna*); a ringed plover (*Charadrius dubia curonicus*); a tern (*Sterna hirundo tibetana*) fished in the river at Kashgar. One would expect this to be a sea bird, but it is common in Central Asia and breeds in Tibet and Kashmir. The carrion crow (*Corvus corone intermedius*) and starling (*Sturnus vulgaris porphynotus*) were common.

Rainfall in Kashgar is in the neighbourhood of one inch a year. In countries as dry as this, when the rain does come it is very unpleasant. All sorts of undesirable and hidden sights and smells are revealed. The water stands about, and in Kashgar the roads become so slippery that they are almost impassable. Once we were caught out at dinner on a night like this; a ride in the dark through slushy country would have been impossible; and our hosts took us in for the night.

One day Sir George was surprised to receive through the post in quite an ordinary way a letter from Mr. Tredwell, newly appointed Consul-General at Tashkent for the United States, who wished to establish contact with the nearest Allied representative. Tredwell and I were, later, to have a great deal in common.

CHAPTER II

KASHGAR TO TASHKENT

THE position in Russian Turkestan was obscure. We knew that Bolsheviks were in control but no one quite knew what a Bolshevik was or what were his aims and objects. It seemed that it would be useful to go and see them, and find out what sort of people they were and to try to persuade them to continue the war against Germany, or at least not to help the Central Powers in the war against us.

It seemed that this could best be done by consultation with the Russians themselves. So, on July 24th Blacker and I left Kashgar for Tashkent, the capital of Russian Turkestan. We were accompanied by Mr. Stephanovitch and his wife, who most efficiently took charge of the catering for the journey. Mrs. Stephanovitch had shopping to do in Tashkent and also wished to see a dentist.

There are two roads from Kashgar to India, the longer one via Leh takes a traveller thirty-eight days, and the shorter one, via Gilgit, which we had ourselves followed, twenty-six days. Letters by runner took about eighteen days to reach the railway at Rawal Pindi in the Punjab. Russia was much closer, but a twelve days' journey over high mountains followed by a couple of days in a train, to reach your shopping centre, will give an idea of the remoteness of Kashgar. We hoped that Stephanovitch would be able to help us on our arrival in Tashkent, but this plan failed for reasons which will appear. The fact was that very little was known in Kashgar of the situation in Tashkent and all accounts of the political conditions were biased one way or the other.

Etherton did not accompany us as he had been appointed Consul-General in place of Sir George Macartney who was retiring.

26

We had a great send-off with the usual *chajans*, which on this occasion included an outsize specimen which might with some reason have been called a banquet. This was given about two miles out from Kashgar by the Russian community and lasted till five o'clock so that we did not arrive at the end of our march till ten-thirty. We had, however, a good moon and travelled some of the way in Sir George's spring 'Mapa'. This was a Chinese cart to which springs had been added to make it more comfortable.

Blacker made this first day's journey on the motor-cycle, doing the twenty-eight miles to Mingyol in three and a half hours. The motor-bike and the 'Mapa' were taken the first two and a half days of our journey. The road then got rougher and we sent them back to Kashgar before crossing the first pass, the Kizil Dawan, 8,350 feet above sea level.

After leaving Kashgar we crossed some stretches of desert on which very wary gazelle were grazing; later we entered the beautiful green mountains of the Alai, inhabited by hospitable Kirghiz whose *yurts* could be seen in most valleys and who sent us bowls of curds and of *kumis*. The latter is a slightly intoxicating liquor, made of fermented mares' milk, which I thought tasted like *chang*, the Tibetan barley beer. Kumis is mentioned by Marco Polo.

In some places the Kirghiz had enclosed and irrigated fields where they were growing crops of lucerne mixed with grasses — the first beginnings of settled cultivation by a nomad grazing people. They grew no food crops but only enclosed grazing for their animals. These fields were a great attraction to numbers of butterflies, many allied to our British forms.

Once, near Shorbulak, we passed through a marble gorge so narrow that loaded camels had to struggle through, their bales of cotton actually brushing the sides of the defile. The traffic of centuries had given a fine polish to the marble.

A couple of days out from Kashgar, Blacker developed a curious illness. It was rather alarming as we had no doctor and only carried the simplest remedies. The local people made a very serviceable litter carried tandem between two ponies. We carried him for two days, then rested a day and sent a messenger on to Irkeshtam, the nearest telegraph office, to telegraph to Kashgar for a doctor.

At Ulugchat we passed a fort with a Chinese garrison a couple of hundred strong. The officer in command had been relieved and ordered to return to Kashgar, but as he was a relative of the dreaded Ti Tai, he refused to go and his unfortunate successor was living in the adjoining village and could do nothing about it.

Irkeshtam, just under 10,000 feet above sea level, was the frontier post between Russia and China. We reached it on July 31st and were entertained by the Russian customs officers. We spent a cheery evening dancing to the clarinet of a military cadet and playing cards — the usual *Deviatka*. The Russians had made themselves very comfortable. Roses, willows, and a pine tree had been planted near the post. They were certainly not in sympathy with the Bolsheviks and were living in a state of great uncertainty, judging by the fortifications of bales of cotton they had prepared. They showed me the skin of a freshly killed bear and told me that wild sheep and ibex were to be had on the surrounding hills. The Russians didn't go in much for shooting; I felt that many a British subaltern would have enjoyed this isolated but sporting post.

The highest pass on the road was the Terek Dawan, about 13,000 feet. We crossed on August 3rd, and although this was the hottest time of the year it froze on the ground the night before we crossed, and there were patches of snow in the hollows round the pass. Among them were the bones of countless animals and even of some men who had lost their lives on this dangerous road. I collected many butterflies here, including some rare *Parnassius* and *Coleas* and others.

At Sufi Kurgan we passed Russian troops, details of the 2nd Siberian Regiment, on detachment from Kharogh post, one of the garrisons of the Pamirs. The post was in process of being taken over by the Red Army and the new detachment

consisted of Czech and Austrian prisoners of war. Only two
of the party were Russians.

We passed a farm near Langar which must at that time have
been the furthest Russian colonization in this direction. These
signs of European civilization were followed by a cart road
and telegraph line, and the next day at Gulcha we came on
more Russian farms and some empty barracks. Here also we
were joined by Dukovitch, head of the Russian bank in Kashgar,
who was going to Tashkent on business. His Armenian clerk,
however, had written to Tashkent to say that he did not
favour the Soviet regime and the poor man was arrested on his
arrival at Tashkent. He thus gained first hand knowledge of the
inside working of a Soviet gaol before he saw Kashgar again.

On August 7th we reached Osh after a very hot march, and
halted the next day to get ourselves straight and tidy after
our journey. The most fantastic rumours about our party had
preceded us. We were the vanguard of a force of twelve thousand men sent from India to capture 'Ferghana and Turkestan';
our servants were all sepoys in disguise. Mr. Stephanovitch,
on our behalf, explained matters to the local officials and after
making a list (Bolsheviks, or perhaps I should say bureaucrats,
love lists) of our men, horses and baggage, we were allowed to
proceed. On the 9th we drove in *tarantas* forty-six versts (thirty
and a half miles) into Andijan, paying one hundred and fifty
roubles for each *tarantas*.

In Andijan we stayed at a bathless hotel. The place was very
hot, with no facilities for keeping cool. The town was full of
released Austrian prisoners. Orchestras of prisoners played at
the tea-houses and restaurants and all the servants in our hotel
were Austrians. The imperial Austrian uniform, which I was
later to wear so much myself, was much in evidence. We spent
three days here before we got permission to proceed. We had
to interview our first komissars, picturesque fellows in Russian
blouses and top boots, with a revolver conspicuously worn in the
belt or placed on the office table. In the streets they walked
with a busy purposeful gait with a portfolio tucked under the

arm. They were evidently out to impress us but failed entirely to do so. We saw a play, *Mazeppa*, in an open air theatre and went to the cinema. The first European shops seen since we first left India were an attraction, though they would not have been thought much of anywhere else.

In Andijan were a number of Hindus from Shikarpur. It is curious that Hindus from this town in Sind have spread over Turkestan. I do not think that there was any business firm actually in Tashkent, but Hindus certainly visited Tashkent occasionally and were well established in Bokhara. A deputation of these men came to see me in Andijan. They complained that they were in danger of losing all their money and possessions as the Bolsheviks regarded them as speculators of the most virulent type. They asked me if I could help them to get their money out of the country; they had between them about two million roubles. Owing to the fall in the exchange rate (at this time from about one and a half rupees per rouble to about ten roubles per rupee), they had lost enormously, but if they could get their money out at once they would be saved from absolute ruin. I told them I could not immediately deal with such a large sum but to oblige them I would take fifty thousand roubles from them and give them a draft on India, at the rate of exchange of the day. I would further do my best with the Russian authorities in Tashkent to help them. They professed to be pleased to get at least some of their money safe, but later, just as we were leaving, they sent word to me to say that after all I was only a traveller and they had no guarantee that I was what I professed to be, and so, as I had no letters from their friends in Kashgar, the deal was off. Eventually of course they must have lost everything.

The Russian consular officers at Kashgar as at all other places were men of the old imperial regime and were, we understood, maintained by the Russian Embassy in Peking, out of the Boxer Indemnity which was paid by the Chinese Government to Russia until renounced by the Bolshevik Government.

Stephanovitch was warned in Andijan that it would be most

dangerous for him to go to Tashkent and that he would certainly be arrested there. The danger was not considered great for his wife. Accordingly when we finally left Andijan, Stephanovitch started back on the fortnight's journey to Kashgar. The journey to the frontier at Irkeshtam was about one hundred and forty miles and would take him five or six days, and we were to try and avoid any questions about him in Tashkent until he had time to recross the frontier.

Railway services had been suspended for two weeks owing to a shortage of oil and other fuel. The result was a waiting list of passengers five or six times the capacity of the train. We were, however, given preferential treatment in this matter and left Andijan at three-thirty in the afternoon on August 12th in an old wagon-lit carriage which had been given over for us three — Mrs. Stephanovitch, Blacker and myself. We reached Cherny-ayevo early next morning and our train remained here the whole of a hot and dusty day to await the arrival of a train from Samarkand and Bokhara. We reached Tashkent at three a.m. the next morning, August 14th, and drove to the Regina Hotel.

CHAPTER III

TASHKENT

AT the time of our arrival Tashkent had been under the Bolsheviks for nearly a year. Trams and horse cabs plied, and a few things could still be bought in the shops. In our hotel we could get quite good meals, and life generally at this time was not very different from what it must have been before the revolution. But the position rapidly deteriorated. Hotels and restaurants were closed or turned into Soviet institutions meagrely patronized by the proletariat. All motor cars had been commandeered for the Bolshevik officials. Theatres were still open. While we were in Tashkent an Englishman passed through with a troupe of performing elephants! These he was taking to Kashgar over the none too easy Terek Dawan. Everywhere one saw Austrian prisoners of war. Many still in their uniforms with F.J.I. on their hats. In all cafés and restaurants an orchestra of Austrians played. The most fashionable restaurant was the Chashka Chai (Cup of Tea). We were very soon known to the band here and they used to break off their tune and play 'Tipperary' as we entered! Under the deep shade of the karagach (a kind of elm) or acacia we would eat ices and drink beer, or one of the substitutes for tea or coffee, to the pleasant sound of running water in the street gutters.

Tashkent was a well wooded town. Streets were lined with double avenues of trees — poplars, elms, chenars, oaks, mulberries and acacias. Down the gutters of the streets ran water turned on from the irrigation system. This flowing water under the shady trees gave a cool and pleasant impression on hot summer days, a characteristic which Tashkent perhaps shares with no other city. Men with cans and the universal kerosene tin used to sprinkle this water over the dusty roads.

All trees were measured up and cut down for fuel in the late summer of 1919. You were given a coupon for fuel on your ration card. When you asked for your share of fuel you were shown a tree standing in the street and told to take it. Fortunes in paper money were made by the lucky owners of saws and axes. I hope these acacias, poplars and mulberries have since been replaced as the absence of trees quite altered the town and ruined its amenities and special character.

The capital of Russian Turkestan consisted of a large native city of over two hundred thousand inhabitants. Adjoining it was a modern Russian city of fifty thousand. On the outskirts of the city was a fort, wireless station, and the White House, once the residence of the Governor-General, in a fine park.

The permanent Russian Consul-General at Kashgar was Prince Mestcherski, who for many years had been a friend of Sir George Macartney. Prince Mestcherski had an aunt, Madame Ugrekhelidze, who was superintendent of a girls' school in Tashkent. Sir George Macartney had stayed with her several times on his way to and from Europe, and our first visit was to her. Here we met a Mr. and Mrs. Edwards. He was a school teacher. They later both disappeared and were probably killed by Kirghiz, as will be recounted further on.

We also got in touch with Mr. Roger C. Tredwell, the United States Consul-General, and his temporary assistant Mr. Shaw. Tredwell was in every way an ornament to his profession and a credit to his country. His conduct of affairs could not have been bettered. Tredwell had rooms with a family named Noyev. The family consisted of father, mother, two girls aged about fourteen and seven and a boy of about eight. The children were in charge of an Irish governess, Miss Houston, resourceful and brave, whose assistance to me and others, and whose courage in sticking to her charges in times of great danger, was beyond praise. The elder girl and the boy are now British subjects and doing well in their professions. The boy is a captain in the Royal Engineers and the girl was secretary to Edgar Wallace up to the time of his death.

Although only a child when I knew her in Tashkent, she was, in spite of her age, reliable and of the greatest use in emergencies.

Mr. Noyev had previously got himself into trouble with the Imperial Government on account of his political views, but he had no sympathy with the people who had now seized power. He managed to keep clear of politics, which meant that though occasionally suspected and sent to gaol for a few days he was not otherwise molested. There was also in Tashkent an English teacher called Smales whom I met once or twice. He had been fourteen years in Tashkent and was married to a Russian. He did not concern himself with the political changes, and he also, beyond occasionally being suspected and spending a night in gaol, was not interfered with.

In Tashkent was a very old widow lady of English birth, Madame Quatts. She had come out as governess to the children of General Kauffmann, the conqueror of Turkestan, about fifty years before, and had married a Russian. She had almost forgotten English and spoke with hesitation and made mistakes in words and grammar, but with this had no trace of a foreign accent. Even this old lady was suspected and arrested. I managed to obtain her release, but later she was again arrested for stealing and was eventually sent to a lunatic asylum. This was really a kindness arranged for her and was the best we could do to mitigate the senseless persecution of this poor old lady.

In many ways the Russian revolution followed the course of the French revolution. Many of the actual revolutionaries were youths, maddened by a little temporary power to commit fearful atrocities. In 1792 the *sans-culottes* were mostly youths.

Many of the early revolutionaries, both in Russia and in France, eventually became victims. We all know of the Russian purges. In Russia especially, people advocating Liberal reforms, whom the Imperial Government punished in various ways for their advanced views, were 'liquidated' by the Bolsheviks who considered them reactionaries. Rising prices, the refusal of peasants to sell food in the towns at the prices fixed by the Government, and many other things had all happened before. But the Russian revolution did not produce a Napoleon!

When the first revolution led by Kerensky occurred in Petrograd in February 1917, the population of Turkestan, both Russian and native, accepted the situation with delight, and most of the government officials served the new provisional government.

In November 1917 when the Bolsheviks brought off their *coup d'état*, they really only obtained control of the centre at Tashkent, but the officials of the previous provisional government in other districts worked for them, not quite knowing what to do and being economically dependent on whatever government was in control at Tashkent. Gradually in the beginning of 1918 unreliable officials were replaced by Bolsheviks.

In November 1917 fighting broke out in Tashkent, and after four days the Bolshevik party gained the upper hand and many adherents of the provisional government were killed.

In the beginning of 1918 a similar movement against the Bolshevik regime had been attempted, and one day an enormous number of unarmed Mohammedans, estimated at two hundred thousand, came from the native city and surrounding country to the Russian town and released from gaol eight members of the provisional government who had been imprisoned by the Bolsheviks, the gaol guards offering no resistance. This enormous crowd was then faced by a small detachment of the Red Army who fired on them. The native Sarts scattered and the prisoners were recaptured and immediately shot in the street.

In the summer of 1916 there had been an attempt at revolt by the native population. This had been repressed with the greatest severity by the Imperial Government and the village of Jizak had been destroyed. Natives from other parts of the country had been brought to Jizak and shown the ruins with corpses lying in the streets and had been told that if they gave any trouble they knew what to expect. The 'Jizak event' as it was called was effective and the native population was completely cowed.

The population of Russian Turkestan was ninety-five per cent native Mohammedan and five per cent European Russians, the total being nearly seven millions. The Russians invariably refer to the natives as 'Sarts' and their language (Turki) as *Sartski* or even *Mussalmanski*. 'Sart' is a word which strictly speaking applies to the town dwellers as opposed to the peasants and the nomadic population, but the word is used by Russians rather loosely. Sart writers sometimes refer to themselves as Turks but this word is, I think, misleading; Turkestani and the even more clumsy word Turkestanian has also been used. On the whole I think it is best to follow the Russians and use the simple word 'Sart', although purists may object that it should not be used for country folk.

Though not born in the saddle (who is?) the people of Turkestan, especially on the farms and small villages (*kishlaks*), never go on foot if they can go on horseback. Outside quite small and mean houses you will see a saddled pony tethered and to go even fifty yards a man will prefer riding to going on foot. They seldom ride fast, a jog of four or five miles an hour is the usual pace. I once asked a man at what age he had learned to ride and he frankly did not understand me. You don't learn to ride — you just ride. I found the same with Tibetans, but they were quite useless at polo in their high saddles and short stirrups, and had really to start again from the beginning to compete with us in rougher sorts of riding.

Russian Turkestan is in one way a curious country. Railways were made before roads — at least before respectable roads. The result is that when the railway line was cut by the enemy there was not, as one might have expected, any possibility of communication by car. In fact, motor cars could only travel short distances from Tashkent.

The other forms of transport were various carts. The native *arba* is a simple cart on two very large and heavy wheels, suitable for passing over rough country. The driver sits on the horse with his feet on the shafts. The *brichka* and *telyeshka* are large Russian country carts for farm work. The *tarantas* is something in the nature of a victoria and less uncomfortable for the passenger than any of the above-mentioned vehicles.

The usual mode of transport, however, is the camel, and numbers of these could be seen in the streets of Tashkent.

The Central Government had announced that the Bolshevik programme included self-determination, and the native Mohammedan population considered that this referred to them with their ninety-five per cent majority. They soon discovered, however, that self-determination in the Bolshevik view did not refer to Turkestan, Finland and other countries under the domination of Russia, but only referred to India and countries in the British, French and other *bourjoui* dominions.

The Sarts relied on the Moscow announcement and believed that the five per cent Russian population had usurped the power against the wishes of the centre, and that Moscow would soon put things right. About June 1917 they formed an autonomous government in Kokhand and asked Moscow to dissolve the five per cent Russian Government and grant them autonomy within the Soviet Union. Moscow replied in effect: 'Do it yourselves, by force if necessary.' On this the five per cent Russian Government who controlled the army, munitions, etc., took the hint and under Kolesov at once attacked the Sarts at Kokhand, defeated them and plundered the city, massacring several thousands, and profaned and destroyed the mosques. So much for self-determination in Turkestan.

The situation was economically very bad. The managers of cotton, wine and other concerns had been eliminated and the workmen were running things badly and dishonestly. A cloud of uneducated komissars were a dead weight on commercial undertakings. Besides being expensive in themselves their corruption added to overhead charges. Unemployment was serious, food very scarce and expensive. The position was not improved by pressing requests from Moscow for the dispatch of large quantities of cotton, cotton oil and fruit. Turkestan had a supply of these commodities but not enough to spare, and in any case the receipt of anything in exchange from Moscow seemed problematical. Before the revolution cotton oil had not been a necessity, but now it was used for lighting and, in spite of the unpleasant flavour, in cooking. A few pieces of twisted cotton wool in a saucer of cotton oil was the usual illumination in Turkestan. There was electric light in Tashkent but it was uncertain and bulbs were hard to come by.

There were also inconveniences caused by the very necessities of the situation when a small minority attempts to coerce the majority by force or fear, and once the Bolsheviks had secured power they had no hesitation in forbidding many of the things they professed to be fighting for, especially for example freedom of the press and freedom of public meeting.

We visited the Foreign Office on August 17th, by which time we calculated that Stephanovitch must have reached the Chinese frontier. We were put off for two days as the foreign komissar was busy. This was in some ways a relief to us and especially to Mrs. Stephanovitch, as it gave her husband an extra two days to get to safety.

On August 19th Blacker and I had our first interview with Damagatsky, the foreign komissar. Before the revolution he had been a draughtsman in the colonization office of the Ministry of Agriculture. In politics he was a left social revolutionary, or L.S.R. They were considered to be milder than the true Bolsheviks though it was hard for an outsider to distinguish between them. I started off badly with Damagatsky by referring to the 'Bolshevik Government'. When we left the room the interpreter said to me 'Remember the foreign komissar is not a Bolshevik but a left social revolutionary. It is wrong to refer to the Bolshevik Government and Damagatsky was offended by it. It is the "Soviet Government", though you may refer to the "Bolshevik Party".'

Unfortunately for us, the British troops from Meshed who were supporting the anti-Bolshevik government of Trans-Caspia had had their first clash with the Bolshevik troops on August 13th. Our arrival that very night put us in a difficult position when confronted with the statement that British troops were fighting against the Red Army. I realized that it was most probably quite true; we had had no news from India or the outside world for about two months. Had the first contact between our troops and the Bolsheviks occurred a few days earlier I would have been warned and would most probably have been recalled. I think that the Bolsheviks would have been justified in interning the mission which had arrived at such a curious time. Internment for any length of time would, as I realized later, have meant almost certain death. There was nowhere to keep us except in the gaol, and unauthorized executions of people in gaol were of very frequent occurrence. A party of drunken soldiers would go to the gaol, take people out and shoot them. Once as we were walking down the street we heard cries and shots from a house. One of these murders was being perpetrated. In excuse it was said that these victims had been so roughly handled by the men who had escorted them that they were shot to put them out of their misery. Slightly more justifiable executions took place when the gaol was full and it was necessary to make room.

The line I took in my discussions with Damagatsky was that it was incredible that the mission should have been sent to Tashkent while at the same time in another part of Turkestan my countrymen were actually at war with them. There must be some mistake. How did he know the troops fighting there were in fact British and British-Indians? The answer was simple and flattering. The artillery was good, far better than anything in Russia. There was also English writing on the shells. I retorted that we had sold shells to all sorts of people and had sent large quantities to Russia to help them in the war; quite possibly they would find English writing on the shells they were using themselves in the Red Army! Neither of these reasons was any proof and until he could produce something more convincing I could not accept the statement. On this Damagatsky said he would try to get a prisoner to convince me, and at many subsequent interviews I always commenced by asking if he had yet succeeded in capturing the proof I desired.

One of Damagatsky's first demands (the first demand made by all Russian officials whatever the business) was 'Show me your documents'. It was hoped I would produce papers which would indicate recognition of the Soviet Government by the British Government. Tredwell had papers appointing him to Tashkent signed by the United States Ambassador, besides his consular commission signed by the President of the United States. We had no such papers. I was hoping that we should be able to obtain some sort of recognition from the Turkestan Soviet and so be a means of contact and communication between the Indian Government and them. We did not in the least know their attitude or intentions, and it was important to find this out. When we were unable to produce the much desired papers we were accused of being spies. I told Damagatsky that he could find out about our status by a wireless message to India. This he said he would do, and in the meantime he was prepared to hear what we had to say.

I told him that we were entirely occupied with winning the war. Nothing else mattered at present and for this end I had three main and important requests to make.

First, the prisoners of war should be controlled. There had at one time been one hundred and ninety thousand prisoners of war in Turkestan. Conditions had been terrible for them, largely owing to defective arrangements. One reason for sending so many prisoners to Turkestan was, doubtless, the remoteness of the district and the difficulty of escape; but also a consideration was the quantity and cheapness of food. In spite of this the rations of the prisoners were so meagre that disease broke out, while medical arrangements were so scanty and inefficient that thousands died. By far the larger number of the prisoners were Austrians who had been captured at Pryzemsl and in other parts of Galicia in the early months of the war; but there were also many Germans.

Captain A. H. Brun, of the Royal Danish Artillery, was in Tashkent doing all he could to mitigate the sufferings of the poor Austrians. His book, *Troublous Times*, gives a harrowing account of their miseries and of his difficulties with the Russians in his attempt to help them. He also describes his own arrest and detention in hourly expectation of being led out to execution, when his companion, Mr. Kleberg, a Swede in charge of similar arrangements for German prisoners, was actually taken from the very same cell and executed.

The agonies of these prisoners have been described by one of them, Gustav Krist. In one barrack the *whole* of the prisoners, two hundred and eighty in number, died of typhus. He also describes the wonderful effect, both moral and physical, which a visit from the Danish Commission produced among the prisoners of war. At the time of our arrival many prisoners had already been transferred to Siberia, while between forty and fifty thousand had died, and in the summer of 1918 there were thirty-three thousand left in Turkestan.

At the time of the Bolshevik revolution all the prisoners had been released. This simply meant opening the gates of the camps and ceasing to issue rations. The prisoners suddenly had to fend for themselves. In many cases at first, conditions were worse than when they were confined in the *lagers*. One officer told me that he had had to eat tortoises at this time.

Numbers of prisoners obtained employment working on farms for the Russian and Sart inhabitants. All Czech prisoners seem to have been musicians and Czech orchestras played at most cafés, as we had seen in far-off Andijan, though where their instruments came from was a mystery. Prisoners were also seen begging in the streets. A number took the places of Russian soldiers who had disappeared or perished in the war or the revolution. They married the widows or deserted wives and adopted the farm or business. Many of these ex-prisoners of war have permanently settled in Turkestan.

There was once a scene in the Roman Catholic cathedral. A Polish-Austrian prisoner of war was being married to a Tashkent girl when one of his companions got up and said that the bridegroom already had a wife in Austria. The priest stopped the ceremony.

Gustav Krist describes how some of the prisoners started considerable industries, and the extreme difficulty of such activities under the Soviet system of government.

While Captain Brun was doing his best for the large number of Austrians, Mr. Kleberg, a Swede, with two assistants, was performing a similar service for the German prisoners who numbered about three thousand. Besides this, Lieutenant Zimmermann, himself a German prisoner of war, was bravely endeavouring to keep these Germans decently organized and looked after, and to prevent them from joining the Red Army. He even issued a proclamation forbidding German prisoners of war to enter the army and threatening them, if they did so, with punishment in Germany afterwards, should they ever return there. This proclamation was stifled by the authorities.

Under the command of an ex-sergeant-major with a fierce moustache, a detachment of about sixty Germans could be seen at the big parades in Tashkent, smartly dressed in black leather. In every way they were a cut above the other troops on parade. I used to hear the German words of the 'International' sung as they marched along, the last word rapped out with great emphasis: 'Und International das macht das Menschenrecht.'

From our point of view it was very important that these prisoners should be controlled. If Zimmermann and the Germans had had their way, a formed body might have entered northern Afghanistan with possibly very grave effects for us on the course of the war. It has been stated that the Amir of Afghanistan had agreed to join with the Central Powers in an invasion of India if a formed body of a stipulated strength could be produced in Afghanistan. This danger seemed very imminent and serious when we heard that a German staff sent expressly to organize these prisoners had actually reached Astrakhan and were only prevented from coming to Turkestan by the interruption of the railway.

The pressure of Tredwell and myself on Damagatsky to control these Germans did not make us popular with them.

Tredwell was justifiably angry when the mother of the interpreter who had translated when he was pressing Damagatsky
to keep control of the prisoners of war, told Mrs. Noyev in
a hairdresser's shop the next day what he had said. Reports of
this sort would not make the Germans more friendly and the
war was still on, which would justify any acts of violence. I
once found myself in the waiting-room at the Foreign Office
with Zimmermann. I am sure he must have known who I was,
but we did not speak.

Damagatsky told us that it had not been possible to keep
touch with all the prisoners after release, though they were
endeavouring to establish a bureau where they would all be
registered, but they had information of about twenty-six
thousand, while he estimated that there must be several thousand more in the country with whom they had lost touch. In
any case there was, he said, no danger of the prisoners arming
and combining in any way. It was the hope of the Government
to revolutionize them and to enrol them in the Red Army.
This was done to a great extent, though it was directly against
various conventions signed by the Imperial Russian Government. Captain Brun mentions how he had obtained a document, signed by Lenin, Trotsky and Chicherin, forbidding the
enlistment of prisoners and even ordering the discharge of any
already enlisted. The Turkestan Government refused to obey
this. The prisoners could not be blamed for joining the Red
Army as any government in Russia which might replace the
Soviet would have interned them until the end of the war.
Damagatsky added that any who did not join the Red Army
would be sent back to Europe as soon as the Askhabad front
had been 'liquidated', which he expected would be done in a
few days. It seemed to me that if such a thing were done we
would find these men fighting against us again, perhaps in
Turkey, and that this should be prevented at all costs. There
was also a danger that we visualized, of energetic officer
prisoners getting into Persia or Afghanistan and joining the
German organization already there under Wassmuss, Nieder-

meyer, von Hentig, and others, and working up feeling against us and even of organizing forces.

The second important matter was the question of cotton; the Central Powers were very short of this essential constituent of war munitions. Turkestan was overflowing with it. Barricades of bales of cotton were used in the fighting. The frontier post at Irkeshtam was, we had seen, fortified in this way; armoured trains were so protected. It was estimated that there were twelve million *poods*, about two hundred thousand tons, of cotton in Turkestan lying available for export. There were only two railways connecting Turkestan with the outside world — the Transcaspian line, blocked by anti-Bolshevik Russians (for a short time with the support of British and Indian troops) and the line north to Orenburg, which was blocked by Cossacks under General Dutov. As long as these two railways remained cut, no appreciable quantity of cotton could leave the country. So great was the need, however, that an attempt was made to remove the cotton by camel caravan and one such caravan of seventy camel loads actually left the country via Emba, a place situated between the Caspian and the Aral seas. It was the intention to organize a regular system of caravans by this route, and this would possibly have been done had the war lasted longer. I asked Damagatsky to see that the cotton was not removed for the benefit of German munitions. His reply to this request was that the war among the imperialist powers was of no great concern to Soviet Russia, and anyone could have the cotton who would pay for it and take it away. In any case, all imperialist powers would soon be swept away by the World Revolution. He added, as a small comfort, that all the cotton that was leaving the country (the small quantity by Emba) was going to Russian commercial firms in Moscow.

The Government wished, and still wishes, to force the population of Turkestan to grow cotton, in order that Russia might be quite independent of supplies from foreign countries. Even before the revolution compulsion was used, but since the last war the pressure has been increased. The native cultivators resisted this. There was always an innate uneasiness at the absence of visible food and a desire to grow food crops. Pressure was exerted in various ways, such as concessions in regard to taxation; supplies of manufactured goods to cotton growers; deprivation of irrigation water for other crops; while cotton growers were helped in every way.

The Russian Government insisted, and now the position in Turkestan is quite satisfactory from their point of view.

· The final completion of the Turkestan-Siberian, or, to use the usual Russian abbreviation, the Turk-Sib railway, contributed to this state of affairs. Through running commenced on this line at the annual May Day festival in 1931. The Bolsheviks took great credit for this but in reality all the plans and a great deal of the work had been completed before the revolution. Practically no technical difficulties remained; some bridges over the larger rivers remained to be completed.

The completion of the railway gave the final blow to any hope of independence to Turkestan. This fertile country was forced to grow cotton to be exchanged for the Siberian food crops brought in by this railway. Mademoiselle Maillart, the well-known Central Asian traveller, has explained how this compulsion was exercised; the peasants were only given corn in proportion to the amount of cotton produced. Thus, a country that had been self-supporting in food was made dependent on food from outside, and could at any moment be easily cut off and starved into subjection in any matter in which the populace might prove difficult to their rulers. Mademoiselle Maillart also mentions that negroes from America were brought in to give instruction in cotton growing.

A third important point was the question of religious propaganda among Mohammedans. The Germans were using their alliance with Turkey in an attempt to raise a religious standard among the Mohammedans in favour of the Central Powers. The Kaiser was reported to be a Mohammedan. The raising of this religious feeling in Central Asia might have effects in Afghanistan and among the tribes of the North-West Frontier of India, and finally among the Mohammedan population of India itself, where the Mohammedan Punjab and North-West Frontier Provinces were our largest and most reliable recruiting ground for the Indian Army. This danger seemed to us, at the time, not only to be very real and of immediate urgency, but also we envisaged the danger of awkward complications after the war. Damagatsky said that any form of religious propaganda would be suppressed by the government, as it was contrary to the policy of the Soviet Government.

In all these requests I was in close co-operation with Mr. Tredwell, the United States Consul, and we frequently visited the foreign komissar together.

There was also the question of the difficulties and losses sustained by British subjects in Turkestan. These men were mostly in the south of the country; it will be remembered that I met a deputation of them in Andijan. These merchants were, of course, capitalists and, as such, fair game for the alleged Marxist Government.

Life in Tashkent at this time was not unpleasant: we lived in the Regina Hotel and had our meals in the restaurant. There were some cinemas and a circus. But we were followed everywhere by spies, and when we returned home at night after going to a concert or cinema, electric torches flashed mysterious signals, and bells were rung to report our safe arrival. The police made frequent searches by day and night, and once came to us at two o'clock in the morning. I protested strongly both at the time and later to Damagatsky at the foreign komissariat. He was polite and sympathetic, but he really had no control over the police in its various forms.

As to these, first there was the militia. This semi-military organization was under a Lett baker, named Tsirul. Tsirul's brother had been executed by the Imperial Government and he himself had done time. He was a violent revolutionary but friendly to us and later, when Tredwell was imprisoned and about to be shot, it was Tsirul who forcibly removed him from gaol and saved his life. He did the same for Captain Brun on another occasion. Tsirul even once proposed to Brun that they should *both* escape together. He was quite frank with Tredwell and once told him that if he helped him in Tashkent he hoped that, if necessary, Tredwell would give him an asylum in America. Tsirul had at one time been obliged to fly from Russia, and had lived in Whitechapel, but knew no English.

Another organization was the ordinary police, and a third the Cheka. This latter on our first arrival, had been called the 'Special Department' (*Osoboi Otdyel*). It later became the 'Enquiry Commission' (*Sledstvennaya Kommissia*), to deal with counter-revolutionaries, hoarders and speculators. Then one day we were informed that it had changed its name to the 'Extraordinary Commission' (*Chrezvoichainaya Kommissia*), abbreviated to Cheka. The full title, 'The Extraordinary Commission to Combat Speculation and Counter-revolution', required some abbreviation, especially in Russian. The Cheka later became the Ogpu, another abbreviation.

Once secret agents of the counter-espionage section of the militia, who were watching me, arrested the Cheka agents engaged in the same employment in the belief that they were secret agents of mine! This caused great amusement throughout the town, the inhabitants of which were finding very little to amuse them under the early Soviet conditions.

CHAPTER IV

CONDITIONS IN TASHKENT

THE position of the Government in Turkestan was at this time hard. They were fighting on four 'fronts', besides having to face danger, which in January 1919 culminated in an armed conflict, on the Home Front, in Tashkent itself.

On the north they had a force facing Dutov who, with his Cossacks, was holding the railway line. This was known in Tashkent as the Aktobinsk Front. South-east of here was a peasant rising in Semirechia, where the Government had about one thousand men engaged. South of this there was a serious Mohammedan rising in Ferghana, under a man named Irgash. They had been strongly reinforced when the Bolshevik Government had suppressed the autonomous government at Kokhand in 1918. The directors of this movement had at times considerable success and large areas in Ferghana were under their control. But like many similar movements there was rivalry among the leaders who, one after another, fell. Irgash, the leader at the time I was in Turkestan, was killed in 1920. He was succeeded by Madamin Beg, who was treacherously murdered, when a guest at a meal, by his host. At the time of our arrival Irgash was in command of about sixteen thousand men, among whom were White Russians and, it was rumoured, some Turkish officers. This movement was later taken on by various men in succession and developed into the *Basmachi* movement which survived up to the present war in a latent form.

These leaders were always described as 'robbers' or 'ex-convicts', but I often thought of the passage about rebellion in 'Lalla Rookh':

> Rebellion! foul, dishonouring word,
> Whose wrongful blight so oft has stain'd
> The holiest cause that tongue or sword
> Of mortal ever lost or gain'd.

How many a spirit, born to bless,
Hath sunk beneath that withering name,
Whom but a day's, an hour's success
Had wafted to eternal fame!

Then there was the Askhabad Front, on the railway line to
the Caspian, where they had a much larger force engaged with
their enemies who had the support of British and Indian troops.
This was the most important from every point of view, for
besides giving communication with Moscow it led to Baku, and
the industrial life of Turkestan depended on the Baku oil.

In addition their position in Tashkent itself was most in-
secure. There was a large Mohammedan town of about two
hundred thousand inhabitants who hated the anti-religious
activities of the Bolsheviks. They would have preferred to get
all Russians out to the country. They were quiescent but, even
though unarmed, always a danger.

Had these 'Fronts' acted together I think Bolshevism would
have been crushed in Turkestan. It was almost impossible to
co-ordinate these movements from inside Turkestan owing to
the difficulties of communication, and the extreme watchful-
ness and severity of the Bolshevik authorities. Though these
difficulties seemed insuperable I always thought that the co-
ordination of these different 'Fronts' could have been arranged
for outside the country. I could not help feeling that there was
something unfair in the way the Bolsheviks acted! In our
country or Dominions, and especially in India, where a man is
suspected of action against the State he is given a long trial
with every chance of wriggling out, and even if found guilty he
is lightly dealt with. This seems to be wrong and too idealistic
in a country where such movements are rife and dangerous, and
are a cause of risk to the law-abiding and peace-loving citizens
who form the bulk of the population. The Bolshevik method
goes to the other extreme. For instance there is a suspicion
that the staff at the wireless station is unreliable. What is the
procedure? Not a long trial with its attendant publicity. No!

Shoot the whole lot at once, and get a fresh lot in. This made it very difficult for those who wished for a change in the regime!

The same with the employment of *agents provocateur*. These were so extensively used that no one trusted anyone else. One has only to return to a free country like ours to realize the immense benefits we live under in freedom from these ever present anxieties which seem to be accepted as a natural state of affairs both in Soviet and totalitarian countries. There is one story of the success of a *provocateur* in the Tashkent wireless station which I believe is true, but owing to the secret methods employed no confirmation was ever possible of such incidents. A girl worker was asked by the *provocateur* to obtain copies of messages for a 'counter-revolutionary' agent; this she did. Later a code book was deliberately left where she could find it; she took it and gave it to the *provocateur*. She was never heard of again.

Adjoining the large native city of Tashkent was a European town of fifty thousand Russians. The majority of these were at heart against the Bolsheviks. They were, however, unarmed and were cowed by the severity of the Bolshevik rule.

Among them was an underground organization. It was difficult to gauge the strength of this owing to the extreme secrecy necessary. The head of the organization knew personally only five others who formed a sort of staff. Each of these six men had enrolled six more and each of these six more and so on *ad infinitum*. The point of this was that a traitor could only give away his own group, i.e. his six companions, and the man who enrolled him, and, of course, any he had enlisted himself. This organization by its very nature lacked cohesion, and it was difficult to say how many people were in it, but it was believed to amount to about three thousand. They were, in fact, so cautious and secret that at the critical moment they failed to function. They were said to be in touch with Irgash, but I could not make out the relationship between them. It seemed to be improbable that Irgash with a strength five times that claimed by the Russian organization in Tashkent would, if successful in turning out the Bolsheviks, put himself meekly under another Russian Government. The White Russians seem everywhere to have been complacently optimistic in this matter. Similarly, when Field-Marshal Mannerheim freed Finland from the Bolsheviks the White Russians expected that the Finns would willingly go back to the pre-war state of affairs.

Had all the different 'Fronts' moved at the same time, say in conjunction with Kolchak's final advance on Tula (south of Moscow), there is in my mind no doubt that Bolshevism would have been crushed in Turkestan. But these forces never acted together; difficulties of communication and lack of unison were the causes. When our troops appeared on the Askhabad Front the people of Tashkent sat down and said: 'Thank God the British are coming to get us out of this mess.'

The Russian counter-revolutionaries considered the state of affairs so fantastic that it could not last. I well remember comparison being made with the Paris Commune which lasted seventy days and the surprise that the Russian Communists had lasted longer.

On the Askhabad Front the Bolshevik troops were no match for our trained and disciplined men. They were soundly defeated every time they met and were terrified of them. Had this small force pushed on resolutely, and been used with determination and energy, there is no doubt in my opinion that they could easily have reached Tashkent and would have been supported by the populace both in the capital and along the route. Had Kolchak at the critical moment, when he was on the point of success, received reinforcements, supplies and encouragement from Turkestan up the railway on his left flank, instead of having the anxiety of enemies there, who can say how different the history of the world would have been?

The Turkestan Red Army at this time consisted of about sixteen thousand men distributed as follows: on the Askhabad Front nine thousand, on the Orenburg Front three thousand; in Tashkent, ready to resist any threat from Irgash and to keep order at the centre, three thousand; in Semirechia, where the Cossacks were in rebellion, one thousand.

The equipment of the Red Army was in a very bad way. They had little ammunition for their guns and what they had was bad. Their rifles were worn out. They were short of oil and coal. Any oil fuel that could be obtained was used on the railways on the Askhabad Front in Transcaspia, where fuel difficulties were very great. On the Aktobinsk Front the engines were adapted to burn fish which were caught in the Aral Sea and dried for this purpose. Troops spent the winter in railway carriages heated in this way. A good supply of fuel for the railways was furnished by saxaul (*Haloxylon ammodendron*), a bush that grew almost universally in the steppe. Parties of so-called counter-revolutionaries, speculators, or merely *bourjoui*, were sent up the line to cut this.

About half the Red Army were Austrian prisoners of war — mostly Magyars. These men really wanted to get back home, though propaganda had turned a few into enthusiastic Communists. There was, however, one famous purely Russian corps, the Jhlobinski Regiment, commanded by a Jew called Rubenstein. This was formed of released convicts and the scum of the Russian towns. They were a terror wherever they passed. They went through Tashkent when we were there. Tsirul, the head of the militia, himself thought it wise to hide, and our Russian friends also prepared a hiding place for us.

The Government was largely Jewish and this led to discontent, especially in the army. The soldiers said: 'Here in the army we have Russians, Magyars, Germans, Sarts, Kirghiz and Armenians, but no Jews. The Jews are living on the fat of the land in Tashkent, while we all come out and fight for the revolution.' This was not strictly true. There were Jewish soldiers and the higher command was Jewish, but the Jew was certainly scarce in the lower ranks of the front line.

In October 1919 Appin, one of the Bolsheviks sent from Moscow to set the Government on true Soviet lines, issued a proclamation declaring a state of war in Turkestan and calling on all ex-officers of the Tsarist army to report themselves. Any who failed to do so by a certain date were to be treated as deserters. These were required as instructors, but, to prevent any unauthorized or undesirable conduct, they were only used in a school of instructors at Tashkent, so that they had contact solely with what were considered reliable and incorruptible Communists. Attached to each unit of the Red Army was a political komissar with a small staff. These people did not interfere in tactics or military training, but dealt with the supply of suitable news, songs, theatres, and other forms of propaganda. They also dealt with discipline, watched suspects and many such general questions.

Apart from unexpected and casual dangers, such as the arrival of the Jhlobinski Regiment, there seemed every prospect that we might all be arrested by the Government. Once a telephone message came to the house where we were dining to say 'Those two engineers will be taken on by the firm from to-day'. Such messages had to be searched for their hidden meaning which was liable to be misunderstood. This one meant that Blacker and I were to be arrested, but we took no action and nothing came of it.

One day a Tibetan doctor called at our hotel. I always regret that I was out at the time and so missed a most interesting interview. His name was Badmaiev (a Russsian form of the Tibetan word *padma*, a lotus, which comes into the invocation *Om Mane Padme Hum*), and he had a lucrative practice in St. Petersburg. This Badmaiev came to some prominence when Dorjiev led the mission from the Dalai Lama to the Tsar of Russia in 1901, which was the fundamental cause of our quarrel with Tibet and laid the foundation of our policy towards that country. He had been a friend of Rasputin and is mentioned in various accounts of that sinister individual. Badmaiev treated people with herbs from Lhasa. I knew one Russian who had consulted him. He told me that Badmaiev's waiting-room was crowded with all the *élite* of the capital; when his turn came to have an obstinate skin disease treated Badmaiev examined the place with a lens, chose some herbs out of a partitioned drawer, told my friend to mix this with vaseline and apply it, and pocketed his fee. My friend did as he was told, but the magic herbs produced no cure! Later when I was in Lhasa I made inquiries about Badmaiev, but no one had heard of him there.

Another visitor was an Afghan doctor whose name or alias was Ibrahim. Blacker saw him and we came to the conclusion that he was one of the many Bolshevik agents who came to us in various guises. It turned out that we were wrong and the poor man was arrested by the Bolsheviks, who suspected him of untold villainies because he had had the temerity to visit us. He was released from gaol by the White Guards during the 'January Events', which we will come to in due course.

A Turk calling himself Suleman also called on us. His story was that he had held an appointment in the Turkish Embassy in Teheran, but had been dismissed for being too friendly with our legation. I managed to find out by telegram from Kashgar that this story was untrue. I never knew who he really was or the object of his visit.

Ten days after our arrival at Tashkent Sir George Macartney joined us. He had been twenty-eight years in Kashgar and had in fact initiated the consulate there under many and grave difficulties and dangers. He was now retiring and wished to return to England. So, before his retirement, it was arranged that he should go to Tashkent to introduce and help the mission with his great and valuable local knowledge and influence. He could then return through Russia or through India, either via Askabad and Meshed or, as he actually did, via Gilgit and Kashmir. Sir George had passed through Tashkent several times before and was well known there. We had several interviews with Damagatsky together. His influence and support proved invaluable to Blacker and me.

One day, Sir George, Blacker and I went to the White House, the residence of the former Governors-General of Turkestan, to see the chief komissar, the head of the Turkestan

Republic, a man named Kolesov. He had been an oiler on the railway until the revolution threw him up to this exalted position. Damagatsky was also present.

Sir George explained the purposes we had in view and also emphasized that we were not spies but had come with definite objects, and that we hoped that our informal contact with the Soviet would prove mutually beneficent.

Kolesov asked us how it was that, in view of our attack on the Soviet Government at Archangel, a mission should have arrived at Tashkent. We replied that we had no information about this and had not been able to communicate with our own Government.

As regards our specific requests which we had already presented to Damagatsky, Kolesov said that he was as anxious as we were that the prisoners of war should not return to their own countries; they were wanted for the Red Army.

As to cotton: that and other commercial matters could be better discussed when the situation in Archangel had been cleared up.

Regarding the disabilities and losses of the British Indian traders, he said that any British subjects in Russia would receive exactly the same treatment as Russian subjects. He added that he had not the power to allow the mission to remain in Turkestan as all relations with foreign governments were conducted through the central government at Moscow.

Kolesov deliberately avoided any reference to the presence of British troops on the Askhabad Front, but after he had left the room, Damagatsky mentioned this, which was perhaps the most important factor of all.

In March 1918 this Kolesov had commanded the Bolshevik force which had attacked Bokhara. After five days' fighting he had been obliged to retire defeated and eventually made peace with the Amir. There was an amusing story about Kolesov which was possibly true. He had been sent twenty-two million roubles from Moscow for the armies fighting in Turkestan and was asked to account for it. He said he had not kept strict accounts but had spent five millions on the Orenburg Front, the rest on the Askhabad Front, and had a little left — the small change which he took out of his pocket.

As his journey home through Russia was impossible, it had been arranged that Sir George should return a few days after our interview with Kolesov, but at the last moment the necessary permits were withheld and it appeared possible that we might all be forcibly detained.

All this time the Press was very bitter against the Allies for the help given to the enemies of the Bolsheviks; more especially was this directed against Great Britain, as in addition to the troops at Archangel we also had troops much nearer home, in Turkestan itself. Violent speeches against the bourgeoisie were daily reported in the papers. 'Red Terror' and wholesale executions were advocated in revenge for the attempt on Lenin's life. Every day the papers contained bulletins of the temperature, pulse and respiration of 'Comrade Lenin'.

It was becoming clear that the Bolsheviks had no intention of helping us to defeat the Germans in the Great War and it was becoming necessary to see what could be done with other Russians who claimed to be ready to step into their shoes.

One night after curfew hour a knock came at my door. This I knew must be the police or someone in authority. A man entered alone. He told me his name was Manditch; he was a Serb. He said he had come on behalf of the police to ask if he could be of any service to me. I said to myself, 'Here is a most obvious *agent provocateur*. I must be careful how I deal with him'. This man was later of immense service to me and without his help it is probable that these lines would never have been written. The following is his story told me in detail later on. He came from Serajevo and had been a friend of Princip and of those who killed the Archduke in July 1914 — the action which started the first world war. Manditch had been a student at Vienna University and had been mobilized in the Austrian infantry at the outbreak of war. He held the rank of lieutenant.

His sympathies were entirely anti-Austrian, anti-German, and pro-Slav, so he took an opportunity during the fighting to desert with thirty-six other Serbs. The lines were at that place four or five miles apart, and he and his companions just walked off in the direction of the enemy until they met a Russian patrol to whom they surrendered. Manditch had at first been kept in a prisoners' camp and later had been appointed to a high position among the prisoners in this camp. The position of senior Austrian military officers having to apply to this young and truculent lieutenant cannot have been pleasant, and I gathered that Manditch had not made it easier for them. The interests of German prisoners of war were in the charge of a Swedish Commission who travelled about the country to the different *lagers*, and for a time Manditch was attached to them on behalf of the Russian intelligence service. When the revolution occurred he readily transferred his services to the new rulers of the country, and now he was prepared to help me in the same way. During a friendly talk I told him that I was the head of an accredited mission and had no intention of doing anything against the Turkestan Government.

CHAPTER V

ALONE

ABOUT this time one rather unpleasant incident occurred which might have led to serious consequences. Mrs. Stephanovitch, who had come with us from Kashgar, wanted to return, and had been refused permission. The Bolsheviks wished to arrest her husband who had returned to Kashgar from Andijan, and had an idea of using her as a decoy. The Armenian assistant in the bank at Kashgar had written to the Soviet authorities in Tashkent denouncing certain Russians in Kasghar as counter-revolutionaries, among them, not incorrectly, her husband. Mrs. Stephanovitch decided to try to slip away from Tashkent without permission. Though I had frequently asked Damagatsky for permission to send messages out of the country, I had been given no opportunity to do so. I therefore decided to send a short message out by her. The message was on a tiny piece of paper. I had given it to her, but I did not know where she had concealed it.

The railways were by this time completely disorganized. Officials travelling were given passenger coaches, as indeed in our own case when we travelled to Tashkent from Andijan, but the public, when allowed to travel, got in or on to goods wagons or anywhere they could. No one knew when any train would start, but the rumour was that this one would go on a certain evening, and I went to the station with Mrs. Stephanovitch at about three that afternoon. We found the train and she and her Sart servant got into a corner of a goods wagon and settled down. She then came out and walked about the platform with me and then we sat down. Suddenly two men came up and asked us to follow them. We were taken to a guard-room full of soldiers, with racks of rifles round the walls. They asked who we were. We told them. As soon as they heard I was 'Angliskiya Missiya' (English Mission) they said I could go but they would detain Mrs. Stephanovitch. I could not of course leave her and remained to see what I could do. I was terrified lest the message should be found, in which case she would certainly have been shot. She behaved in the most cool and disarming manner. Nothing could have exceeded the admirable way she kept her head, chatted with the guards and laughed the whole incident off. I managed to ask her where the small piece of paper had been concealed. She told me that it was in her servant's old cotton quilt. The careful search of her belongings was done by one of the two men who had arrested us, a Jew named Rakmelivitch, who afterwards came into some prominence. While this was going on I was strolling about the guard-room and, when near the door, the other man who had arrested us went outside and beckoned to me. I went out to him and he said to me in Persian: 'Do you speak Persian.'

'I do a little.'

'Do you know a Serbian named Manditch.'

'No,' I replied.

'I am Gegoloshweli,' he said, 'and I know that you have met Manditch.'

This Gegoloshweli was head of the police and had sent Manditch to see me. I was suspicious of him and feared a trap. It was essential to avoid doing anything which might give the Bolshevik Government an excuse to arrest us. I then replied, 'Yes, a man named Manditch did come to see me, I had forgotten his name.'

'I wish to help you,' he said.

'Then get this useless search of the lady's belongings over as soon as possible and let us get away.'

'I will do my best, but the man who is conducting the search, Rakmelivitch, is a most brutal man and one of Pashko's friends. I can do little with him.'

This Pashko was a sailor whom I knew well by sight. He had been one of the leaders of the mutiny of the Black Sea Fleet at Odessà when the sailors tortured their officers and threw them into the sea. He was one of the most bitter and cruel of the komissars. The worst that could be said of a man was that he was Pashko's friend.

I was watching the search from the doorway and I saw Rakmelivitch feeling all through the servant's clothes, especially the padding round the shoulders. The servant's new quilt was subject to the most minute search short of cutting it open. I then saw him pick up the old and tattered quilt which I knew contained the message. He looked at it in a most perfunctory way, shook it, turned it round, and shook it again, and from where I was standing I actually saw the piece of paper sticking out of a rent. He did not see it and threw the quilt on the ground. Imagine my relief.

Mrs. Stephanovitch was wearing a scarf over her head and carrying a straw hat in her hand. Curiously enough the police never even looked at this hat, and it was fortunate for her that they did not. The Soviet of Syzran, a town on the Volga, had issued a proclamation nationalizing women. All the best and most beautiful women, the proclamation stated, belonged to the bourgeoisie, while the peasants and workers had to put up with the second best. Therefore all women were to be public property. This was too much for Lenin and the Bolsheviks at the centre, and the order was withdrawn and possession of even a copy was forbidden. It would have been dangerous propaganda against the Bolsheviks, especially abroad. Mrs. Stephanovitch had a copy of the order in her hat. The mere possession of this might have led to her being shot. While this was going on Sir George and Major Blacker came in. They had also come to see Mrs. Stephanovitch off by the train. After the search had proved fruitless Mrs. Stephanovitch was released and we all drove back to our quarters. I was more than relieved and determined never to risk getting women into trouble in such a way again.

Gegoloshweli afterwards told me that one of the police agents on duty at the station had reported that two people sitting on the platform were talking in a foreign language. These were

Mrs. Stephanovitch and myself. Rakmelivitch had at once ordered our arrest.

The Cossacks under Dutov were keeping the railway line cut north of Tashkent. After considerable argument Sir George Macartney had been given permission by the Bolsheviks to go by rail as far as possible and then to walk into Dutov's lines if he could. The risks, however, were very great, mostly, I think, from the undisciplined Red Army who would have been quite capable of removing him from the train and shooting him. He consequently decided to give up this project and to return to England through India. After considerable difficulty he obtained permission to return to Andijan *en route* to Chinese Turkestan. Major Blacker, who had not been in good health, accompanied him. It had been difficult to arrange this but the mission, consisting of Khan Sahib Iftekhar Admad, our servants and I myself, remained behind. Mrs. Stephanovitch also went. A spy travelled on the train with them, a man I afterwards knew. Gegoloshweli later told me he had to send one but had sent a man who would not annoy them!

After their departure on September 14th, just a month after our arrival, I was left very much on my own, but had a tower of strength in the presence of Mr. Tredwell, the United States Consul-General. We saw a great deal of each other, had most of our meals together in the hotel, and had many joint interviews with Damagatsky to press the interests of the Allies in the matters mentioned above.

Shortly after the departure of Sir George Macartney and Major Blacker, I left the Hotel Regina and obtained a *mandat* for half a single-storied house, No. 44 Moskovskaya. This belonged to a rich Jewish merchant named Gelodo who had disappeared during the revolution in some other part of Russia. His wife spoke good English. I had my own front door but shared the garden with the other inmates.

There was a Natural History Museum in Tashkent and one day I went with a few butterflies I had collected on the journey between Kashgar and Andijan. I found an Austrian prisoner of war in charge and asked him if he would allow me to compare my insects with the museum collection in order that I might get their correct names. He regretted that the Tashkent Museum had not a single specimen of a butterfly from Turkestan, but they had some fine things from South America! He agreed that this was absurd but, of course, he had only been a very short time at the museum. Later I went again and was shown the nucleus of the local collection on setting boards. My request had subsequent results, for the schools next summer were sent out on excursions and given butterfly nets wherewith to enrich the national collection.

In Tashkent was a world-famous ornithologist named Zarudni with whom I made friends. He had a valuable collection of twenty-eight thousand skins of Central Asian and Persian birds, and a library of the best ornithological books in English and other languages. He died in March 1919, and I made such efforts as were possible, from the position in which I was at the time, to buy these collections for the British Museum, but they were 'nationalized' and removed to the Tashkent Museum before he was buried. His widow was given a job. Her duty was to take sticks and umbrellas from visitors to the museum.

Tashkent was still at this time comparatively gay. The country was, of course, completely cut off from the world. In such matters as cinemas we were reduced to three or four films which were moved round from one theatre to another, and were freely interspersed with pictures of Lenin, Trotsky and other prominent Bolsheviks. Films I saw several times were 'The Prisoner of Zenda' and 'Sherlock Holmes' (Holmes spelt Xolmes as there is no H in Russian). There was quite a good opera company, largely amateurs, which gave us *Rigoletto*, *Eugeni Onyegin* and other operas.

The whole of this time we were watched by spies; Tredwell and I were each honoured with the company of three of these gentlemen. They took rooms opposite the houses we were occupying and spent many hours looking out of the windows in a bored way. They followed us to the theatre in the evening. Once we protested to Damagatsky that our friends were shy of coming out with us on this account and he promised to see that they were less obtrusive.

I had left some of my baggage and my servants at Osh. We had half expected to be sent back, perhaps even from Andijan, and had not thought it wise to be embarrassed with too much. I sent to bring some essentials of this up and, on its arrival at Tashkent, the police insisted on searching this baggage. I protested on principle and Damagatsky promised to arrange that it should be delivered without interference. However, he had no power to do this and after a fortnight I allowed the search under protest, while Tredwell took photos of the operation much to the discomfiture of the police. The remainder of my things, mostly camp kit, was eventually lost when the man with whom I had left them at Osh was shot as a counter-revolutionary.

The authorities were always trying to trap us with *agents provocateur.* These men were all turned away with the information that we were not there to engage in any activities against the Government. Once a man rushed into Tredwell's room in a state of great excitement. He had been sent with a message to Tredwell from the British General at Askhabad. He had had the most fearsome adventures and had been arrested three times and had been obliged to swallow the message. Tredwell expressed his astonishment that a letter from a British General should be sent to him in this way. Afterwards he recognized the supposed messenger as one of the clerks working in the Foreign Office.

Our visitors were not all of this type. The Greek consul called. An Austrian prisoner named Zipser, who was a manufacturer of explosives in Manchester and who had an English wife, asked me if I could have him sent to India. Internment there till the end of the war would be better than life in Turkestan. He said he had refused to make explosives for the Turkestan Government, alleging the lack of materials and machinery. His visit was reported and he was arrested and asked what he had said to me. Rakmelivitch had threatened to shoot him and had even fired a revolver past his head.

Our news of the war was derived from the several papers published in Tashkent: *Nasha Gazette* (Our Gazette), *Isvestia*, *Krasni Front* (Red Front), *Turkestanski Komunist*, and *Sovietski Turkestan*. This news was usually relegated to a small paragraph in an obscure corner and headed 'imperialists' War'. Later the Peace Conference was referred to as the 'Black Paris International'. The important events were the progress of revolutionary movements in other countries and speeches of various komissars. A favourite word with the journalist, was 'nakanune' (eve). It was always the 'eve' of some event advantageous to them. The eve of the downfall of Imperialism or the eve of the end of exploitation by the world's bourgeoisie, or more simply of World Revolution, or of Victory of the Red Army, etc. One headline ran: 'Eve of General Strike in all Entente Countries to prevent interference in Russian affairs.' Owing to shortage of paper these newspapers were brought out on brown paper on which the print was almost illegible and later, very suitably, on red paper. The writers of the leading articles — at least of those which I read, on the iniquities of my country — were ignorant men with little knowledge of history or geography. The writer would take a few facts from an out-of-date book of reference, cut out what did not suit his argument, distort the rest so that it did, and add a few rhetorical expressions and slogans.

In other ways also these papers were not run on precisely the lines we are accustomed to. One day the *Isvestia* failed to appear. The next day the following notice appeared at the head of the paper: 'No. 92 of the *Isvestia* of the Turtsik (Turkestan Central Executive Committee) of May 7th, 1919, did not appear solely because Comrade Fedovev, the responsible head of the Tashkent Printing Press, did not consider himself obliged at the proper time, to take the trouble to arrange the delivery of kerosene at Press No. 2. This, in spite of the fact that requisition No. 1199 was given to him on May 3rd by Comrade Fink in charge of the Technical Department of the Press.' News of the fighting with our troops in Transcaspia also came from the local press. It was all very depressing reading — so much so, in fact, that had I believed half of it, I should probably have given up and turned Bolshevik myself! Continual Bolshevik victories were reported, while the Indian troops ran away or deserted at each contact with the wonderful Red Army. Here is a translation of one of these effusions: 'Telegram from the Askhabad Front, September 29th. To-day Popof reported that Squadron-Commander Butchenko got into the enemy's stronghold and was surrounded there by Indian cavalrymen; he ran them through with lances and took an Indian officer prisoner, but afterwards they killed him, relieving him of his papers and Nikolai money. Butchenko returned with his party, having suffered no losses.' I hoped that some day it might have been possible to settle with Comrade Butchenko for this callous murder, but probably the whole incident was fictitious.

One morning at daybreak I was awakened by the excited calls of newspaper boys in the streets. This was so unusual an event that I bought a copy of their paper. This was called *Anarchist*. It had been brought out secretly and was full of abuse of the komissars, giving awkward details of their former activities. It was immediately repressed and possession of a copy was severely punished. Needless to say the paper which had optimistically been numbered 'one' never got beyond this first copy. Occasionally Armenian newspapers printed at Baku were smuggled through the Askhabad Front. These gave more unbiased news of the war. Damagatsky inquired whether it would be possible to get some reliable foreign newspapers. I told him that all my post including daily papers was lying in Kashgar. At his suggestion I telegraphed for them to be sent. My private letters were also sent and these were not delivered to me but kept back by the authorities. I managed to get some at least of these a few months later.

One night after curfew I had another visit from Manditch; again he asked whether he could help me. By this time I felt that I could trust him a little. I told him again that I had not come to act against the Government, but that there were two matters which could hardly be considered in this light in which he might be of use to me. First, I realized that at any moment Tredwell and I might be arrested. It would be quite contrary to all diplomatic usage, but still it might be done. Should this happen, could he arrange that we should not be sent to prison. The prisons were dirty and conditions there were very unpleasant and life uncertain. Manditch agreed with me about the conditions of the prisons and said that he thought this could be done. My second request was perhaps more dangerous if he were really a *provocateur*. It was that I should be given a little notice before arrest. This he promised to do. He then said that Gegoloshweli, the chief of police, would like a private interview with me. This could be arranged as follows: Three spies had been ordered to shadow me. There were no taxis in the town as all motor vehicles had been taken by the Soviet officials; but a few horse cabs still plied. One of my spies had a bicycle, and if ever I got into a cab he had orders to follow me. Gegoloshweli would arrange that on a special afternoon, to be arranged beforehand, the bicycle spy should be given other duty. The other men had orders that, in the absence of the cyclist, if I took a cab, they were to take another and do their best to follow me. Manditch therefore told me to take a cab, but not one off a rank; I was to wait till I found one elsewhere and alone, so that the spy could not get another and follow me. I was to drive anywhere as fast as possible and then, having thus shaken off my two dismounted spies, I could walk back to the police headquarters. This I did several times. I was even shown the spy reports on myself and made useful corrections. I found that they reported each house I visited and the length of time I stayed there. Apparently sometimes they lost me, in which case they invented a programme for me, sometimes quite an attractive, though scarcely respectable one!

About September 1918 the Soviet Government wished to send a mission to Meshed in North-East Persia, the head-quarters of our troops under General Malleson, and asked me for a letter of introduction. Considering the way I was being treated I thought this rather an extraordinary request. I could not, however, neglect such an opportunity of sending out a message, which unknown to themselves, the mission carried and delivered. This mission was headed by a man named Babushkin. One member was an ex-officer called Kalashnikov who was Damagatsky's assistant at the Foreign Office.

Once when I was at the Foreign Office I was speaking to Kalashnikov alone. He told me that the present regime was going far beyond anything he had contemplated and he wished to leave the country and was trying to get posted to the mission to Meshed for this purpose. I asked him why he wrote and signed such violent articles in the local newspapers. He said he was forced to do this, but the articles did not represent his true opinions and, in any case, were much milder than those that other journalists were writing. Sveshnikov and Galsch were much worse. It was the presence of many people of this type, ready to do anything for an easier life, which led to the success of the Russian revolution. I gave Kalashnikov a separate private letter to the British authorities in Meshed who did not arrest him but sent him off to join the Menshevik Force who were fighting against the Bolsheviks on the Trans-caspian railway. Presumably they had also seen his signed articles and at once shot him as a revolutionary.

Babushkin and his assistant, Afanasiev, were arrested and kept as hostages for the safety of Mr. Tredwell, myself and the other members of the mission.

Life in this Communist paradise was in many ways unpleasant. It was not nice to see people, both workmen and men of other classes, even though you had no idea who they were, being arrested and led off to what you knew was almost certain execution.

The German practice of persecuting Jews by making women

of the upper classes scrub the streets in public was not exactly original. The Bolsheviks arrested numbers of the upper classes, many of whom were actually working for the Government in clerical posts, and made them carry bricks in a place where clearing and building operations were in progress, while the proletariat looked on and jeered. Later, those over fifty-five years old were exempted. It was said that the more humane soldiers of the Red Army, out of pity for these old men, insisted on this in face of the opposition of the fanatical komissars.

CHAPTER VI

ARRESTED

I HAD been continually pressing Damagatsky to allow me to communicate with Kashgar and at last I was told I could have one courier sent from Kashgar on condition that no cipher messages were enclosed. I telegraphed to Etherton in Kashgar and on October 13th a sealed bag arrived intact, much to my surprise. The courier was an ex-soldier from the 11th Bengal Lancers. He had had some adventures on the way. In spite of his papers, showing him to be a British courier, he had been arrested in Kokhand and had spent two days in gaol there. He was detained for a day in the guard-room on Chernyayevo station but he had again been allowed to proceed. Arriving at Tashkent at daybreak, he had walked out of the station without anyone questioning him. I am certain that it was the intention of the authorities to inspect this bag before delivering it to me, but the police were slack and lazy at that early hour.

About this time a wireless message addressed to me was received ordering me to return to India. The authorities never told me of this and I could not let them know that I knew of it. This would have got my informants into trouble. 'Trouble' in Tashkent at this time meant, not the firing squad, but having your brains blown out with a pistol.

It was curious and even awkward to know secretly of matters which the Bolsheviks were trying to keep from me. Sir George Macartney had been allowed to send one short message in code by wireless from Tashkent; this had been received in India, but could not be deciphered. The Indian Government sent a wireless message to me asking me to repeat the message in another code. I knew of this and asked Damagatsky whether any reply had been received to Sir George's message from India. I expected him to tell me of the reply. Damagatsky told me that no reply had been received and I could not tell him that I knew he was lying, that I had seen the reply and had even brought the answer to it ready in my pocket. This would have given trouble to my sources of information, so my reply to the telegram from India could not therefore be sent.

After the receipt of these letters from Kashgar I went to Damagatsky and thanked him for facilitating the arrival of my courier, and said that I had received orders to return; he could hardly suppress his astonishment. The orders for my return had actually not come in the courier's bag but in the telegram of which I knew, but which Damagatsky was withholding from me. He said he would see about it, and the next day, October 14th, I presented an official request for my papers. This was never answered.

Tredwell had engaged a Cossack colonel as his interpreter. His position was difficult and dangerous, but no one of this kind could afford to let an opportunity slip of earning a living. He was paid to help Tredwell by translating the Russian Press and in other ways, but was in no way working against the Bolshevik Government. He told Tredwell that he must give up the work, and it transpired that he had been told by friends that all Allied officers and their staffs were to be arrested 'as had been done in other parts of Russia'. The orders, as we subsequently learned, were to 'destroy' them if they could not be safely kept. The telegram conveying this order was signed 'Karakhan'. Karakhan was the assistant komissar for Foreign Affairs under Chicherin in Moscow. He was an Armenian from Tiflis and was one of the early revolutionaries, but no one in Turkestan had ever heard of him! He had been three times imprisoned by the Tsar's Government for his revolutionary activities. He was at one time Ambassador to China and was eventually himself destroyed in a 'Purge' in December 1937. He was a violent enemy of ours and had ordered the Soviet Minister to Kabul to arrange a supply of arms to the tribes on the North-West Frontier of India who were as usual giving us trouble. The Turkestan Government telegraphed to Moscow for confirmation and further details of the orders for our arrest. I was certain to hear of the reply to this, and also felt sure that I would get a warning through Manditch if we were to be arrested.

Late on the night of October 14th Manditch visited me and told me that Tredwell, Edwards, Iftekar Ahmad, my clerk, and I were all to be arrested at six o'clock in the evening of the next day. I knew that Tredwell was dining with people a few doors away, with a special permit from Tsirul to be out late. I took a chance of infringing the curfew order and ran out and told him.

We knew that the Turkestan Government had not, so far, received a reply to the telegram they had sent to Moscow about us, and we were rather puzzled at this approaching arrest, but decided to let events take their course. In any case, an arrest of our persons would put us in the right in any subsequent steps we might take.

The next day I told Edwards; I destroyed certain papers, put my private correspondence into a safe place, leaving a few letters from tradesmen to be found. Had there been no letters at all suspicions might have been roused and further more intense searches made. I concealed an Austrian uniform which I had obtained in case it should prove necessary to disguise myself. I also wrote a letter to Sir Hamilton Grant, who was Foreign Secretary in Delhi, which was intended to hoodwink my captors. In this I wrote that I was finding it impossible to come to any understanding with the authorities; they were suspicious of me and pestered me with spies and might even be so stupid as to arrest me in defiance of diplomatic procedure; unless I could persuade the Government to treat me in a more reasonable and friendly way I could see no object in remaining and would take steps to leave. If allowance were made for their failings they were really not so bad. I added a few true words on the situation, which included the statement that one of their chief troubles was Irgash, who was leading a rebellion of about sixteen thousand Mohammedans in Ferghana, 'assisted and financed by Turks and Germans'. It must be remembered that the war was still going on and it seemed to me that it would do no harm to increase the tension between our enemies and the Soviet Government. This sentence in my letter was to make all the difference to me and probably even saved my life.

About six o'clock in the evening of October 15th, the time I expected to be arrested, I went over to see Edwards. Thinking Mrs. Edwards might be left at liberty, I wished to see that she thoroughly understood a secret method of communication which might be of use to us.

While there the front door bell rang, and in walked my old acquaintance, Gegoloshweli, his assistant and some soldiers and members of the *Sledstvennaya* commission. They, like their successors, the Cheka, had power quite independent of the Government. They took me back to my own quarters. I expressed surprise at this outrage, and demanded to know under whose orders they were acting. 'Under orders of the *Sledstvennaya* commission,' they replied.

'Do Kolesov and Damagatsky know of this and do they approve?'

'Yes, they do.'

Later I asked Damagatsky about this and he denied it, saying that the commission had power to do what they liked and that neither he nor any member of the Government knew. It will be realized that I knew myself, and that Gegoloshweli knew that I knew, but, of course no glance of recognition passed between us. I am convinced that the commission had not informed the Government. This is clear from their actions in regard to Tredwell. My captors told me that Tredwell had been arrested and showed me a letter of protest that he had given them at the time. I said that I would also give them a written protest to be handed at once to the Government. I said that I knew that they were only subordinates carrying out an unpleasant duty of which they must disapprove and which was bound to lead to serious consequences, and that I bore them no personal grudge. Would they each have a glass of wine and a cigar? Gegoloshweli, who knew that this was a play, could hardly keep solemn. He knew that I was fully aware that these were no subordinates but the heads of the *Sledstvennaya* commission itself in full force! They, on their part, rather sheepishly accepted my hospitality.

In the meantime the soldiers searched carefully through all my things and took every scrap of written paper. I asked them to leave me a notebook in which I had written Russian words and notes on grammar, but this was refused. They also took my revolver (but I had another one). They left everything else behind. They left an armed soldier in the small lobby who watched me unceasingly as I sat in my room. I tried to make friends with him and offered him tea and cigarettes and promised not to run away in the night, and assured him he might sleep without anxiety. He was a surly beast. He told me that he had been wounded in the imperialists' war and, pointing to his rifle, told me I had better not be up to any tricks. Later at night he was joined by another who remained in my bedroom all night. This second was a more pleasant youth of seventeen who had been a waiter in the Regina restaurant. The next morning he was alone on guard while my surly friend went, I suppose, for his breakfast. He fell asleep and I took the opportunity to go for a stroll in the small garden and could easily have left the house. He woke up in some alarm and called me back; I told him that I wished to buy some apples at the fruit kiosk at the street corner. He said that I could not do so. I insisted, opened the door and went out into the street, he following with his rifle and protesting. I walked the necessary fifty yards, bought my apples and gave him some and we returned.

The whole town knew of these arrests, and many people believed that Tredwell, the others and I myself had been shot. I had a visit from two girls who lived with Madame Ugrahelidze at the school who were anxious to know my true situation. My sentry answered the door and threatened them with his rifle and bayonet, and I was not allowed to speak to them. My next visitor was Captain Brun who received the same treatment. A short time later I was sitting at the table in my room, the two sentries on chairs against the wall opposite me. The door into the garden was open but from where they were they could not well see out and I saw my landlady in the garden making mysterious signs. I did not know what she wanted but was ready for anything. The next instant a lady whom I had once met with Tredwell walked briskly into the room from the garden as though she knew nothing of the sentries and held out her hand. I was ready and jumped up and met her and we just managed to shake hands before the two sentries could stop us and drove her out. She did this act very well and I found a small piece of paper in my hand. This was a note from Tredwell to say that he had been arrested the evening before and had at once telephoned to Tsirul who had immediately driven to see Kolesov and Damagatsky and he insisted on Tredwell's release. Tsirul pointed out that he was a properly authorized consul and that this arrest might end in grave trouble and prevent what they wanted more than all, the recognition of the Republic by other countries. In his note to me Tredwell said that Kolesov and Damagatsky had come to him that evening and personally released him and apologized on behalf of the Government. He would leave no stone unturned to get me released.

My next visitor was Gegoloshweli himself who told me that the commission would come at one o'clock to question me.

They arrived punctually in a motor car and two carriages. The chief was a youth called Siderov, and there was also a sulky brute called Lobov who had been the most unpleasant of those who had actually arrested me. Altogether there were six of the commission, all carrying revolvers, while behind each stood an armed soldier. The conversation was partly in Persian with Gegoloshweli; partly in French with one of his assistants and partly in imperfect Russian. This proving unsatisfactory my landlady, Mrs. Gelodo, was later brought in. She told me that she had listened at the keyhole from her half of the house to the whole proceedings, and was very puzzled to know what the language was in which I had been speaking to Gegoloshweli.

I commenced by protesting very strongly at my arrest. I said that when the news of this was received by the House of Commons I would not care to be the people who had ordered it. I had learnt that, in the eyes of the type of man in the employ of the Bolsheviks, the House of Commons was an assembly of riff-raff who were almost Bolsheviks themselves; the name itself lends colour to this idea. The House of Lords, on the other hand, was a kind of counter-revolutionary White Guard; the two coming to some sort of compromise over the Government of the country! They badly wanted the good opinion of the House of Commons.

I insisted on being told the reason for my arrest and demanded permission to report it at once by wireless to India. This was refused. The speaker of the commission then said: 'The charge against you is that you paid two million Nikolai roubles to Irgash who is in rebellion in Ferghana.'

I laughed and said: 'It is foolish for you of all people to make such a stupid charge against me. I did not pay anything to Irgash, but I know who did. In fact, all Tashkent knows that Irgash's agent got the two millions from Germann (the Russian way of spelling and pronouncing Hermann), the German agent at such and such a number of such and such a street at six p.m., on such and such a date.'

I knew the address of Hermann, invented the date and hour and used their own figure of two millions. This detailed statement caused considerable astonishment among them and a good deal of talk. Finally Lobov said:

'That is all nonsense and you have invented it.'

I replied: 'I may have invented it but if so I did not invent it to-day as I have put it in a report to my Government.'

Their spokesman said: 'Have you a copy of that report?'

'No,' I replied, 'I know that the authorities of the Turkestan Republic have very little knowledge of, or consideration for, diplomatic usage. I am always followed by spies, police disturb me at night and search my boxes; every day articles printed against my country and myself appear in the Press and I have been expecting a breach of my diplomatic immunity and an insult of this kind for some time. I keep no copies of anything.'

This caused a snigger of triumph from Lobov. 'You never wrote such a report.'

'Yes, I did, and, although for the reasons I have given you, I have no copy, the report itself is in your hands. The courier whom Mr. Damagatsky promised I might send to Kashgar has so far not received his passport and the actual report is among the papers you stole from me last night, about which act of violence the House of Commons will hear in due course.'

They then sent a soldier out to the cars who brought in my suitcase containing all my papers; these had not been touched since they had been taken the night before.

'Which is the report you refer to?'

I took up a letter in an official envelope with a large red seal (I rather feared I had overdone the seal).

'That is the report I refer to.'

'Open it.'

'I refuse to do so. This is a privileged document written to my Government; you are twelve armed men in my room and I certainly cannot prevent you from breaking that seal, but I would not care to be the man who had done it when the news reaches the House of Commons and they protest to Moscow.'

Gegoloshweli, who knew that I had been warned, guessed that this was some trick and could hardly keep a straight face. The letter was passed round, the seal examined, but no one dared to open it. At last one of the members of the commission said: 'Let us be reasonable! We have made a charge against you. You say this document contains evidence that the charge is untrue. Will you not in your own interests open it?' I was beginning to fear that I had overstressed the danger to anyone who should open the letter and that it would never be opened at all; this would have been a pity after the trouble I had taken to write it especially for these visitors of mine. I replied:

'Of course I will, since you ask so nicely; but I refuse to do so when my house is invaded by twelve armed men who order me to disclose the contents of privileged documents. I must, however, make conditions. You have made a charge against me, and I say that the contents of this letter prove it to be without foundation. Have you any other charges? It is possible this letter may also have reference to them, I do not know.'

'No. We have no other charges.'

'Then I must make this condition. I will only allow you to see the portions of the letter referring to your charge that I paid money to Irgash. Do you agree?'

After some discussion they agreed and I opened the letter. I covered up the portions which did not refer to Irgash, and the man who spoke some French came round and I translated the sentence about Turks and Germans financing Irgash word for word into French. He was satisfied that my translation was correct.

It was at this point that Mrs. Gelodo, who had been listening at the key-hole from her part of the house, was brought in and she translated from English into Russian. They were apparently convinced and opinion veered round in my favour; only Lobov remained sulky, suspicious and discomfited.

While this talk was going on I took another envelope out of the drawer, addressed it and resealed the letter and laid it on the table.

One of the commission then said: 'We are very sorry to trouble you but this is a most important matter. May we take an exact copy of the English of that portion of your letter?'

I agreed, reopened the letter and Mrs. Gelodo copied the important sentence. As soon as this was done I resealed the letter in a fresh envelope.

The commission then said: 'We are sorry to trouble you again. We want to see the whole letter.'

'I certainly cannot allow that. You agreed to my conditions. Of course I must submit to force by twelve armed men, but it will only be the worse for those responsible when the news reaches the House of Commons.'

'Then will you open it once more just to let us see the date?'

'I give you my word that that was written yesterday. I cannot open it again, as at this rate I will use up all my envelopes and I find such things almost unobtainable in Tashkent at present.'

The matter rested there and the letter remained sealed. I then demanded to see my clerk, Khan Sahib Iftekar Ahmad, who had also been arrested. This interview was granted on condition that I spoke to him only in Persian in the presence of one of them. No word of English or Hindustani must pass. I agreed, under protest, and the interview was arranged for five p.m.

They then all went out and carried on a long conversation on the pavement which I watched from my window. They then returned to the front door and called my sentries out and shouted to me, *Voi svobodni* (You are free). I went to the door and asked them about Iftekar Ahmad and Edwards, who had also been arrested, and they said they would also be freed at once.

They had been kept in a special lock-up of the *Sledstvennaya* commission. Here a fellow prisoner told Iftekar that he had been sent to me with a message from Irgash but had been arrested before he could deliver the message. I had warned Iftekar of the possibility of this. He, therefore, replied that I took no interest in Irgash's movements or intentions. I hope this obvious *agent provocateur* took the news back and that his masters were duly impressed.

Another of Iftekar Ahmad's cell-mates was a man who had been caught changing Nikolai (imperial) paper money for Soviet money at a premium to the disadvantage of the latter. This was a thing that everyone including myself was doing.

I afterwards learnt that when the *Sledstvennaya* commission reported the result of my interrogatory to Kolesov, he was very upset and said: 'We have been watching the wrong people all the time and wasted ten thousand roubles on a dancing girl in the National Hotel to watch them.' This girl was in a room opposite Tredwell's when he and I were living in the National Hotel. She was an obvious spy as she sat reading a book with her door open watching his room. She told a friend of his that she had been paid to try to get into touch with him, hated the job and would do him no harm.

The authorities now redoubled their surveillance over Tredwell and myself and we were each of us accommodated with six spies to watch our movements and to make sure that we did not disappear before the expected reply from Moscow.

The next day, October 17th, I went to the Foreign Office and interviewed Damagatsky. I asked him for a reply to my letter presented to him on the 14th, in which I had asked for the necessary documents authorizing my departure for Kashgar. I said that astonishing events had recently prevented my seeing him before about this. He said he had nothing to do with that 'stupidity', but made no apologies as he had done in Tredwell's case. Damagatsky told me that he had not been to his office for four days and had so far done nothing about my demand for my papers. I knew, of course, that he was awaiting a reply to his telegram to Moscow. I saw him again the next day and pressed for a reply of some sort to my letter. He then said he could do nothing in the matter, but I should see Kolesov, the chief komissar. I there and then made him telephone to Kolesov asking for an immediate interview. The latter replied that he could not see me that day, but would see me at the White House the next day, October 19th, at any time between ten and two. (He was still hoping that the expected orders from Moscow would come before he had to meet me.) I went at ten-thirty and met him driving out of the gate in a motor car. He saw me and Miss Houston, who was accompanying me to interpret, and waved us aside, but I stood in the gateway and the chauffeur had to pull up. I said: 'You have given me an appointment and I have come to keep it.' He said he had been unexpectedly called away and would see me at five p.m. I knew that he would give me no permission pending the receipt of further orders from Moscow, and would probably avoid an interview until he had received his instructions from 'the Centre'.

I said: 'My business is very brief and can be settled on the spot. Are you going to give me my papers and allow me to return in accordance with orders received from India or not? I sent an official letter to the foreign komissar a week ago which has not been answered, and the foreign komissar has sent me to you as head of the State.'

'I cannot let you leave. My Government have grave suspicions of you, though personally I have none.' (The komissar always said this kind of thing so that they would escape personal blame if the tables should be turned.) 'I will let you know definitely in three or four days' (i.e. when he had received the answer from Moscow).

'I suppose you know the result of keeping the official representative of another government against his will.'

'I am not satisfied that you have any official position.'

'May I communicate with India by wireless to explain my position?'

'Yes, you may send a message but in clear not in cipher.' With this he drove off. It was obvious that I would be given no permission to go and that, if the reply from Moscow was unfavourable, Tredwell, Edwards, Iftekar Ahmad and I would again be arrested. I had not really expected to be given my papers but I thought it would go far to justify any further action I might take if I had asked for them and been refused. I talked the matter over with Tredwell. The position for him was fairly satisfactory. He had been sent by the United States Embassy in Petrograd as Consul-General in Tashkent and had proper diplomatic documents. The heads of the Turkestan Government had immediately released him and apologized when he had been arrested and he had been recognized as an official person in many ways. The feeling against America was not so bad as against us. It is true that American troops were fighting on the Murman coast but that was a long way from Turkestan. On the other hand our support of the Mensheviks in Transcaspia had prevented the Red Army from 'liquidating' this 'Front' and so clearing the way to Krasnovodsk and Baku with its oil and communication with Russia *via* the Caspian and Astrakhan, whence further military supplies might be obtained. The Press had not been backward in inflaming the army and populace on these lines. Even if I were not executed by the Government there was always the probability of soldiers (drunk or sober) taking the matter into their own hands. It had frequently happened that parties of soldiers had gone into the gaol and shot prisoners apparently at random. I still thought that our troops who were opposing the Bolsheviks in Transcaspia were advancing to Tashkent and thought that I would be less of an embarrassment if free and that I might help them with information. Further, Tredwell and I hoped that we would have more opportunities of assisting our cause — the cause of the Allies in the war — if one of us were free, though in hiding, than if both of us were imprisoned or under surveillance. I therefore made the following arrangements to be carried out at once if the answer from Moscow made it advisable.

I was to change into Austrian uniform and walk out of Tashkent at dusk — of course before the curfew time — and to continue walking ten or fifteen miles that night. I was then to lie up near the road, and a friend of mine, Petrov, was to drive down the road in a cart the next morning and pick me up and drive me on to a meteorological station where I would be safe for a few days and could make arrangement to cross the mountains to Ferghana and China.

CHAPTER VII

I DISAPPEAR

On October 20th I was lunching with Tredwell at his house with the Noyevs when a ring came at the front door. Noyev's young daughter went to the door and was given a small note by an unknown white-haired old lady. It was written in English in red ink and was to say that we were all to be arrested again, and ended with the unpleasant sentence: 'For Bailey the position is especially dangerous and shooting is not out of the question.' This was not a nice dish to be served up at lunch. The message was dated October 18th, i.e. the day before my interview with Kolesov in his car. I am sure that had Kolesov received the message at the time of our interview, he would have ordered my arrest; but such things moved very slowly in the Turkestan Government, and it was usually a couple of days before a message had been decoded and brought up for action. This was the 20th, and events might be expected at any moment.

These were the days of no secret diplomacy, and it was the custom of the Soviet Government to publish correspondence which in other countries would be classed as confidential. The following appeared in *Nasha Gazetta* on November 1st:

WIRELESS FROM MOSCOW

With reference to your telegram concerning the advance of the British troops and the repressive measures you have taken, it is necessary to take the following steps:

(1) Intern all subjects of Allies between ages seventeen and forty-eight, except women and children and workmen, who support the Bolsheviks, also making exceptions for others if political considerations require it.

(2) Stop all payments to British subjects and their allies.

(3) Arrest all official representatives, seize their correspondence and send it to us.

(4) Take strict measures against all those who have intercourse with the British or their allies.

Your second proposition of declaring all Englishmen hostages is not convenient and is sufficiently covered by point number one. There must be no exception for official representatives of the Allies, as their pretended partiality towards the Soviet authorities is a trick well known to us for the purpose of deceiving local authorities.

Consider these instructions as issued by the Central Government and let us know when you have carried them out.

What about Colonel Bailey? Your former considerations are now worthless. He should be arrested immediately.

For the People's Komissar,

(*signed*) KARAKHAN

In spite of the above the *Sovietski Turkestan* a few days later declared that all British subjects were to be held as hostages until the British troops had left Turkestan.

I had been most careful that no one should know my plans. The scheme prepared for my escape was known only to Petrov, who was to drive out and take me on, and to the person who was to help me to change into an Austrian prisoner of war. While continuing our lunch Noyev said to me: 'I do not want to interfere or to pry into your affairs, but it seems to me that your position is critical and I think you should make some arrangements to hide yourself to-day.'

'I have already done so,' I said.

'That is very prudent of you. Perhaps with my knowledge of the situation I can be of assistance.'

I then told him of my plans, but of course did not mention Petrov.

'I think,' he said, 'that you will certainly be caught on the Salarski bridge.' This was a bridge leading over the Salar River at the outskirts of the town. 'There is always a guard there and in the evening they frequently hold up suspicious people for inquiry the next morning. If it were my affair I would strongly advise you to hide in Tashkent itself for ten days or so and let the hot search for you burn itself out; then you will be able to move more safely.'

It turned out that this advice was sound. I did not, of course, know the country and would have been obliged to follow the main road. I afterwards found that at the village of Nikolskoe, four versts (a verst is a little more than a kilometre — say two-thirds of a mile) from Tashkent, was a guard whose duty it was to examine all people passing through the village at night. Even if I had been allowed over the Salarski bridge I should have been held up here.

We discussed the situation with Tredwell and decided that this was the best thing to do. It made no difference to the immediate project of becoming an Austrian. The plan, of course, depended on finding a suitable hiding place in the town at very short notice. Noyev said he could do this. It had to be an inconspicuous household and one with which I had had no connection. All the houses I had ever visited would, of course, be searched. I then left for my own quarters to make final arrangements. I got out my Austrian jacket and kepi and carried them to a certain house where I left them. The house was one of a row in a street and my plan was to enter the house in the usual unsuspicious way, to change with great rapidity, to run through the gardens behind and to come out into the street further down in such a short time that, even if the six spies were sufficiently wide awake, they could not suspect that an Austrian walking out of a house some way down the street was the man they were watching, whom they had *just* seen walk into another house, dressed entirely differently.

In London, and most towns in Great Britain, the small back gardens are separated by substantial stone walls, but in Tashkent there were wooden partitions in which were usually doors. It was arranged that these doors should be open and that a man should wait at a friendly house down the street to let me out.

The essence of this plan was speed. After leaving my uniform at this house I returned home and destroyed certain papers. At the time of my arrest a list of my property had been prepared by the police. I felt that there must be grave risks to anyone found with any of these things, and I thought that they might make a special search for any articles that were missing from this list. However, a risk was taken with a few valuable and useful things, such as my field glasses, telescope, cameras, etc. Long afterwards my telescope was found concealed in a bag of flour and confiscated, but it was not recognized as mine; the man who had my field glasses was shot by the Bolsheviks in the subsequent 'January Events' and I lost them.

Most of my things, for the above reason, were left in the house and I never saw any of them again. My cameras I recovered and they were used a good deal at first, I am afraid, rather nervously, but later, as I got used to my position, with more confidence.

My private letters were burnt, but a copy of a diary was kept by a friend. This was subsequently burnt when his house was about to be searched. As soon as I learnt this I rewrote it as well as possible from memory.

I also told Khan Sahib Iftekar Ahmad to disappear. This was not difficult for him. He spoke Turki and was able to disguise himself as a Sart. On leaving Tashkent and travelling across country he was caught and detained for a short time by Irgash's men, but eventually reached Kashgar safely on December 7th.

I had two servants, Haider, a typical good Punjabi, and Ibrahim, a Turki boy whom I had obtained from Shahzada Abdul Rahim Beg. The latter was nervous and I did not trust him not to give me away if threatened, and so I told him nothing. Haider, on the other hand, I confided in.

I had previously given each of them a considerable sum of money in case of my sudden and unexpected arrest. This was sewn into their clothes. I told Haider that after my disappearance he would be arrested and questioned. He was to say that

I had told him some days previously that we were returning to Kashgar; that later I had been very angry at the delay in our departure and that he supposed I had deserted him and gone off by myself. He was a workman and his only desire was to go back to his home in the Punjab. I told him that if he did this he would not be troubled beyond some threats and questionings. Of course, he did not know where I was. I told him that as far as possible he should stay on in the house and in any case keep in touch with Mrs. Gelodo's house, so that I could find him to give him further orders. I impressed on him the necessity of taking on some work and earning money. If he did not do this the authorities would wonder where he obtained his living expenses and would suspect that he was in touch with me and give him further trouble.

For a time in the summer Haider got employment throwing paraffin-tins full of water from the flowing gutters on to the dusty roads. At another time he sold soda water and lemonade in the streets. My final instructions to him as I left the house were that the next morning he was to come to call me as usual and then to report at once to Mrs. Gelodo that I was not there and that the bed had not been slept in. He was then to allow events to take their normal course.

I put on a pair of Austrian top-boots. My grey trousers I wore outside these and not tucked into the boots as was usually done by the prisoners. My spies were with me but, perhaps owing to my protest to Damagatsky, at a discreet distance and would not notice the boots. I took off my jacket which I left behind in the house and wore a light overcoat and hat. I walked at dusk to the Noyevs where I was given a meal and a small bottle of brandy. While I was here Noyev, who was a lawyer, received a telephone message 'I will take up the case to-morrow'. This meant that arrangements for my hiding place were ready. I then walked to the house where preparations for my change of personality had been made. I rang the bell: it was answered, and I asked in the normal way whether anyone was in; I entered and the street door was closed. Immediately all was hustle. I tore off my overcoat, pulled on the Austrian tunic and kepi which were lying ready on the hall table, tucked the trousers into the boots, wrapped my overcoat round the civilian hat, and taking these with me dashed out into the garden, through the open door into the next garden, and so on. One of the doors had been shut and locked since my friends had opened it. A couple of good kicks breached the pallisade and I ran on. A few houses down I was met by Petrov who had been involved in my first plan of escape. He hurried me through the house and I walked out into the street. The plan had worked well. I had been an incredibly short time doing all this, and as I walked into the street I saw the six spies watching the house from the other side of the road.

It is a curious feeling to walk about in a foreign uniform; I was very conscious of the F.J.I. on my hat. I knew there were some thirty thousand Austrian prisoners about who had been together for four years, and was not sure whether a strange face would be noticed, and, though I met a few in the street, I never looked at them.

Later, when I had access to secret police reports, I found out that my six spies had reported that I had returned home just before the curfew hour and I can guess what actually happened. I am sure that as soon as they saw me enter the house where I had been several times before, they concluded I would be there some time; probably I was taking tea or supper there and they could with safety leave me for a few minutes and themselves indulge in a cup of tea at the chai-khana (tea-house) round the corner. I can only say that after the few seconds it had taken me to come out again into the street they were still there, and that later they reported wrongly to the police that I had returned home.

It was, of course, of the utmost importance to my friends that there should be no trace of their having helped me, so I took the following precautions: I walked to a certain house where a man was to be smoking a cigarette by the open door. I had met the man once only and would not have recognized him.

I was to walk right in and he would follow me. This was done, and here I left my civilian coat and hat which I had carried. Had these been found in the house through which I had filtered it would have been known that I had changed my clothes there. This man took me through his garden, we climbed over a wall into another garden, and were led by a lady through her house into another street — much as had been done on the first occasion, but now there was no need for haste. (People were frequently asked to help unknown fugitives in this way and the unknown lady took it all in the day's work.) This man and I then walked about rather quiet residential parts of the town. Presently, as curfew hour approached, the streets became more and more deserted until at last we were the only people in the street. We then walked round the corner and after a few yards turned round and came back; the street we had left was still empty. We were quite sure that our plans had succeeded and that we had not been followed. Perhaps all these very great precautions were not really necessary; but the consequences to those helping me and to myself would have been fatal if we had underestimated the sagacity of those put to watch me. It was only people who took the greatest precautions who survived.

My companion and I then entered a humble, inconspicuous house in a street. The small family (we will call them Mateveev) greeted me with the greatest kindness and gave me supper.

The first thing I did next morning was to go over my whole head with a fine hair clipper and to cut off my moustache. I then let everything grow, hair, beard and moustache.

The Mateveevs had a little girl who was given lessons each morning by her mother. Her father would read to her in the evening. The child had a passion for the card game of 'Old Maid', called in Russian 'Truba chist' (Chimney sweep), and we played many a game. Whenever she won, as she usually did, she was overcome with disgust, pointing at me and saying: 'Filthy, black, dirty chimney sweep!'

I found this homely life very useful in learning Russian. For the first couple of days I never left the house at all. Later, I walked a little in the tiny garden after dark. A place was prepared for me under the floorboards where food and water were stored, but this was never used.

I now had to adopt in every way I could think of the habits and manners of an Austrian prisoner. I thought of the advice old Peter Pienaar gave David Hannay in *The Thirty-Nine Steps* and how he fell into his background, and I tried to melt into the field-grey mass of Austrian prisoners of war. Among other small things, I noticed that a Russian has a distinctive way of putting on his coat. It is lifted over the left shoulder before the arm is put in. I do not know what Austrians do, but I thought I would be less conspicuous if I acted in the Russian way. After all if *I* noticed a difference it was quite possible that *they* would too.

Later, I got quite into the way of clicking my heels and bowing when I met anyone outside the peasantry, though it was among humble folk that I was to spend most of my time.

There was a French archaeologist, M. Castagné, in the town, whom I had met on several occasions. Some time before my arrest I had heard from Manditch that Castagné was to be arrested and had warned him, but had no idea whether he had taken any precautions. He was an acquaintance of my kind host and I met him in the house somewhat to my consternation, I must admit; but it turned out that he was also on the run. I had been reading *Raymond*, by Oliver Lodge, and could not help comparing his experiences after death with mine after disappearance. There was a kind of social circle 'on the run', and I met several other *Byejhnyets*, as we were called in Russian; no names were ever exchanged among us.

So alarmed was I at my secret hiding place being known to Castagné that when he came again a couple of days later he was told that I had left Tashkent; I hope he has since forgiven me for the deception.

Once Miss Houston came to see me. She had been to my house and had managed to save a pair of boots and a pair of my riding breeches and a few other clothes. I thought these might be useful later, and it turned out that they were invaluable, for boots especially were unobtainable. I received several letters from Tredwell. These were sent through two people who did not know for whom they were, nor by whom they were sent. This would make it difficult to trace any connection from him to me.

Tredwell told me that the day after I left a sealed letter was received for me from Solkin, the President of the Ispolkom or Executive Committee. The writing was partly legible through the envelope, which was very thin. It was apparently an invitation for me to come and see him at the White House at eleven the next morning about my departure from Turkestan. I have reason to believe that this was an attempt of the Bolsheviks to get me out of my hiding place. Solkin was intensely anti-British and I had never met him.

On my disappearance the town was searched for me. Notices were placarded in the streets of the town and in every village and railway station, not only offering a reward for my arrest (an insultingly small one I thought) but also threatening with death and confiscation of property (as though any property had not already been confiscated), anyone who helped or harboured me in any way. The whole block in which Tredwell and the Noyevs were living was searched so that nothing would have escaped. The block through which I had filtered was searched and the occupiers questioned. Miss Houston was called up before a court of inquiry; my servants were arrested and threatened with death if they did not disclose where I was; but the arrangements made proved satisfactory and after a few days in gaol they were released. One newspaper reported that I had been found in Samarkand and was being brought to Tashkent. A man believed to be me was arrested there, but I knew nothing of him nor what happened to him.

I had disappeared on October 20th. On 24th Karakhan's telegram of the 18th, the purport of which had been communicated to me on the 20th, had struggled through the routine and reached the rulers of the Republic of Turkestan, and an order was issued for the arrest in seven days' time of all Allied subjects as a reprisal for British atrocities at the capture of Merv. The order stated: 'The imperialists use explosive bullets, destroy hospital trains, mercilessly exterminate the civil population, European and native, not excepting women and children.' On seeing this, Edwards and his wife hid themselves. A French artillery officer, Capdeville, did the same. He actually came to the house I was in and asked my host to hide him. Mateveev said he could not do so but made other satisfactory arrangements. I saw Capdeville on this occasion, but he did not see me. I think it was a pity that Mrs. Edwards disappeared. The Bolsheviks had, as a rule, not molested women, beyond the usual threats and interrogations.

Tredwell was arrested on October 26th and suffered five months' internment in his quarters with two visits to the local gaol where his life was in very great danger. One very curious thing happened: Damagatsky, the foreign komissar, himself approached Mateveev through a third party, asking if in certain eventualities he would help him to escape!

The concealment of Tsirul when the Jhlobenski Regiment of Rascals passed through, and this strange request of Damagatsky showed how uncertain the position of the Government was.

Even the President and principal officers of the Government of the Republic once got into their cars and fled. No one knew why. The rumour was that some wit had sent a telegram to Kolesov the President: 'All is discovered, fly at once.' However, the alarm was soon over, and having got to the end of the motor car road a few miles out of Tashkent, they turned the car round and turned back, and having recovered from their fright, carried on as before.

A Roumanian officer, Captain Bolterno, with whom I had made friends, once came to the house and recognized me.

I had obtained the passport of an Austrian prisoner of war. I was Andre Kekeshi, a cook by profession. I carried this document for about four months.

About this time rumours reached me that wireless messages

had been received from the Government of India and Sir George Macartney, asking the Bolsheviks to send me back, saying that the unfortunate 'coilision' between our troops and theirs near Askhabad had occurred after I had been sent off from India. There was also said to have been a message from the British Mission at Meshed in Persia to say that the Soviet Mission under Babushkin, who had taken the letters of introduction forced from me, had been arrested and were being held as hostages for the safety of Tredwell and myself. I never saw these messages but only heard of them.

The Bolsheviks themselves were puzzled by my disappearance. Of course, they did not suspect that all their telegraphic correspondence with Karakhan and Moscow was known to me and had, indeed, been in my hands several days before it had been deciphered and communicated to the government officers to whom it was addressed.

Tredwell's interpreter had a good knowledge of English and was taken to my house to read the papers and books I had left behind. He told friends of mine that, at the time of my disappearance, the Bolsheviks thought that I had been done away with by the Germans who naturally resented my continued requests to Damagatsky to keep them under strict control.

CHAPTER VIII

TO THE MOUNTAINS

I HAD been in Tashkent more than two months before these events happened. Apart from the soldier of the 11th Bengal Lancers who only brought private letters, I had received no communication from India or Kashgar except the wireless message ordering my return, and even this had been kept from me by the authorities and I had only heard of it secretly from not entirely reliable sources. I believed that the British force which had been supporting anti-Bolshevik Russians near Merv was coming on to Tashkent. How easy it would have been and what a welcome they would have had! I had received no news of any kind from them, consequently I was in the dark as to their intentions.

I made the following plan: I proposed to leave Tashkent when the hot search was over and make my way to Irgash's forces, see what he was doing and what his intentions and prospects were, and then either remain in Turkestan until the British force from Transcaspia arrived or go and join them.

A young friend of mine, whom we will call Markov, had a bee-farm in the mountains whence tracks led into Ferghana. It was my intention to make for his hut and thence to make my way to Irgash as soon as possible.

On November 5th I left town, taking the road to the northeast. I drove a cart with some hay loaded behind, on which sat Markov. I was wearing my Austrian uniform in public for the second time, the first being the night of my disappearance. I still felt rather shy and queer in it. One Austrian came up to me and asked me to give him a lift as far as Nikolskoe, a village four versts from Tashkent. This I refused rather bluntly. We reached Nikolskoe at dusk and stopped for a few minutes at the house of a relative of Markov's where his wife was living.

She gave us nice hot *perojhki* of apples — kind of tartlet. This was very welcome as the evening was freezing cold. Nikolskoe is the village where a Bolshevik military post examined all travellers, especially at night. Our friends showed us the fire this guard was burning in the veranda of their quarters and led us through by-lanes to avoid it, an easy matter when assisted, but I believe that, had I adhered to my earlier plan of leaving Tashkent at once on the night when I disappeared, and blundered on to this post in ignorance of its existence, I might have been subjected to awkward and perhaps fatal questionings.

We travelled with our cart until about ten p.m. when we had covered twenty-four versts from Tashkent and had reached the village of Troitskoe. Here we put up with a peasant whom we will call Ivan. He was a friend of Markov's. Markov and I slept together in the livingroom-cum-kitchen, which I was later to know very well. Our bed was a bag of hay from our cart. We were to start at daybreak so as to get the dangerous part of our journey over quickly.

Troitskoe had been one of the largest camps for prisoners of war and also one of the worst. Captain Brun in his book states that there were eight thousand graves of prisoners of war here.

The village was still full of Austrians. I did not want to stay here for there was the danger that some of them might meet me and question me in the course of casual conversation. I then learnt one of the intensely annoying failings of Russians of some classes. I was awake and ready early, but instead of starting they lighted a samovar and made tea. This went on till about nine. They then said that it was too late to reach the journey's end planned for that day so we would start at noon and make a short journey to Iskander village and spend the night there. This, of course, meant stopping in another house and giving more people the chance to talk to me and notice me. I could not do much. Markov was the only man who knew who I was and any undue haste or pressure might have made the others suspicious. At noon someone put up another samovar and my impatience was getting unbearable. Markov then said that there was a guard on the road and that we could not pass this till after dark, so it would be unsafe to start till four. At four someone started another samovar and then it was decided that it was too late to start at all and that we would go next day! I later got used to this sort of thing, but at first under the peculiar circumstances of my case it was somewhat annoying.

The next day was November 7th, the first anniversary of the Bolshevik revolution. After more of the samovar business we got away at nine and travelled nineteen versts to Iskander village finding no dangerous guard on the road. Here we stopped a couple of hours and had dinner with the local komissar. He was a relative of Ivan's. The inhabitants of the village, to the number of about fifty, mostly children, were marching up and down the village street singing the 'Workman's Marseillaise', the 'International' and other revolutionary songs. The Bolsheviks went in a good deal for musical propaganda. They had on this occasion sent men from Tashkent to organize it. The Sart population were taught the tunes with Turki words.

After our meal we continued our journey. A few miles from Iskander we crossed the Chirchik River and drove up the left bank. I saw a flock of large bustards here and also many sand-grouse. At dusk we passed the large village of Khojakent, twenty-two versts from Iskander. Some distance on, when it was quite dark except for a small moon, we reached the hamlet of Yusuf Khana.

I had extracted a promise from Markov and Ivan that we would reach the bee-farm that night and not run further risks in villages. We could not go further with the cart in the dark but in order to keep their promise my friends offered to walk with me to the farm that night. However, we decided to spend the night where we were. I was taken to a house where I met a Tartar, Colonel Yusupov, and a Polish-Russian captain of cavalry named Lipski. Both were, like myself, 'wanted'. I had to declare who I was to them. The next morning Markov, Ivan, Lipski and I left together, passing Brich Mulla village at the mouth of the Kok Su Valley. Nearly all the rivers in Turkestan are called Kok Su — blue water. It is true that you come on an occasional Ak Su — white water; Kara Su — black water, or even Kizil Su — red water; but the blue is the favourite. We were now getting to the end of the road and one might say of civilization. This meant that one attracted more individual attention locally, and I was no longer merged into a background of Austrian prisoners.

In Brich Mulla was a Polish officer prisoner of war who was noted for his hospitality and curiosity. He was, I was told, sure to invite me in if he saw me, so Colonel Yusupov went in to see him to arrange that he should not be in a room facing the road and so see us as we drove past. At Brich Mulla we left the cart and climbed steeply up for two hours till we reached the bee-farm. This consisted of a couple of huts situated in a small valley surrounded by steep hills on which was a certain amount of snow. The hills were sparsely covered with small juniper bushes with a few larger trees. On the road up we disturbed many very tame chukor, which were having a prolonged close time as no one in Turkestan was allowed to possess arms.

At the bee-farm I found a Russian General whom Tredwell and I nicknamed 'Garibaldi'. He had held an important command in the Great War and had had something to do with the Underground Army which has been mentioned. He had been obliged to fly and had come to this hut where he had lived alone for ten days before our arrival.

The only other inhabitant was a Tajik with his wife, his grown-up son and a baby. They occupied the second hut. His name was Eshan. Eshan was, I found, almost as common a name for men as Koksu was for rivers.

We three, Garibaldi, Lipski and I, settled down to our simple life. My two companions had had very little to do with the British — one of them, I believe, had never seen one of us before. Until we got on more familiar terms I was always addressed as 'Mister' — 'No, Mister' — 'Yes, Mister'. Once they were discussing me. With my limited understanding of Russian I could not understand all they said, so I asked them. It turned out that they believed that we lived permanently in a dense sea fog and never saw the sun, which resulted in a morose temperament; and yet here was I who did not differ very much from themselves.

We knew that we would be talked about in Brich Mulla before long and it was essential to get on before suspicious reports about us reached the authorities. So it was advisable to act quickly. On November 9th, the day after our arrival, we sent Ivan and Eshan off to obtain information about the road to Ferghana; while Lipski and I reconnoitred our surroundings to decide what to do if we were found. We climbed a hill twelve hundred feet above our hut whence we got a good view of the country. Here in a cave Lipski had concealed some rifles. The place could easily have been defended, but in the end we decided to use another cave in a different direction and made the following plans for our safety:

We had six rifles of three different bores. We had Troikhlinieka, i.e. 'three lines', which corresponded to our .303 rifles; Berdanka, which corresponded to the Martini-Henry of our army, and a sporting Winchester. Three of these were always ready, hanging in the hut with a haversack of food hung on the same peg. My own haversack contained a small primus stove. We would not be able to light a fire once we left the hut as smoke would have given us away. If any Bolsheviks made an attack on us we were to resist and, if obliged to leave the hut, we were to go off in different directions and make for a rendezvous where an overhanging rock gave some shelter, about three miles away to the north. Here we concealed another primus stove, some supplies, and three rifles and ammunition. The idea was that we would only be in immediate danger from a small party. We might kill them or drive them off and then bolt, but if this did not happen they could not easily follow us in three different directions. They would presumably concentrate on one and perhaps get him, but the other two might escape. Whoever succeeded in reaching this rendezvous was to wait there forty-eight hours for the others and then make for Auli

Ata or Chimkent to the north, a distance of several days journey. Here the situation would be as dangerous as at Tashkent, but there would be a fresh, though slender, chance. It would be difficult if not impossible to explain one's arrival to the authorities with documents, to say the least of it, not in perfect order!

Our hut consisted of a single room about twelve feet square, a quarter of which was taken up by a huge brick and mud stove. Here we three settled down to a rather monotonous life while awaiting the return of Ivan and Eshan who were reconnoitring the road. Every day we had to collect fuel, cook meals and clean up our room. Our water came from a delightful crystal clear spring a few yards from the hut.

The small valley must have been very beautiful in summer with countless wild flowers. I collected some of the seed and eventually brought it home.

Outdoor work was done by Lipski and myself. We found it hard work cutting wood and dragging it in. We also went out most days either to reconnoitre or to make arrangements in the event of our being discovered and having to fly. We also climbed the hills in search of wild pig; though we occasionally saw some, we never got a shot.

In the hut we made ourselves as comfortable as possible. We brought in some wooden packing cases from the honey store and on these placed springy juniper branches, and this made a large and fairly soft communal bed.

Garibaldi put me to shame in the matter of cooking and baking. During the ten days he had, like I myself, lain low in Tashkent to allow of the inevitable intense search, he had learnt some cooking and, especially, baking. I blamed myself for not having done the same.

Our cooking was simple and perhaps lazy. We only cooked every other morning. One day we would cook *pilau*. This was eaten at midday, warmed up in the evening, warmed up again the next midday and evening. We then cooked 'soup'. This soup had an enormous lump of meat in it when available, and we warmed it up in the same way, so that it lasted two days, after which we cooked a *pilau*, and so on.

This is how we made the *pilau*. We had a semi-spherical iron cooking pot. This was put on the fire and we cut up the fat of the tail of a fat-tailed sheep into little cubes like dice and threw them in. While they were melting we cut up some onions. We then removed the small hard bits of the fat which had not melted from the pan, and these were later put into our loaves of bread. We put the onions in to cook in the melted fat and while this was going on we cut up some carrots. We then threw these in and cut up our meat. This was then put in and we washed our rice in cold water. When this was ready, some sultanas were put into the pan, if we had them, and then the rice was added. Then, immediately, before the rice could burn, we poured in water until it was the depth of the top little finger joint over the rice. The whole thing was then allowed to cook until the water had boiled away and the surface of the rice was dry. The dish was then ready, but it was improved by being covered and kept hot (but not cooked) for a few minutes while we got our plates and spoons. Then, and not till then, did we stir it, bringing up all the earlier ingredients to the top and mixing it thoroughly. I can only say that done in this way the dish was excellent.

There seems to be a provision of nature that onions take just so much longer to cook than carrots as it takes to cut up the latter, and both of these so much longer than the meat, and so on. There is a school of thought which insists that the carrots should go in before the onions and I have listened to heated controversies on this important subject. In addition to the above we had bread which Garibaldi baked every few days and an unlimited quantity of honey from the three hundred and sixty pounds in large zinc containers lying in the store-room ready for market. We also had such things as tea, sugar, salt, etc., which Eshan brought up periodically from Brich Mulla.

Eshan could neither read nor write, consequently he had a good memory, but sometimes he missed things from the long lists of our requirements. So we used to give him a pinch of each thing we wanted as a shopping list. He would take a little flour, a little fat, a piece of string or paper, the stub of a cigarette, a peppercorn, a pinch of salt, a piece of carrot, etc.

I had lived a good deal in camp in my previous appointments in Tibet and elsewhere and thought I knew most of the tips about camping, but here I picked up a few things I did not know. Here is one tip, perhaps not of great practical value, but which I have used since. A small piece of gun-cotton about the size of a walnut is an excellent thing to start a fire when the firewood is damp. It is, of course, not explosive unless detonated and burns quickly with intense heat, and seems literally to drive the dampness out of the fuel.

One night we had an alarm. Markov had brought his ponies up to graze and had lost one. While searching for it at dusk he came on a man hiding in the bushes who jumped up and ran away. Could it be that we were being watched? We spent that night doing sentry-go by turns but nothing happened and we never heard any more of our strange visitor. He was perhaps a thief, or perhaps some poor fellow like ourselves, fleeing for his life.

To ordinary inquirers Garibaldi was to be Markov's wife's grandfather just looking after the honey. Lipski was to be a hunter and I, with my cook's passport, a sausage maker. Lipski hoped to kill some wild boars which I had come to turn into sausage to be sold in Tashkent. On one or two occasions parties of hunters arrived and this was the story told them.

This account of ourselves was not the happiest, and both Garibaldi and I were somewhat inconvenienced by the roles we had adopted. The General had to pretend religious sectarian restrictions which he did not really profess, and I was obliged to do some unpleasant *charcuterie* in the snow.

One day when Lipski and I returned in the evening we noticed ten ponies grazing near our hut. At first we were afraid that the Red Guards had come and taken Garibaldi and were waiting for us. We approached very carefully and found that a party of Tajiks had arrived from a village below. They had brought their valuables up and were going to hide them. We helped them to build a rough hut partially dug out of the hillside, in the back of which they dug into the hill a winding passage three or four yards long. At the end they dug a pit and into this put several very heavy sacks. This was all filled in and the entrance concealed by the hut. In helping them to move a heavy beam I strained a leg which had been damaged in Gallipoli and was laid out for a couple of days. This would have upset our plans for dealing with a Bolshevik attempt to take us but I was soon fit again without any trouble. Our Tajik friends remained several days and made us welcome presents of milk and *kumis* in return for the help we had given them.

On November 21st Ivan and Eshan returned. They reported that apart from a good deal of snow there were no physical difficulties in getting through but every possible track was guarded by Bolsheviks who were anxious to prevent any communication between Irgash and Tashkent. They had been stopped and questioned at four or five places.

This news caused me so much disappointment that I searched for excuses to disbelieve it, but I did not like to take grave risks by going against the information which I had taken so much trouble to obtain and, in the end, I was convinced that the report was true. It was further confirmed in a book, *Les Basmachis* by M. Castagné, published in Paris in 1925, in which he says that the passes between Ferghana and Syr-Daria province were occupied by the Red Army to isolate the counter-revolutionary elements in Tashkent from the Basmachis — the followers of Irgash — in Kokhand.

Later we intended to send Ivan by rail to Irgash with letters from Garibaldi to Kornilov, the most active White Russian with Irgash's force. He was to report on the conditions there and try to get Irgash's people to bring us over the range, avoiding the Bolshevik pickets. This plan was never carried out, owing to circumstances which will be related. However, I sent Ivan off at once to Tashkent to join Markov who had taken letters from me to Tredwell.

Colonel Kornilov was a brother of the famous General Kornilov whose differences with Kerensky allowed Lenin to accomplish his Bolshevik revolution. I had once met General Kornilov in China, when I had to spend ten days in quarantine in Shan-Hai-Kwan.

General Kornilov was later killed by a shell which came into his room. He was in command of the Turkoman Detachment of the *Dikkaia Divisia* or 'Wild Division', consisting of non-European Russians under the command of the Grand Duke Nicholas.

I later got to know Colonel Kornilov well. He was eventually arrested and shot by the Bolsheviks in circumstances which will be recounted later.

Markov had gone to Tashkent to get news and, I hoped, letters from Tredwell. He had promised to return by November 18th. We were without any news from him until on December 4th we heard that he had been robbed on the road and had had to return to Tashkent. I feared for what he might have been carrying in the way of messages. I also had lent him my second pistol. It will be remembered that one had been taken by the Cheka at the time of the arrest.

CHAPTER IX

THE BEE-FARM

WE had several falls of snow about November 23rd and the following days. This made it easy to track the wild boars, but Lipski and I had no luck. Besides these wild pig there were said to be ibex in the higher hills, but I never saw any. There were also flocks of the very tame chukor.

On December 6th, during our midday meal, we were startled by the persistent barking of dogs. I went out and saw, half a mile away, several dogs barking at something in the bushes. I ran back for my rifle and met Lipski in the door of the hut running out with his. He said Eshan had told him that some dogs were baying a pig. We ran out through the deep snow and soon came on four dogs round an enormous boar. We ran on and then noticed a man about ten yards off the boar aiming at it. I thought by what I knew of the etiquette of sport that it was none of my business so I stopped and watched. There was a noise like a toy pistol from the hunter — a bad cartridge. He fired again with the same result. The pig then decided to change his quarters and ran towards me with the four yapping dogs on his heels. A couple of shots laid him low. The man came up; he turned out to be a one-armed Russian. He had come with his dogs to try to get a pig for meat and sale. He had fired seven shots at it but all his ammunition was bad. He was very glad I had killed it and we decided to cut it in half and each take half. It was a huge boar by Indian pig-sticking standards and measured thirty-nine inches at the shoulder. We dragged the heavy beast with great difficulty through the deep snow until one of the Tajiks came up with a horse. Being a Mohammedan he would not touch the unclean animal but took the end of a rope with which in due course we dragged it to the hut. When our one-armed friend heard that I was a sausage maker he took no further part in the proceedings beyond remarking that it was fortunate to find a professional in such an out of the way place, and I was left to clean out the pig myself! There were certainly unexpected disadvantages on a cold day in having a cook's passport! I also had to tell him how we handled pigs in Hungary. A few days later we sent him his half of the pig, and in that cold our share lasted us till we left more than a month later.

Bez-Ruki in Russian means 'without hand' and this is the name we used for our fellow hunter. No one asked or gave names in those days. He spent the night with us, and the next day we went out with him and his dogs again but had no luck.

Several parties of Russian hunters visited us at various times and occasionally they spent the night with us; but the slaughter of this pig was the only success registered. These Russian hunters were hard on their dogs; they were left out on the cold veranda and given very little to eat. Every time one tried to get into the warm — overwarm — hut, he was driven out with angry cries. So hungry were they that they had already eaten some of the pig we had killed during the short time we were away getting a rope.

Communication with Tredwell and my friends in Tashkent was proving very difficult and uncertain, and so I decided to return there and to attempt to go to Irgash from the town. Nothing could be done, however, until the return of my messengers who were due on November 18th. Markov and Ivan actually did not arrive until December 7th. This delay was very annoying to me. I was keen to get on to Irgash as planned. The explanation of this delay of nineteen days was that Markov had started back on the 23rd, met Ivan on the way and had gone back to stay with him — more samovar, I expect. Then he had started again and had been held up by Red Guards who had taken all his property, including my camera which he was bringing out to me from Tashkent, and the pistol I had lent him. He told the Red Guards that he was himself an officer of the Red Militia and they gave him back all the property.

I was very glad to have my things back and to get news of the world. Tredwell wrote that the war had been over for nearly a month and a revolution had broken out in Germany. Later, inaccurate reports of the peace terms were spread about.

Constantinople, Smyrna and the Dardanelles were to go to Greece. Italy was to have Syria and Armenia. South Africa was to have the German possessions in East Africa.

The German islands in the Pacific were divided between Japan, Australia and New Zealand. We were to get Arabia, Mesopotamia, Palestine, West Africa, the Caucasus and, above all, Turkestan!

A correction was put about later that Turkestan was only to go to Great Britain for twenty-five years as a guarantee for loans we had supplied to Russia. Revolutionary risings were reported from Holland, Belgium, Switzerland, Denmark and Sweden. The prisoners of war in Tashkent had formed revolutionary councils.

I decided to return to Tashkent as soon as a suitable hiding place could be arranged. I had been unable to get to Irgash through the mountains by this route and my messengers to Tashkent and other places were so slow and unreliable that it was difficult to do any good where I was. I had, however, to wait in the mountains until the necessary arrangements could be made. I spent the next day deciphering Tredwell's messages, and then occurred an accident which upset all our plans. Markov and Ivan were very anxious to get another pig. Meat was very scarce and they both had families to feed. The deep snow made it easier to track and find them, so on December 9th we three went out. We went some miles up the Kok Su Valley and then up a steep side valley where we were told there were numbers of pig. We climbed up steeply over snow disturbing hundreds of chukor which flew off down hill. Presently out of some willow scrub the chukor kept getting up, indicating the presence of a wild animal, and presently a large boar came out of the bushes above us, looked at us and came towards us. We were standing on a steep snow slope and could not shoot, and after the first yard or two we could only see the top of his back owing to the lie of the ground. We crossed the snow slope and picked up his tracks. I was wearing a pair of native boots called locally *chukai*. The *chukai* is really a sort of raw hide bag or sock. Instead of wearing socks on your feet you tie a small bandage in a special way; you then pull on your *chukai*, having first put a little hay in the sole. The *chukai* has to be well greased every day, and this was one of my duties each evening when we returned. They are the warmest footgear imaginable for snow but have the great disadvantage, as I found out, that there is no hard heel or sole to get a grip of steep snow. I was crossing a steep slope of fairly hard snow, with my rifle slung, when I slipped. The snow sloped about two thousand feet down to the bottom of the valley where it ended in rocks and bushes. A few feet below me was an island in the snow, covered in bushes, and about two hundred feet lower some rocks stuck out of the snow from the left side. I could not stop myself, but as I passed the island at a terrific rate I seized some of the bushes only to tear the skin off my hands without checking my fall. I expected in a few seconds to be dashed against the rocks and instinctively tried to guide myself clear of them, though I foresaw that this only meant a worse smash at the bottom. After sliding a couple of hundred feet I must have come on a patch of softer snow. I was still struggling to stop and avoid the nearer rocks when the surface broke. I went head over heels and pulled up deep in the snow with something wrong with both of my knees. The leather strap of my rifle had snapped without my feeling it, and the rifle was in the snow ten yards above me. Markov and Ivan had not seen this, though I had whizzed past close to where they were tracking the pig. I called and they came to me. One knee was in great pain and one quite numb. We were a very long way from home and had the most difficult country to cross. We decided that we must go straight down the snow slope to the Kok Su Valley where there was a small road which would eventually lead us back to our hut by a very round about way. Markov went straight back to the hut about six versts off to get a pony. The Tajik treasure-burying party were fortunately still there. Ivan pulled me down the steep snow by my painful leg while the other was of use as a brake to stop another uncontrolled glissade. After an unpleasant hour of this, during which I got very wet and cold, we reached the bottom. Here Ivan could not pull me any more, so he cut two forked sticks which we padded with clothes and tried to use as crutches, but I really had no sound leg and even if I had it would have been impossible to use crutches in the rough boulders and undergrowth. In the end he carried me, taking frequent rests until we reached the path. Here there was no snow; we were almost frozen and Ivan got some brushwood and we made a fire, hoping that Markov would soon come with a pony. After some hours Markov and a stranger, a hunter from Nikolskoe village, came and told us that Eshan was bringing a horse soon. This arrived in due course and I was put up. The slope of the hill was on my right — my painful leg — and the track was so narrow that it kept touching bushes and each time I got an agonizing twinge in my knee. This made it particularly difficult and unpleasant after it got dark. The next day a Sart doctor was obtained: an old man with a long white beard. He explained that my knee was dislocated and must be pulled straight. This he said would be painful and I believed him. The whole knee was fearfully swollen, and he said that it was full of water and that he would take the swelling down with salt which was the 'enemy of water'. He made a paste of salt and eggs which luckily we were able to get from the Tajiks. Then after a short prayer he seized my leg, pulled it out and pressed it down. I have never felt such pain. He then put a wooden splint behind it and covered the knee with the egg and salt paste and we bandaged the whole thing. I paid him seventy-five roubles. I would gladly have given more, but it would not have been in keeping with my role to have shown that I had plenty of money or was careless of it. I asked the doctor if he could do anything for the pain and his only suggestion was *kumis* of which we got some from our Tajik friends, but I do not think it had any effect. I had several sleepless nights but eventually managed to get some opium which enabled me to sleep.

This accident upset all our plans. In the first place our arrangements for fighting any small party who might try to capture us at the hut, and retiring to our cave, had to be altered. My companions took the rifles and ammunition away and buried them. Had they been found we would, of course, all have been shot at once without any inquiry, but if we were unarmed we might conceivably be the people we purported to be, living harmlessly in this hut. The risk they thus took was a great sacrifice on their part for which I could not be sufficiently grateful.

We had now been in this hut over a month and many people had seen us; first the unknown stranger whom Markov had seen when looking for his pony; then *Bez-Ruki* with whom we had shot the pig. Then this party of hunters from Nikolskoe; the Tajiks and one or two others. It was quite likely that some news of a suspicious character might have reached the authorities. We even heard that a communistic forester (*lyes obschenik*) at Brich Mulla had reported that we were suspicious people. Also I was anxious for reasons already stated to get back to Tashkent. Nothing could be done, however, until I got better.

On December 13th I was still in bed and in addition had fever, when a man, Lukashov, arrived. He had taken letters from me secretly to Etherton in Kashgar. On his return he had to pass through territory controlled by Irgash, who had delayed him a fortnight. I was very disappointed with the message I received. There was nothing of importance and no answer to questions I had asked, and no instructions or information as to our policy and intentions. Lukashov also brought a packet of cheap American cigarettes, a luxury after having only Russian ones. Lukashov, though a very brave man, was afraid, and we did not think it safe for him to stay with us more than one night. I had prepared several messages at the time of my arrest. These were with Tredwell who had not been able to get a reliable messenger. I told Lukashov that I would prepare some more messages when free of the fever and would send them to him to Tashkent. He was also to get the messages which Tredwell already had and go off to the British Mission on the Transcaspian Front.

Markov and Ivan also returned from a pig-shooting expedition on the 13th, having shot four. This made the meat situation satisfactory. In his rather aimless way Markov went off on the 15th without waiting for my letters; he was to return the next day. It snowed heavily on the night of the 15th and Markov sent a message to say he was ill and could not come. This was very annoying as Lukashov had to take an early opportunity to go off and I feared he might go without my later messages. It was difficulties like this that made me so anxious to return to Tashkent where I could control actions of this kind.

Lukashov with two companions eventually enlisted in the Red Army and was sent to the Transcaspian Front. Instead of confining himself to the job he had to do, that of getting my messages through, he, entirely on his own, also took some anti-Bolshevik pamphlets which he had had secretly printed and which he conveyed to the troops of the Red Army. Before the revolution Lukashov had been a station-master and knew how to telegraph. In some way he got hold of the instrument in Karaul Kuyu station behind the Bolshevik lines and telegraphed up to the Front that a British force had appeared and were about to capture the place he was in, and that the army should retire at once. The Bolshevik headquarters must have known that this was impossible. Anyhow, instead of retiring they sent a message to the nearest troops ordering them to find out what this meant, and Lukashov was arrested. The pamphlets were found on him and he was shot at once. He was a very brave man but would have done more for his side if he had stuck to what he was told to do. Tredwell had given Lukashov a small note to help him through the British lines. Later, in March, two men, Tsvetkov and Agapov (neither of whom did Tredwell or I know at all) were tried for counter-revolutionary activities. During this trial, which was reported in detail in the newspapers, it was stated that a British passport had been found on Lukashov. This he certainly did not have, but Tredwell's note may have been interpreted as some sort of passport. Later, I was able to get at Lukashov's dossier and saw a list of property taken off him when he was shot. The list contained the book in which my messages were concealed. I also learnt that they had found on him a cipher message believed to be in English. This was certainly not mine. The message was sent to Moscow to be deciphered, but the experts there could make nothing of it.

The party of hunters from Nikolskoe who had been with us for several days, Lipski and Markov, all left together with Lukashov leaving Garibaldi and me alone. Eshan also remained in the neighbouring hut. Garibaldi had very hard work looking after me, getting in firewood, cooking and keeping our small quarters clean and tidy. He was not a young man. Later we persuaded Eshan to get in our firewood on payment.

Our valley was very sheltered. It was, I think, about four thousand feet above sea level. One morning a thermometer in the veranda registered fourteen degrees, but at eight in the morning the usual temperatures were above this, but always below freezing point. I found the villages about fifteen hundred feet lower down to be really colder as they were more exposed and caught the winds.

On Christmas Day four more hunters, this time from Troitskoe village, arrived to try for pig, but after a couple of unsuccessful days returned. These visits were annoying to Garibaldi in a peculiar way. He was supposed to be the grandfather of Markov's wife. Her family were Tolstovtsi — followers of Tolstoy. They lived in the most simple way and were not even allowed to drink tea. He found it very trying to keep to these rules for the sake of appearances.

After about a fortnight in bed I got up and, with the aid of improvised crutches, went into the veranda where I helped by sawing up firewood.

The world-wide influenza epidemic reached Brich Mulla about this time. We heard that a mysterious disease was sweeping through the countryside claiming many victims, but had no idea what it was or that it was so widespread.

One day we heard that searches and requisitions were being carried out in Brich Mulla and Khojakent and that the forester had told Bolsheviks that there was a quantity of honey in our hut and that the people living there were fugitives. All this made us anxious to leave. This was impossible for me. The country was under four feet of snow and by no means could I, with my bad leg, get through that. Eshan told us that a further heavy fall of snow would close the road between us and the rest of the world until March. We accordingly got up supplies to last us for two months. Our frozen pig was still going strong. We had a fine spell on January 5th, 1919, and I hoped that I could be got down, but heavy snow fell again the next two days. Then Lipski unexpectedly returned. He had joined a party of hunters in a neighbouring valley who had shot twelve pigs. The Russians drove the pigs towards the natives who actually shot them.

At the foot of the hill in the Kok Su Valley was a bridge up to which Lipski told us horses could come, and Eshan was persuaded to carry me up to this point, about three versts from our hut. We did not want to pass through Brich Mulla in broad daylight as it would have done us no good if the communist forester had seen us pass and had known that we had evacuated our hut. It was better in every way that it should be believed that we were still in our bee-farm, for a few days at any rate.

Just as we were starting Garibaldi had a quite unnecessary row with Eshan, who thereupon refused to help at all. However, a little tact brought him round and at one o'clock, after wrapping myself up as warmly as possible, I got on to his back and we went off down the hill.

Eshan had great difficulty in carrying me through the deep snow and both he and I arrived at the bridge frozen. Here were no ponies, but Lipski himself was there and he took a turn at carrying me as Eshan was done in. We reached Brich Mulla about six in the evening. Four versts beyond Brich Mulla was the hamlet of Yusuf Khana with its meteorological station. I had hoped to spend a night there, but without a pony, and at this late hour it was not possible to reach it. We therefore slept in a room where Lipski's shooting party had put up. Markov, who was on his way back to the hut, also turned up unexpectedly and spent the night with us. We had intended to start before daybreak but as usual we could not get off. The excuse made was that the high wind of the day before had caused deep drifts of snow on the road which would be impassable for us until it had been beaten down by traffic. So I spent an impatient morning drinking tea for, as usual, the samovar seems to have been the real cause of our delay. Lipski and I rode off about midday in a strong and bitterly cold wind. I had obtained from Tashkent a black leather suit such as most Russians wore in winter. The Austrian uniform was not warm enough for the winter cold in the Turkestan mountains.

After two hours — some of it floundering in snow when I feared a fall and further damage to my leg — we reached Yusuf Khana. Here we learnt that a man who was to have taken me in his sledge to Tashkent had just left without me. I was very disappointed as I was anxious to reach Tashkent as soon as possible. Had I not just missed this man, or had I not had the accident to my leg which delayed me so long, I would have been in Tashkent during the Ossipov rising which was just about to break out. I might have been able to influence the issue in some way or I might equally likely have been shot along with Kleberg and the other four thousand in the reprisal which followed Ossipov's failure.

I found an Austrian officer prisoner of war in charge of the meteorological station at Yusuf Khana. He was a Czech called Merz whom I again met some months later. Here also was Edwards in hiding. He had been here ever since he had escaped from arrest. His wife was hiding in Tashkent.

CHAPTER X

IN TROITSKOE

I STAYED a few days in the meteorological station, trying to make arrangements to go to Tashkent. One day Garibaldi passed through. It is an instance of the care we took to keep our business concealed from others that although we all had our midday meal together neither Edwards nor Merz knew who he was, nor that he had been in the mountains with me. We were very comfortable and well fed here, though the bread was not as good as Garibaldi's baking. The Soviet bread was a mixture of maize and other flour and was suspected to contain a proportion of sawdust. We had the luxury of paraffin oil to burn. In our hut up the hill our only light had been pieces of cotton wool laid in a saucer of cotton oil. Later this was all anyone had in Tashkent when, as frequently happened, the electric light was cut off. One day some hunters arrived with four camels. They were part of a kind of commercial company which had been formed to kill pigs and other game for sale in the town. One of these was Colonel Yusupov with whom I had stopped on November 7th and who, of course, knew me. I was not to see him again till we met in Bokhara ten months later. We had a lot of snow here and it was very cold and windy. The temperature sank below zero, Fahrenheit. In fact it was much colder than at the bee-farm in our sheltered valley three thousand feet higher. While staying here we heard rumours of disturbances in Tashkent. The news was that the Bolsheviks had been overthrown. I did not believe this, but my companions were on the top of the wave and already looking forward to the joys of a free normal life with its many pleasures.

After a stay of a week I left at seven on the morning of January 17th with the temperature sixteen degrees Fahrenheit and a bitter wind. In Yusuf Khana I had been enrolled on the staff of the meteorological station and when I left I was given some of the very inferior bread which was my ration as a Soviet worker. It is lucky for me that I did not obey my first impulse which was to leave the horrid stuff behind, as some weeks later, when it had not improved by keeping, it was all I had to eat.

I expected to be searched on the road, so I left my diary and some other papers with Edwards. I hoped to get an opportunity to recover them later. However, they were all burnt and for the second time I rewrote my notes from memory as soon as I heard of their destruction. Perhaps I stressed too much the importance of secrecy. I never let anyone know who I was unless it was absolutely necessary. In the same way I protected other people by not claiming acquaintance or talking about their affairs. I was somewhat annoyed later to hear from my friends in Tashkent that Edwards had written to his wife to say that I had arrived at Yusuf Khana with a broken leg. Everyone at Brich Mulla knew that an Austrian had broken his leg in the mountains and that the native doctor had gone up to him. If it had ever been found out that I was the Austrian many people would have been shot. I had told no one that I was going to stop at Yusuf Khana, but told Eshan that I was going to Khojakent so that if anything were found out the people of the Yusuf Khana meterological station would not be suspected. Had Edwards' message to his wife been intercepted we would all have been caught and certainly shot. I never spoke to Edwards again though I once passed him in the street and recognized him through his disguise. He did not know me in mine. I saw his wife once. Later they both lost their lives, perhaps owing to some similar lack of caution.

We rode along the road to Iskander, now under deep snow. Ivan happened to know that his relative the komissar of Iskander was travelling that morning by the usual road along the left bank of the Chirchik River. We consequently avoided meeting him by taking a different road up the right bank of the river, but we had our midday meal in his house in Iskander. Here we picked up Ivan's *brichka* (cart) and in it we drove to his house in Troitskoe. The next day, January 18th, we were to go to Tashkent.

I had made arrangements for the Mateveevs to receive me again for a few days. I did not want to go to them till dusk, and, on account of my bad leg, I wanted to spend as little time as possible tramping the streets of Tashkent until it was dark enough to enter his house. I was able to limp about a little by this time, but I did not want to put an undue strain on my leg. I might have waited in a tea-shop, but this would probably have led to awkward, and perhaps dangerous, conversations. We, therefore, decided to start at two p.m. which would, we calculated, get me to Tashkent at the right time.

In the morning Ivan told me that there had been trouble in Tashkent between the Bolsheviks and the L.S.R.s, or, to give them their full title, seldom used, Left Social Revolutionaries. This gave an inadequate idea of most serious events.

These events were reflected in the affairs of this small village. The politics of Troitskoe were amusing, though apt to be violent. The peasants, in fact, knew and cared nothing for politics. Only two political parties, which were almost indistinguishable to ordinary mortals, counted at all after the revolution. These were the Bolsheviks and the L.S.R.s. Emissaries from each of these parties had visited the village and told the people that they should belong to their particular party. The result was that one end of the long straggling village considered themselves L.S.R.s and the other end Bolsheviks. The Government at Tashkent had sent men to disarm the L.S.R.s of Troitskoe. The L.S.R.s of Tashkent had warned their sympathizers in Troitskoe to hide their arms as they were to be taken from them. In the morning twenty-five Bolshevik soldiers arrived. They had a list of L.S.R.s known to possess rifles in which was entered Ivan's name; they were searching the whole village for arms, especially the houses of the marked men. We saw them coming down the street, visiting one detached house after another. I had very little property at this time — only one very small bundle of a spare shirt, toothbrush, writing materials, camera, etc. These I took and hid in the steep bank of the river which ran a couple of hundred yards behind the house. When the Bolsheviks were about to enter the house I took Ivan's pony to the stream and gave it water. They did not actually search the house. Ivan said that he had no rifle, he had sold it three years ago and occasionally borrowed one from the Kirghiz in the mountains. They accepted this story. I saw them pointing at me and Ivan told me that he had explained to them that I was an Austrian who was living with him and looking after his pony and doing other service. To our relief they moved on to the next house. All day a Bolshevik post was maintained on the road at the entrance to the village and everyone was searched. We consequently could not travel, but the next day, the 19th, the post was withdrawn and we left for Tashkent in Ivan's sledge at two o'clock.

After travelling about ten versts we met a sledge coming from the direction of Tashkent. The driver asked us where we were going. We replied that we were going 'to town'. He told us that fighting was going on there and that it was impossible to enter the town. Ivan wanted to turn back. I would not hear of it on the evidence of one man who had not himself been up to the barrier. So we went on, meeting others with the same story. Soon we heard the sound of artillery and later, as we got nearer, the crackle of musketry. We then met some people who had actually been turned back. They told us that on the Salar bridge was a post of Red Army soldiers who held up all travellers. They either arrested them and kept them for inquiry or turned them back. On this we returned to Ivan's house at Troitskoe, passing lorry-loads of the soldiers who had been disarming the peasants, returning to Tashkent.

The next day, the 20th, we heard gunfire all day and the rumour was that the L.S.R.s were fighting the Bolsheviks and had won a victory. The L.S.R.s of the village held a meeting at which a considerable quantity of liquor was consumed and at which it was decided to murder all the Bolsheviks at the other end of the village. Hidden weapons were taken out and a move was made to carry out this decision. The Bolsheviks heard of it and fled to a Kirghiz village five miles away, and the L.S.R.s returned to cool their heads. They then decided to send a man to Tashkent to find out what was happening there before making another attack on the Bolsheviks. The next day, the 21st, the man returned with the news that there were no longer any such people as Bolsheviks or L.S.R.s, but all were united in one Communist party who were now called upon to wipe out the White Guard who were trying to bring back the Old Regime. The would-be murderers and their intended victims kissed and made friends and started off in a body to fight against the counter-revolutionaries who were retiring to the mountains. The poor villagers of Troitskoe were still very uncertain and did not know what to believe. I listened to many discussions. It emerged from these that the thing that would save them from the present tyranny was called a 'Constitutional Assembly' (*Uchreditelnoe Sobranye*). No one knew what sort of animal this was till a wiseacre explained that it was another word for the Old Regime. I was astonished at the way these peasants were definitely against *that*.

The reason for the dislike of the peasants for the Bolshevik regime is easily explained by the programme advocated and actually attempted. Every man had his work to do. Some were coal miners, some railwaymen, some factory hands of different kinds. Some served in co-operative stores, some were actors or musicians, some were soldiers and some conducted the government in its different branches, and some were peasants. The idea as explained to the peasants of Troitskoe was that all these people in their various tasks worked about eight to ten hours a day. When the *bourjoui* parasites had been eliminated they would find that four hours a day was all that was necessary and the rest of the twenty-four hours would be for rest, leisure and enjoyment, but up to the present a large proportion of the time of the workers had been employed in maintaining the parasites who were now being liquidated. There would be no need for money; the product of the various hours of work would be exchanged in some way. The peasant would do an honest day's work and at the end of the harvest he would be left enough food to keep him and his family until the next harvest. The excess, which would be considerable if he really did an honest day's work, would be taken from him for the other workers. In the same way the product of their work would be supplied to the peasant, e.g. he would be given coal, a railway journey, manufactured cloth or other articles, a theatre or cinema ticket., etc. The idea sounded all right and, as far as the peasants were concerned, was actually put into practice. Parties of Bolsheviks visited Troitskoe village when I was there and removed flour and other food in excess of the requirements of the family without payment. If all the peasants had willingly done what was wanted, the scheme *might* have worked, but here human nature stepped in. A man saw that if he worked hard he was at the end of the year left with no more than a neighbour who might have been lazy. Consequently in 1919 large areas of land were actually not cultivated. Ivan himself had some fields which he looked after in a native village some distance off in the mountains, while his land near Troitskoe was neglected. He used to send flour secretly at night to his relative, the komissar of Iskander, who was not above accepting it. A similar situation arose in other parts of Russia in 1932 when the peasants refused to harvest crops beyond their own requirements.

The interest of the peasant in the revolution took on a different aspect when he had obtained possession of his land. His chief interest now was to prevent the return of the old evicted landlord, further subdivision of land, and too much State interference.

The universal salary was nine hundred roubles a month irrespective of what work was done. This had, to our eyes, curious results. For instance, doctors in the hospitals were paid at the same rate as servants, but the latter being 'workmen' and members of trades unions, had many advantages, financial and otherwise, which the doctors themselves did not get.

The Government eventually saw that it was necessary to pay the peasants something for the produce taken from them. The amount given, however, was disproportionate to the prices of the articles they had to buy, and so they did not willingly sell their produce. Consequently forcible requisitions were necessary and this led to friction between town and country. The necessity for more food than the ration led to what the Bolsheviks called 'speculation', i.e. secret purchase of goods by people who had money. Your nine hundred roubles bought what was allowed on the ration card, and perhaps a little over from the co-operative shops, but this was not enough, and often the shops had sold out before you reached the head of the queue.

These departures from pure Communism, after being suppressed and in some cases tacitly allowed, were later consolidated in the New Economic Policy. This, however, was not inaugurated until 1921, after I had left the country. The real and most pronounced change in agricultural policy was in 1925 when a peasant was allowed to hire labour to help him.

This is what had been happening in Tashkent; known for ever as the 'January Events'. The komissar for war was a youth of twenty-three called Ossipov. I knew him by sight but had never spoken to him. He it was who had made difficulties over my sending a courier to Kashgar. It will be recalled that Damagatsky had at my pressing request promised that I might send a message to Kashgar and a certain Colonel Ivanov had agreed to go with it. His papers were made out and signed and sealed by Damagatsky, but he was not allowed to travel without permission of the military authorities, and Ossipov had not only refused this but had been rude and threatening to Ivanov when he went to get the permission. I protested to Damagatsky at the insults to my proposed courier, of whom Damagatsky had himself approved. This was in October, and goes to show that at the time Ossipov was a pure Bolshevik.

Ossipov now, for some reason, organized a rebellion against the Bolsheviks. The railway workmen and the best Bolshevik regiment, under a man Kolosaiev, an ex-N.C.O. of cavalry, started the affair. Ossipov went to the barracks of the 2nd Turkestan Regiment and telephoned to the White House, the residence of Kolesov, the head of the Government, that there was trouble in the barracks and asked that some of the komissars should come and help him to settle it by talking to the men. Eight of them came, including the notorious Pashko. Ossipov shot the whole lot. He then declared that the Bolshevik regime was ended and proceeded to get drunk. The fort at Tashkent was occupied by released Magyar prisoners of war who had joined the Red Army. They were loyal to the Bolsheviks and the principal fighting was an artillery duel between the guns of the fort and those in the barracks of the 2nd Regiment. The resistance of these Magyars in the fort was largely responsible for the failure of Ossipov's rebellion.

All prisoners in gaol were released. Two were personal friends of mine, and one was taken to the barracks where he actually spoke to Ossipov, who was drunk.

There are several stories to explain why what started with every prospect of success was an eventual failure. The railway workmen and other supporters of this outbreak did not want the old regime back. They wanted some milder form of socialism than Bolshevism. Kolosaiev had addressed Ossipov as 'Tovarish' (comrade) — the usual form of address. Ossipov had replied that they were no longer 'comrades' but they were officers. On this Kolosaiev turned his men against Ossipov, who was left with only such White Guards as had joined him after the initial action of the railway workers.

This coup had been badly and hurriedly organized, no attempt being made beforehand to bring in Garibaldi's secret army, though Garibaldi was asked to join after the outbreak had begun. Had he come out as a leader and called on the organization, the movement might have been successful. The poor natives did not know what to do. A large detachment of them in the Red Army fought for Ossipov, thinking that they were fighting in support of the Government, and suffered in consequence.

After the conventional precaution of shooting all members of the Cheka who were at headquarters, one of the first things Ossipov did was to go to the bank and remove all the money — between three and four million roubles, a considerable amount being in gold. The Bolsheviks later shot the cashier who had handed the money over, though what else he could have done it is hard to see.

Fighting went on in various parts of the town. Several prominent Bolsheviks joined Ossipov; amongst these was Gegoloshweli who had arrested me on October 21st. At length, on January 21st, Ossipov decided that he was beaten and, with his small party (and of course the money), left Tashkent, deserting detachments of his supporters in different parts of the town who were given no warning and were eventually killed.

The Bolsheviks took fearful vengeance for this rising. All people suspected of having had a hand were arrested. Not only those who had actually taken part, but innocent people also. I heard many harrowing stories. It was sufficient to wear a collar to be classed as *bourjoui* and be arrested. One engineer who had come from Bokhara for the Christmas holidays of his daughter was among those arrested and shot. Another victim was an engineer, Kerensky, brother of the Kerensky who had led the first revolution in European Russia. Worst of all, they arrested and shot Kleberg, the head of the Swedish organization in charge of the interests of German prisoners of war, whose only crime can have been the wearing of a collar. In fact, all those arrested, about four thousand, were shot in a most brutal way.

I had the following story some months later from a man who is, I believe, the only one who escaped. I give it for what it is worth, only saying that it was quite possible.

The man, whom we will call Simeonov, had been a member of the Okhrana, the secret police in the days of the Tsar. He was caught in the streets actually fighting with a revolver and his guilt was not in doubt. He, with several hundred others, was marched into a room in the railway workshops. It was very cold and he was wearing a coat with a fur collar; he had spectacles and a moustache turned up at the ends. He had two passports, one his own and a false one in the name of Popov. He had shown the latter when arrested. The prisoners were called up six at a time. There were six judges at desks, all workmen. A soldier standing by said that he had seen the prisoner before the 'court' with arms in his hands, fighting. The 'judge' ordered him to be shot and the name was written on a list. The batch was then marched into another room to await their turn. Simeonov told the five of his batch that he was going to try to get away and asked them when the names of the batch were called out to say that he, Simeonov, had already been shot. Popov was a common name and there was sure to be one on the list. Simeonov himself got rid of his Popov passport by eating it mixed with snow as he was being taken across the courtyard to the second room. He tore the fur off the collar of his coat, threw away his spectacles and turned his moustache down. In fact, made himself look as different as possible. He told me that in his police days he had often disguised himself. There was a kind of cupboard in the room and he got behind this. All worked according to plan. The five men of his batch were duly called out and shot. They said that Popov, the sixth of their batch, had already been shot and the 'judges' were satisfied with this. He himself remained in his hiding place for several days. He never had an opportunity to get away. At last hunger, thirst and cramp decided him to give himself up and he came out. He was at once asked by soldiers who he was and what he was doing. He said his name was Simeonov and showed his passport. He said he had just come in from the street out of curiosity to see where the people had been shot. He was imprisoned for about three months but as they could then find out nothing against him, he was released.

Whatever the truth or fiction there may be in the above story, the indisputable fact remains that these four thousand men were executed after a brief summary 'trial'(!) during which they were not allowed to speak in their defence. Had he been allowed to say one word, surely they would not have shot the Swede, Kleberg, who had nothing to do with the matter? The names of those sentenced were written on a list which was eventually lost. The victims were taken to a large barrack-room where they were stripped naked, as the Bolsheviks wanted their clothes. They were then taken out and shot in circumstances of the greatest brutality, which I will refrain from recounting. The actual executioners were mostly Magyar ex-prisoners of war, but one Russian, Tolchakov, enjoyed this kind of thing and had himself shot seven hundred and fifty-eight people. He afterwards did all the executions himself and was allowed a special ration of wine to help him to do his work! Later, when he wanted a rest, he was put in charge of the convalescent depot of Charvak in the mountains! The chief judge of these so-called trials was a rascal named Leppa. He was caught looting the property of his victims, tried and found guilty and sentenced to three months' deprivation of civil rights!

One lady whom I know had her husband and three sons shot at this time. A few women who had given food to the 'Whites' when fighting were shot, but most women were left alone.

One youth of eighteen was caught with the White Guards and was to be shot. The Bolsheviks offered him his life if he would give a list of men who had helped or sympathized with Ossipov's rising. He gave thirty-six names and these men were all shot. The authorities then decided to shoot the boy himself, but in the end let him off, thinking he might still be useful, and in any case someone would later take their revenge. The poor boy was going about in terror, knowing that the relatives of his victims had sworn to kill him.

Gegoloshweli, who had been caught red-handed, was among those arrested. As his wife had been friends with many komissars, she was allowed to go and look for the body of her husband and bury it. She found him with no wound. He had fallen down dead when about to be shot.

A by-product of the January fighting was the play of children in the streets. They re-acted the street fighting and copied with some faithfulness the sound of a bullet *arriving*! I always think the Pashtu word *Daz* for a shot is more expressive than any of our words. *Daz* is much nearer the sound as it appears to the target, while our words 'bang', 'pop', etc., are coined from the point of view of the firer.

CHAPTER XI

RETURN TO TASHKENT

WHILE this was going on I was living at Troitskoe with Ivan.
The family consisted of Ivan's wife and a little girl of seven
or eight. It was winter and the small room was sealed up. All
windows had the cracks pasted over with newspaper and the
door was bound with felt. Whenever the door was opened for
anyone to enter, everyone in the room immediately shouted
'Shut the door!' We frequently had visitors; sometimes the
neighbours would come in to gossip. On one occasion Ivan's
relative, the komissar from Iskander, came in for the night
with his wife. He was boasting about what he did to White
Guards and how clever he was at spotting them, which made me
feel uncomfortable. He said he could always tell White
Guards by the white palms of their hands. His wife seized his
hand and opened it, showed it to us and said: 'You must then
be a White Guard yourself for you have done no work since
the revolution'. He and I had to share the same bowl for our
dinner and slept on the floor under the same quilt. He asked
me the number of my regiment and whether I was a Magyar.
I said I was a Rumanian in a Magyar regiment, the 32nd. I
knew that many Magyars had joined the Bolsheviks and, as I
had the passport of a Magyar prisoner of war, I feared that I
might be asked questions. I had learnt from Merz at Yusuf
Khana that the 32nd Regiment was a Magyar regiment which
enlisted some Rumanians. The komissar asked me no further
questions. Through his connection with the komissar I had
hoped that Ivan would be able to get me a *mandat* for quarters
in Troitskoe; this would have been a kind of certificate of
identity for the future and would have led to my getting another
mandat in Tashkent. But the komissar was too cautious and
said to his wife: 'Tell your relative, Ivan, that his friend should

apply to the prisoner of war bureau. For all I know he may be a White Guard.'

On my journey out of Tashkent I had paced the room and noted the measurement, ten feet by eleven and eight feet high, because we had crowded six people into this for the night and the atmosphere and the whole idea had horrified me. One night a large party of Ivan's friends came and we slept fourteen in this room. There was no room for any more and a baby was hung from the ceiling in a basket. The place was so stuffy that I could not stand it and spent the night outside in the cold.

After his defeat Ossipov withdrew from Tashkent and, passing fairly near to Troitskoe, eventually reached Brich Mulla. The direct road from Tashkent to Brich Mulla was through Troitskoe village and past the window of our house, and all day long we saw lorry-loads of soldiers, guns and machine guns going up, and several times lorry-loads of wounded passed on their way back to Tashkent.

After all fighting in Tashkent was over, I decided that I ought to try again to go there. I sent Ivan in to make arrangements. He was stopped on the road by Red Guards and would have been arrested had not one of the soldiers recognized him as a 'Troitskoe *mujhik*', and let him go, telling him to go back to Troitskoe. As he was approaching the village it was dark and another patrol tried to arrest him. However, he got away but lost his horse which was recovered the next day.

After the peasants of Troitskoe had been convinced that Ossipov's movement meant a return to the Old Regime, the Bolsheviks returned the arms they had taken from the L.S.R.s. To the surprise of the Bolsheviks the village was already armed to the teeth, all the hidden arms having been taken out. In their confiscation of arms they had not found a tenth.

Ivan was himself ordered to join the force against Ossipov although his sympathies were strongly against the Bolsheviks. This at first meant he was to stand by till called upon. He was given a rifle, with no back sight, which he kept in our house. One night he was put on guard in the street to see that no one passed along the road during the night. He told me that the whole guard sat round a fire in one of their houses and that there was not a single man watching the road.

One day a priest came in to bless the house and sprinkle holy water. He was going all round the village from house to house. Ivan had some religious pictures in the house which reminded me very much of Tibetan 'tankas', both in form and in the subject which included the physical tortures of hell. The Bolsheviks were of course atheists, but religion was by no means dead. Teaching of religion was forbidden in schools and the ikons had been removed from all school-rooms. There was, however, one in the corner of Ivan's living-room, and the little girl used to cross herself before this after every meal, much to the annoyance of Ivan's relation, the komissar, who considered this 'old-fashioned nonsense'.

Ivan was at last sent out to fight Ossipov with his useless rifle and a horse. I was left alone in the house with Ivan's wife and the child. This was a very unpleasant time. The woman was out a good deal gossiping with neighbours and, I imagine, having meals there, for I got very little to eat. Our food in any case was poor; dry bread made mostly of maize and other things, a small quantity of dried fruit, salted cabbage of which there was a cask in an outhouse, the cabbage being held down by an old brick. The little girl used to annoy me by stealing my share of dried fruit and hiding it! This will show the ridiculous state of mind into which I had allowed myself to fall! We sometimes had a little rice instead of bread. Once I was left quite alone for two days, the woman and child going off to neighbours. I had nothing to eat and was obliged to take out the half loaf I had saved for an emergency from the days I was at Yusuf Khana three weeks before and eat it. It had got very mouldy!

Numbers of village women would come to our house and work themselves up into a state of hysteria about the fate of their husbands who had been sent to fight the remnants of Ossipov's force. They would all weep. One woman went almost mad at the sight of a truck-load of reinforcements which passed our window. Then one day a report came that some Troitskoe men had been killed in the fighting. Ivan's wife went off in a terrible state to see the list. She could not read but the list was read to her; she came back with the, to me, amazing statement that she did not know Ivan's (or her own) surname! She had only been with him a few months! The little girl, her daughter by a former husband, however, was able to tell her and all was well. What struck me was that not only Ivan's wife but her friends and neighbours seemed to be more concerned that his death would deprive her of food than that she had lost a dear husband and companion. It is sad to think that conditions of living can make human beings so materialistic.

I afterwards heard that Ivan got into trouble with the soldiers because he was firing his rifle up in the air instead of at Ossipov's men. He pointed out that he had no backsight and even if he had had he knew nothing about it as he had never fired a rifle in his life. One of the other Troitskoe peasants said this was not true as he was the most noted slayer of wild pig in the village!

One day Eshan came to see me. He had been to Tashkent to take some money from Markov to his wife. He had been searched but allowed to pass. All the time we had been at the bee-farm with him he had never suspected who we were. He now told us that he suspected that the White Guards were Garibaldi's and my people. This was not very nice as he would talk among his native friends. However, it was getting too late for news or suspicions up there to do us much harm.

Later we heard that Markov and Lipski had themselves joined Ossipov in the Pskem Valley. The Bolsheviks heard that counter-revolutionaries were living at the hut and sent up a party to see. After our departure other refugees had gone there, including Markov's father-in-law. Red soldiers visited the hut, looted it thoroughly and took all the honey. To see what had actually happened, Markov, Lipski and another man left Ossipov and crossing the ridge from the Pskem Valley into the Kok Su, made for the honey farm. On the way they met two Sarts who told them that the hut had been looted, but that there was no one there now. So they approached the hut suspecting nothing. Markov himself was about two hundred yards in front of his two companions when he reached the house. A dog barked and out came six Red Guards. Markov lost his temper and fired, wounding one in the jaw. The others fired and killed him. Lipski and his companion saw this happen and then retired. The Bolsheviks at the hut did not know whom they had killed but Eshan was still living there and recognized Markov's body and told them.

On their way back they came on the two Sarts who had given them the false information that no one was there. They caught them and learned that they were scouts sent out by the Bolshevik party from the honey farm to get information about Ossipov's men. Lipski and his friend killed these two men.

Markov had been a very good friend to me and was a most charming companion. If he had not acted as he did he would merely have lost his property, which, considering he was with Ossipov, was only to be expected.

I heard that Markov's father-in-law had got into trouble with the Bolsheviks. He had boldly got up at a meeting and suggested that all parties be allowed to vote; not, as by the new franchise rule, only the Bolsheviks and L.S.R.s. They had come to arrest him for this and he had escaped to our hut where he had hidden for some days. Markov had then openly joined Ossipov and so his father-in-law had to leave the hut. He had to pass through the Bolshevik troops who were fighting against Ossipov. He was seen, fired on, and taken prisoner, but after a few days in prison was released. All this had led to suspicion of the house and to the death of Markov.

I decided now again to attempt to return to Tashkent. I had been so long in Troitskoe, and was known to so many people, that I had established here an identity as an Austrian prisoner and many people would have vouched for me as such in any simple inquiry.

But there were difficulties. I had been going under the name of Kekeshi, a Hungarian. Many Hungarians were in the Bolshevik service, in the army, police, etc., and I did not know one word of Hungarian. I had been able to tell the ignorant komissar of Iskander that I was a Rumanian in a Hungarian regiment, but Kekeshi is no Rumanian name, so this alone might have led to suspicion, and I realized that as soon as I was suspected I would be found out. My attempt to get a *mandat* for quarters in Troitskoe had failed. I had by now completely adopted the personality of Kekeshi, and I therefore decided to travel with some peasants who had known me for some time and who would be quite ready innocently to swear that I really was Kekeshi, the Hungarian prisoner of war, and I hoped they would answer any questions and especially testify that I had been in Troitskoe all the time during the 'January Events'.

On February 14th I started out from Troitskoe on foot carrying a few things in a bundle. I expected to be searched and questioned, and left all my papers and everything that could cause any suspicions behind. After going a short distance I was overtaken by the peasants with whom I was to travel, a man and two women in a cart. I had told them that I wanted to go to town, but had been refused a permit as the man who should have given it had quarrelled with me.

We drove to Nikolskoe where we passed the funeral of three men killed in the fighting with Ossipov. Here we had dinner with some peasants and then the man drove the cart back to Troitskoe and the two women and I walked the four versts into Tashkent. This was hard on my leg, it was the first long walk I had done. The women had said that they would see me over the bridge on the Salar River where there was said to be a Bolshevik picquet. However, at the last minute, they left me and went off to the railway station. This made any explanations more difficult, but I decided to go on and to my relief I found that the picquet on the bridge had been removed and was only put on at night. I reached the town about two o'clock. I intended to go to my previous quarters at the Mateveevs, but did not want to do so before dusk. I therefore wandered about for four hours in falling snow; I had tea several times in different chai khana (tea-shops). In one or these two Austrians also in uniform came in and spoke to me. I talked to them a little but they did not ask my nationality or regiment. My modest German was sufficient for them. However, I cut the interview short by gulping my tea and going out before we got on dangerous ground.

The Mateveevs were very glad to see me; they had not heard of me for a long time and thought I must have been killed. During my absence in the mountains three people had been billeted at the Mateveevs. The arrangement was that we all lived together. Our host's wife cooked for the whole household, with occasional assistance from myself or the other lodgers.

They told me that Garibaldi had stopped with them. When the 'January Events' began, some of Ossipov's men came to him and asked him to come out as their leader with his organization — the secret army. He refused. My host was so angry with him that he turned him out. I tried to find him but he had left Tashkent and I never saw him again. I heard that some months afterwards he had made his peace with the Bolsheviks.

The day after my arrival I had a visit from Miss Houston. She told me that Noyev had been arrested and kept five weeks in gaol. He was there at the time of the 'January Events' and was released by Ossipov's men. Had he not been safely put away he would probably have been shot at that time. As it was he gave himself up and was re-imprisoned. He was elaborately questioned about my whereabouts. Neither he nor Miss Houston, nor in fact anyone in Tashkent except my hosts and my messenger, Lukashov, had known where I had been.

I was now obliged to return the Kekeshi passport. I had always imagined that Kekeshi must have been one of the many thousands of prisoners of war who had died, but I now learnt that he was very much alive and was incommoded by the absence of his passport which he had lent to a friend for a short time. The only one that I could obtain at very short notice was that of a Galician, Austrian prisoner, by name Vladimir Kuzimovitch. This was quite unsuitable. As a Galician I should have been able to speak perfect Russian. All Austrian-Slav prisoners — Poles, Serbs, Slovaks, Czechs, etc. — after four years in Russia could speak perfectly. I, therefore, had to avoid passports of prisoners of Slav races.

After a day or two I obtained the passport of a Rumanian officer prisoner called Georgi Chuka. I was glad to get the passport of a Rumanian-Austrian. There were so many Magyars in the town and so many of these had joined the Bolsheviks that my lack of knowledge of the language might have been noticed. There were fewer Rumanians so the risk was not so great. I could pass for a Rumanian prisoner with a smattering of German, without the likelihood of a Rumanian being at hand to show that I was a fraud. Actually I was careful to avoid any such chances. For instance, I never risked being stopped in the street about curfew time. Once I was going home fully a quarter of an hour before the time when I was greeted by a policeman with '*Stoi, Tovarish*' (halt, comrade). He accused me of being out too late. I showed him my watch and he said: 'Well, hurry up then.' A considerable time before curfew hour the streets were practically deserted as people did not like having unnecessary contacts with the police. Once when we heard that the curfew hour had been altered, we rang up the police to ask them. They would have been surprised to learn who it was that wanted to know!

CHAPTER XII

TASHKENT AGAIN

ONE of the first things I had to do after my return to Tashkent was to consult a good Russian doctor about my leg. We had to choose a trustworthy man and to tell him who I really was. This was not difficult and a consultation was arranged. The doctor said that the Sart doctor who had treated me in the mountains had done very well indeed. He recommended massage. There was, he said, a good masseuse in the town. I said that in my peculiar position it was essential that I should see as few people as possible and that my acquaintances should be discreet. Could this masseuse be relied upon not to question me too much and to keep her mouth shut if she had any suspicions that I was not exactly what my papers showed. The doctor said that such people had nothing to do but to chatter when engaged in their work and that a silent and discreet masseuse did not exist, certainly in Russia. I, therefore, had to give up all idea of massage.

After a few days with my hospitable friends, certain reasons made it necessary for me to leave immediately. I did not know where to go. Considerable preparations were necessary before quarters could be occupied.

People took a great risk in putting up anyone in trouble with the authorities. Each house had been visited by the *Zhilischnaya Kommissiya* (Quartering or Billeting Commission). They would enter a house, say, with dining-room, drawing-room and three other rooms. They would find three people living there. They would put perhaps two or more families in the house. One of these would be a reliable Bolshevik who watched the others. One man was appointed head of the house and it was his duty to report the arrival of any strangers. Did he not do so he would certainly be given away by the Bolshevik lodger specially installed there. Everyone had to have a *mandat* or permission to occupy his quarters. These were difficult to obtain. What many people of the upper classes did was to abandon their houses and furniture and go to live with friends. In this way a house could be filled with people of the same class and this was pleasanter than having a Bolshevik agent watching you. The great difficulty of all these combined household arrangements was cooking. There would be only one kitchen range in the house and the different families all had to use it and this led to unpleasantness and quarrels. There were no open fireplaces in any of the rooms. All heating was by large closed stoves which could not be used for cooking.

I decided to go to the house of an engineer named Andreyev whom I had met once or twice in the early days of my time in Tashkent and who, I thought, would be sympathetic. The house stood in a small garden. I walked up and rang the bell. The door was opened by a girl whom I had also met previously. I hoped she would not see through my disguise of beard and Austrian uniform. She gave no sign and said she would call Andreyev. I said to him in Russian: 'Do you know who I am?' He replied in English: 'I suppose you are Colonel Bailey.' 'It is clever of you to recognize me,' I said. He replied: 'The girl who opened the door told me who you were.' This was bad news as she was famous for being the most unrestrained chatterbox in the town.

I explained my position to Andreyev. He said he could take me in but only most secretly. If the other family in the house should come to know I was there the news would rapidly spread. They were quite unable to hold their tongues.

Here at Andreyev's I was to remain absolutely hidden and never go out except into the garden after dark. I went to get my small belongings and as I left the house the girl gave me a sweet smile of recognition from the window. Some years later I met her in Korea.

I lived in a back room and Andreyev brought me my food. I usually joined him and his sister at supper in the evening. Later

I went out into the town occasionally after Andreyev had made sure that all the other talkative intimates were out of the way. At Andreyev's I had plenty of time for reading. I found some of Tolstoy's children's stories very simple in language, easy and delightful to read. There were several good books in French. In English I read the Bible through from beginning to end; also *The Old Curiosity Shop* twice as it was the only book of this kind in English. It did not suffer from re-reading. A flamboyantly illustrated guide to the Albert Memorial showed that this much abused monument contained hidden historic details which had escaped me as I had never been nearer to it than the road.

Once when I was in my room Andreyev's sister came in to say that the house was being searched. There was no possibility of leaving so we hurriedly got some books and writing materials together and sat at a table. When the men entered they asked who I was. The lady replied that I was an Austrian prisoner of war who was giving her lessons in French. They made no further inquiries and did not ask to see my passport, and we found that they were really only the Housing or Quartering Commission seeing that people were not wasting space and were living properly jammed up. Still, the incident gave us a start at the time.

On another occasion there was a search of the house for hidden stores of food, etc. This was a most dangerous affair, but I was warned and went out for a walk, returning just at curfew time, after it was all over.

About this time I discarded my Austrian uniform. Most of these uniforms had been continuously worn for four years — some for more — and were getting worn out, and prisoners were providing themselves with Russian civilian clothes, so that it became rather more conspicious to wear uniform than not to do so. I also obtained a pair of plain (non-magnifying) pince-nez as a further disguise.

In the meantime, Miss Houston had been trying to find me other quarters. The idea was that I should in some way get a *mandat*, which proved very difficult. In the end quarters were found but without a *mandat*.

I received the following note from Miss Houston written in pencil on a small piece of paper which I have by me as I write and which gives a vivid idea of the precautions necessary:

'Now, the arrangement is so: you will be opposite the Foreign Office in the Voronsovsky on the corner where the Town Hall is (you know, where the trams turn round). Well, you stand on the corner of the Romanovsky and Voronsovsky at five-thirty, and you will see a grey-haired lady coming along from our house direction with a bundle wrapped in a red tablecloth under her arm. She will stop at the Town Hall for a minute and light a cigarette, then go on walking. You must follow; then when she will go into her house you pass and afterwards come back and go in yourself.'

I lived in this house with people I am calling the Pavlovs quite openly; I used to help with the work in various little ways. One night a wounded man named Krasnov arrived and I was asked to help to carry him in. This we had to do just before curfew hour which was at that time eleven o'clock, and only after making sure that the other inhabitants of the house were shut up in their rooms and would not see. He had been shot in the leg when fighting with Ossipov against the Bolsheviks. In some inexplicable way he had passed himself off as a Red Guard and had been taken to hospital. Later he was suspected, and made a wonderful escape from the ward when the nurses were out of the room. He just walked out on his crutches and got into a carriage which his friends had ready. Unfortunately his leg broke again. He was taken to a *dacha* (garden) outside Tashkent where he remained safely till the leg got better. It never got a chance to get quite well. I felt very sorry for a wounded man having to hide like this, knowing that he would be shot if found.

One day my landlady said that the head of the house was insisting on a *mandat* for me. To obtain this I had to go personally to the Housing Commission with my passport. I had no idea how safe my Chuka passport was, and in any case I had always avoided such personal contacts with the bureaucracy of Bolshevism. I presumed that Chuka was dead, but like Kekeshi he might not be. We therefore made the following arrangements: I went back to Andreyev for a couple of nights. My hostess took my Chuka passport to the Housing Commission and told them that I was ill and that some Red Guards had been quartered in the house entered on the passport, and that I wanted to leave and move over to her, as I was giving French lessons to her son. They accepted this and gave her a *mandat*. At that moment an Austrian who was a sort of interpreter to the Commission, overheard the name Chuka. He said he knew him well, snatched the *mandat* and my passport out of the lady's hand and said: 'Tell Chuka to come himself to the Dom Svobodni (Headquarters of the Government) for the mandat and at the same time bring the money he owes me.' Thus my plans for a *mandat* broke down and, worse still, I lost my passport. This was a disappointment as not only would I have had a *mandat* for these quarters, but I would have had my identity accepted which would have made further proceedings easier. Later I saw an advertisement in the newspaper that Chuka was giving English lessons at the address on the passport I had been using! I thus learned that Chuka was still in the land of the living. We were afraid that the lady might get into trouble if the supposed Chuka ever turned up for his *mandat*, but we arranged a story to explain her position if questioned. She was to say she had told Chuka to go for his *mandat* with the money he owed, but that he had stopped coming for the daily French lesson and she did not know where he was. However, she was never questioned, though two suspicious characters who we thought might be Cheka agents were billeted in the house probably to clear up these suspicious circumstances.

Passports were not easily obtained and for a short time I used that of a Lett named Justus. A Lett is not a Slav and so need not know Russian, but by my passport I had been fourteen years in Tashkent and would have been expected to have friends in the town and to know more Russian than I did. Also I was seventy-five years old, but we managed to change the 'seven' into a 'four'. I got rid of this unsatisfactory paper as soon as possible. Later, I was Joseph Lazar, a Rumanian prisoner of war and a coachman by profession.

Just before I abandoned the name of Chuka I had to visit a dentist, a lady. I had to wait my turn in the waiting-room, and the assistant used to call out the names as the patient's turn came. I was afraid that as I had lost my Chuka papers the position would have been very awkward if any friend of Chuka's or any Bolshevik who knew what had happened (and such spies were everywhere) was in the waiting-room. The dentist knew me as Chuka and I could not suddenly appear under another name. I therefore told the dentist I had to go to Samarkand. She said I must come back in a month or I would have great trouble, but I never did so.

Talking of dentistry, there was an extraordinary Chinese itinerant dentist in the Old Town of Tashkent, who worked in the streets. He told the patient that he was suffering from a maggot in his tooth; he would remove it. He opened the patient's mouth and put in a pair of chopsticks and brought out a maggot or caterpillar, threw it on the ground and stamped on it, gave the man a pill and took his fee. I can only imagine that the chopsticks were hollow and concealed a maggot. The patient seeing what had come out was well on the way to a faith cure, and an opium pill perhaps confirmed his relief.

Other strange people could be found in Tashkent. I have mentioned the Englishman with his troupe of performing elephants. I saw in the street a very old Serbian whose only stock-in-trade was a parrot, which for a small sum picked an envelope out of a packet and gave it to you. Inside was your fortune; mine was: 'She loves you.' This probably differed but little from all the others. The old man told me he had travelled all over India and largely in China making a living in this way.

My leg was still giving me some trouble and I thought it advisable to consult the doctor again. It happened that the appointment was made just after I had changed to the Lazar passport. On my first visit I had gone to his private house, but now he wished to see me at a small hospital or nursing home. I rang the bell and the door was answered by a nurse who had in her hand a notebook. As she admitted me she asked me in brusque, businesslike way my name. I had only had the name a few hours and was so taken aback that for the moment I could not give it. I then got it out: 'Lazar.'

'Christian name?'

That beat me; I knew it was something in the Bible, so said 'Peter'.

This was written down but when I saw my passport I realized that I should have said 'Joseph'.

The doctor who was expecting me had no idea who Peter Lazar could be, so I had to brush the nurse aside, burst into the room, take off my spectacles, when he at once recognized me.

At the time of the 'January Events' many people who had nothing to do with them had hidden themselves and were trying to leave the country. They were continually being caught, arrested and in some cases, shot. The Sarts had a profitable time. They would take money to help a man to leave and then hand him over to the Bolsheviks and thus get paid twice, while the unfortunate refugee lost his life. Colonel Ivanov, who had been accepted as my courier to go to Kashgar, was re-arrested in this way. On my disappearance he had been arrested and sent to gaol for his connection with me. This was really most unjust. Damagatsky had said I might send a courier and asked me to send the man to the foreign commissariat for his papers. I chose Colonel Ivanov quite openly and above board, and sent him for his papers, which were refused by Ossipov. In fact, I only saw Ivanov once when I had arranged with him to take my dispatches. Ivanov had been released by the White Guards during the 'January Events'. After the defeat of Ossipov he had tried to leave the city with his wife and child disguised as Sarts. He had paid a Sart well to take him out of the city, but on the road the guide had demanded a further sum which Ivanov could not pay. The man therefore informed the Bolsheviks who rewarded him and arrested Ivanov.

This kind of thing made it impossible for me to travel about and to get out of the country or even to send messages. I have explained how Lukashov had been shot. Another messenger got as far as Samarkand and then came back with my messages. Others failed to deliver my messages for one reason or another. Perhaps they never tried.

Owing to the difficulty over the *mandat* at the Pavlovs I could not return to that house permanently, but for a short time I slept in either of two other houses, and in the end returned to the Pavlovs. Had I been found sleeping in a house without a *mandat*, I proposed to give some address and say that I had come for a cup of tea and had stayed too late, and had not been able to return before curfew, so I had been obliged to spend the night where I was. However, this was not necessary, and by good luck neither of these houses was searched when I was in it.

One day a lady told me that she had heard that an Englishman who was very much wanted by the authorities was living in a certain woman's house, but was obliged frequently to go to other houses to avoid danger of searches. This so exactly described myself that I decided I must leave these quarters for ever.

I still visited the Pavlovs occasionally and had several interviews with my servant, Haider, there. He told me that after my disappearance, he and Ibrahim, my other servant, had been arrested, threatened with shooting, beaten and asked to disclose where I was. They did not know and gave the reply I had told them to give, and after some time in prison they were released. He thought Khan Sahib Iftekar Ahmad had gone back to Kashgar and I later heard that this was so.

We had our last fall of snow on March 23rd — a late year. The spring now came on quickly and was very lovely in Tashkent. The streets for many days were scented by the flowers of the acacias which formed the avenues; this is, perhaps, the pleasantest memory I keep of my year in Tashkent. The scented air, deep shade and running water in the streets made one wish that man were not so unkind and that people had leisure and quiet to enjoy it all.

The danger of arrest was still as great as ever. It was impossible not to allow at least a few people to know who and where I was, but I kept the circle as small as possible. It had, however, inevitably grown larger and rumours were spreading. I therefore decided to make a fresh start. I knew that Mrs. Edwards could not hold a secret, so I decided to use her unreliability in this respect for my own purposes. The Edwards were hiding somewhere. Miss Houston was in touch with them and was helping them with quarters and *mandats*, as she was doing for me. One day I arranged a meeting with Mrs. Edwards. This took place in the street. She, dressed as a peasant woman with a kerchief over her head, and I in Russian dress with a beard. However, we easily recognized each other. I told her as a very great secret that I was leaving the country and wished to do what I could to help her before I left. She asked me where I was going. I said: 'To Ferghana, but it must be an absolute secret or I should be caught on the way.' I heard two days later that she had told several people that she had met me and that I had told her I was going to Ferghana, but she thought I would never give away my intentions like that, so that she really thought I must be going in the opposite direction, to Bokhara! Things could not have gone better. I was delighted. The rumour I had started was well on its way. She told me that she and her husband were also making arrangements to go away. I asked if I could help them and suggested that they might give themselves up, but they were afraid to do this. I gave her money and put her in the way of assistance. I never saw her again. I am sure that the rumour I had thus spread had reached the Bolsheviks and they took it for granted that I had left. All this time I had been in touch with Tredwell, but so closely was he guarded that I had not been able to speak to him.

CHAPTER XIII

LOCAL BOLSHEVISM

THE Bolsheviks in Tashkent were cut off (except by wireless) from the outer world; in February or March 1919, however, General Dutov, who held the railway north of Tashkent, was forced to retire and the line was opened up giving communication with Moscow. The authorities in Moscow were becoming alarmed at events in Turkestan. In these early days of the revolution, in out of the way parts of the country, there was not much opportunity of finding efficient leaders, and the early revolutionaries in Turkestan were men of little education or capability.

The principles of Communism were not being followed; the massacres in January gave a bad name to the Russian Government as a whole; the treatment of the native population and their exclusion from the Government was contrary to the expressed programme of Moscow. They felt that if some Mohammedans could be brought in the enormous native population would be reconciled to the new conditions. They sent down a commission of a more able type of Bolshevik to report and advise. These were Appin, Voskin, Vanbar alias Weinberg, Bravin and others. This man, Weinberg, told Miss Houston that he was really a Belgian journalist and was a secret British agent, and was in touch with the British Mission in Meshed. He asked her to help him and promised to take her with him to Meshed when he went there. This was evidently an attempt to trap her, but she was too clever and told him that she thought it a dangerous thing to mix in politics and preferred to confine herself to her work. A man of this name, possibly the same, was some years later secretary of the Central Trades Union Council.

Bravin had been a consul in Persia and, I believe, once acted as Minister in Teheran under the Imperial Russian regime. He spoke both Persian and Hindustani.

These people brought with them a sum of fifty million roubles in imperial notes with which to back up the rotten Turkestan currency which nobody wanted. The imperial or 'Nikolai' note was more valuable than the Soviet money; it is strange that the Moscow Government should have admitted this and acted in direct defiance of their own laws. They were, however, in need of some currency which would be acceptable to the Turkomans and others whom they hoped to bribe to fight against their enemies in Transcaspia and other parts of the country.

They also brought with them a copy of the *Times* of January 29th, 1919, and I managed to borrow this, which, though over two months old, was of great interest and value to me. This was the first English newspaper I had seen since a *Weekly Times* of September, 1918. I think some surprise would have been occasioned among the 'big men' had they known who was reading their paper in the next room. To show how I had been cut off from news I may state that I first learned of the movement of General Dunsterville to Baku from a review of a book by Edmund Candler in this paper.

About this time some Indian revolutionaries appeared in Tashkent. They were headed by one Barkatulla, who called himself 'Professor'. He was a native of Bhopal State in Central India and had been a teacher of Hindustani at Tokyo until expelled from the country by the Japanese, when he moved to America where he had let no opportunity pass of vilifying our rule in India. He claimed to be a German subject, and even stated that he was the German diplomatic agent in Kabul. He held a German passport issued at Dar-es-Salaam in East Africa. He died in 1927. During the war an organization called the Provisional Government of India had been formed in Berlin. The President was Mahendra Pratap (of whom more later) and this Barkatulla was the foreign minister. This government was to be ready to take over the government of India after we had been defeated in the war and turned out. History repeats itself. On July 24th, 1941, the London *Daily Sketch* reported: 'Ribbentrop is forming a "Provisional Government of India" composed of well-known renegade Hindus and Molsems in Berlin.' Associated with Mahendra Pratap and Barkatulla in the enterprise was a Turkish captain, Mohammed Kazim Beg, who styled himself Turkish diplomatic agent in Kabul. He had been a member of the Turko-German Mission in Afghanistan under Niedermeyer. Barkatulla guaranteed to organize a Bolshevik revolution in Afghanistan if sufficiently financed and supported.

These two men claimed to be representatives of Germany and Turkey in Afghanistan, and, after the war, at a time when we were at peace with these countries, they carried out the most violent propaganda against us.

Here are some items from a memorandum issued by these people. Many of us will hardly recognize India under this description:

'In India the British draw large salaries while the people perish of plague and famine caused by extortionate taxation; according to statistics published by the British Government itself, nineteen million Indians had died of famine during the last ten years. Thousands are hanged, imprisoned and exiled for expressing love of their country. Trials are held in English, a language which the accused and others do not understand. Men are punished for carrying pen-knives more than six inches long. Mohammedans may not collect in their mosques for prayer, nor may Hindus come together in their temples. Many parts of India are uncultivated as the yield of the soil is insufficient to pay the enormous taxes demanded. The Government has forbidden education and prevented the establishment of factories. Men are forced to work for twelve hours a day in fearful heat for a wage of from threepence to sixpence a day, and in many cases under a system of forced labour for no pay at all. Men are also sent abroad to work in British colonies against their will. The famine-stricken people are enticed into the army and then forced to destroy their own brothers. On account of this many regiments have mutinied. An army known to the people as the "Army of Murderers" has been especially recruited from the wild frontier tribes (mostly Afghans) with which the people are kept in subjection. India was forced to pay large sums towards the last war. It was further stated that Sir Rabindranath Tagore, "the Tolstoy of India", had been imprisoned. No such uncultured, barbarous, immoral deed had ever been perpetrated in Russia even under the Tsars. England has thrown aside the fig-leaf with which she covers her face.'

One article in a newspaper referred to the Indian Mutiny when thousands of old men, women and children were cruelly murdered. The exact date of the Mutiny was known a year before to two hundred and fifty thousand sepoys, but no single one was a traitor to give the date away. The sepoys at this time formed 'Soviets' in the same way that Russian soldiers did sixty years later. When the new rebellion does break out in India they can rely on the help of the workmen of England.

My servant, Haider, went to these people and told them that I had disappeared, leaving him stranded without money and that I had not even paid him his wages. He asked their assistance to return to India. Kazim Beg read his passport which was in the usual printed form 'To afford him every assistance and protection of which he may stand in need'. He was very angry with him and said: 'If you are on these terms with the oppressors of India you are no friend of ours. Off you go to gaol.' Poor Haider was again imprisoned, but only for one night as the prison authorities had had him before and knew all about him, and released him the next day. It is curious that people like Barkatulla and Kazim Beg, an Indian and a Turk, had the power in Russia to order people off to gaol. This was called 'Internationalism'.

I have a proclamation issued by these two. It began with a list of Mohammedan holy places captured by the British: Mecca, Baghdad, Damascus, Jerusalem, Nejf, Kerbela, Kum and Meshed, and a list of countries oppressed: India, Egypt,

Tunis, Algeria, Morocco, Arabia and Ireland! It went on to say: 'The English are Normans who conquered Britain in A.D. 1066 and the real British people itself are awaiting the moment when the World Revolution will bring them liberty.'

There was also a wonderful travesty of the American Civil War in a speech by Kazim Beg which was published. There had been a war between North and South America because the South Americans wanted to force the North Americans to release their slaves. Eventually the South Americans were successful in the war and the slaves were released. President Wilson is President of North America and was enslaving the Mohammedans of Turkey and ten million Jews! It is conceivable that the half-educated people might have heard of the American Civil War and would believe this sort of thing.

Other propaganda in which Kazim Beg specialized was to the effect that Indians were not allowed in tramcars in India, such luxuries were only for the white people! They were allowed in railway trains but only in special trucks, like cattle trucks. Only Europeans were allowed to travel in passenger coaches. Later, when I was in Bokhara, a man told me that this was certainly true as he had seen photographs of carriages marked 'For Europeans Only'! The explanation is that in some trains a single *third* class compartment is so labelled. There is no such reservation in first, second and intermediate class carriages. This reservation of third class compartments avoids undesirable racial quarrels with the lower classes of India. This fact figured to a large extent in the Bolshevik propaganda, the implication being that the poor Indian was not allowed to enter even a third class carriage but had to travel in something worse! Bravin was put on to help Barkatulla and Kazim Beg and between them they sent men to buy off the Turkomans who were fighting with our troops against the Bolsheviks in Transcaspia.

The Bolshevik plans for India were to start disturbances by any means possible — Pan-Islamism would do as well as anything else, even though this might be contrary to their eventual policy in Turkestan. They would then guide these disturbances into a revolution on Bolshevik lines. It was during the summer of 1919 that the Bolsheviks began to realize that their dream of World Revolution would not be fulfilled. The proletariat of the west were proving traitors to their cause. This annoyed them considerably, and the British Labour Party came in for a deal of abuse. They were 'Lackeys of the Bourgeoisie'!

They therefore decided to turn their main attention eastwards. The professed plan in the East was to exploit countries considered ripe for revolution such as China, India, Persia and Afghanistan, and, with armed Communist forces led by Russians, to turn on the traitorous proletariat of the West and compel them to adopt Communism. There would be no necessity for serious fighting; a few leaflets before or during the battle advising the enemy soldiers not to fire on their fellow workers would be sufficient. In countries ruled despotically such as Afghanistan, Persia and Bokhara, parliamentary institutions were to be helped with encouragement in various degrees. Freedom of speech, writing and public meeting under such institutions would give the people the power gradually to weaken the position of the despotic ruler and give opportunities for working up Communist feeling in the country. The complete Bolshevization of Asia was the key to World Revolution.

Later they realized that India was not ready for Communism and that under British rule it never would be. They therefore advocated and encouraged every movement towards independence, believing that if the British could be turned out the chaotic residue would be ripe for Communism.

Naturally, these attempts to interfere with the Empire of India did not pass unnoticed and in reply to the protests of the Government, the Soviet authorities on May 15th, 1923, said that their actions in the East aimed at the maintenance and development of friendly connections with the peoples of the East, based on genuine respect for their interests and rights. The oppressed people of Turkestan might have another story to tell. The Turkestan Government were especially concerned with the neighbouring province of Chinese Turkestan. They tried to establish diplomatic and consular relations, but the Chinese Government refused to accept such people. They then sent a man called Shester as commercial agent to Kashgar. He was refused permission to enter the country, but later a small commercial mission was accepted and a Sart Commercial Mission from Chinese Turkestan visited Tashkent. I gathered that the latter was really an attempt to save a little from the wrecks of the fortunes of Sart merchants of Chinese Turkestan whose property at their branches in Russian Turkestan had been confiscated by the Bolsheviks.

The Red Army consisted largely of prisoners of war, most of whom were Hungarians; Rumanians for many reasons refused to join. German prisoners were comparatively few in numbers and, owing to the efforts of Zimmermann, very few of them joined.

The British Mission at Meshed had offered to send any men back to their homes in Austria who would surrender themselves. The prisoners as a body demanded to be allowed to return this way. The Bolsheviks refused and there was some tension in the army at this time.

In April 1919 nine hundred armed soldiers came from the Transcaspian front and the Samarkand garrison to enforce their demands. The Soviet authorities dealt with these in a very clever way: the trucks at the rear of the train were cut off by night, one by one, and dropped at different places in the desert. A Bolshevik force then went down the line and dealt with each truckload separately and disarmed the mutineers without any fighting. The train was then joined up again and run right through Tashkent without a stop to Aris station, north of Tashkent. Here the men were taken out. Seventy of them were taken back to Tashkent; of these, twenty were shot. Had this train reached Tashkent without interference a severe blow would have been struck at the structure of Bolshevism in Turkestan. The German and Austrian prisoners of war were really the backbone of the Red Army. They were well trained soldiers with considerable experience. To encourage colonization the Imperial Russian Government had exempted from military service all men born in Turkestan and also all who had arrived as young children and had been a certain number of years in Turkestan before they reached military age; the result was that there were few trained soldiers of Russian nationality in Turkestan.

For the benefit of the prisoners of war who had joined the Bolsheviks a party called 'Internationalists' was formed and encouraged by the Turkestan Bolsheviks. The idea, of course, was to abolish all national barriers and to fuse humanity into one homogeneous whole. However, the party broke up owing to quarrels over the question of the language to be employed. The party split into two main branches, the Hungarian Internationalists and the German Internationalists!

From among these Communist prisoners the authorities organized a committee to control the prisoners (who had all been released at the outbreak of the revolution). This committee by threats and persuasion managed to keep a large number of prisoners in the army. The army was well fed and well paid compared with the civil population, and the committee of Communists was all powerful. Still, it is surprising that there were not more desertions and escapes than there were. Another factor was this: it was now 1919, many of these soldiers called up before the war had not seen their homes for six years and more. They probably had not communicated with their families for years. Their relations must in many cases have thought them dead. Probably a similar state of affairs existed among Russian prisoners in Austria. The Austrian prisoners in Russia were marrying Russian women and working the land relinquished by the Russian husband or father who had disappeared during the war and revolution. These Austrians did not want to return. They found Turkestan a fertile country and conditions not unbearable, especially for those who had joined the Communist party.

As late as 1929 efforts were made to get the remainder of the prisoners from Turkestan and Siberia back to Austria and

Hungary but, I believe, with little success. Those who had been so long away had really settled down and colonized their new country. Alexander the Great's Greek soldiers are said to have colonized the country through which he passed on his way to India in the same way. Roman soldiers did the same in many places.

The Bolsheviks having put down the rebellion against them in January 1919 settled down to run the country according to their own lights.

I have explained how houses were requisitioned and *mandats* given for their occupation. People living in good houses with nice furniture often wished to remove it. The Bolsheviks forbade this, saying that all furniture must be nationalized with the house. One friend of mine had put his winter clothes away and during a search in summer they were all removed. The searcher said: 'If you keep things shut up in a box you cannot want them very much.' In the spring government officials entered all the small private gardens in the town and 'nationalized' the fruit trees. The owner was told that when ripe the fruit would be picked by the Government and no private ownership would be recognized.

A Russian Grand Duke, Nikolai Constantinovitch, had been living in Tashkent. He had been exiled from European Russia many years before on account of an escapade in which the crown jewels figured. He had died a short time before I reached Tashkent. His large house, full of beautiful pictures and furniture and *objets d'art* had been nationalized and was a museum to show the people how the *bourjoui* lived in the bad old days. His morganatic widow, who had been given the title of Princess Iskander by the Tsar, was left in the house as caretaker. As an Austrian prisoner of war I sometimes visited this 'museum piece' and talked with the princess. Later her son was to be my companion in our long desert ride from Bokhara to Meshed.

Among other objects displayed was a fine jewelled dagger which took the fancy of Bravin, who ordered her to hand it over.

This she refused to do. Not knowing that this was the wife of the Grand Duke, he was very angry, but afterwards when he learnt who the caretaker was he was less insistent and finally agreed to give a receipt for the dagger. This the princess placed in the cabinet where the dagger had been. This caused amusement in the town and embarrassment to Bravin who eventually got the notice removed, but stuck to the dagger. Similarly, stuffed birds and animals in glass cases and other natural history specimens were displayed in the Tashkent Museum labelled 'Nationalized from . . .'

In the course of searches photographs were objects of special interest to the police. A photo of an officer of the imperial days often led to arrests and inquiries as to where he was and in any case gave a presumption that the person concerned was not favourable to the new regime.

When we arrived in Tashkent there were no metal coins in use. There were several kinds of paper currency. First the 'Nikolai' (Imperial Russian) money. This was in notes of various denominations from one kopek (a farthing) up to five hundred roubles (fifty pounds at the pre-war exchange). Then there was also money issued by Kerensky's government, notably a thousand rouble note bearing a picture of the Duma building. Both these currencies were considered reliable and it was in them that we brought our money from Kashgar. Kerensky's government had issued small, unnumbered notes of twenty and forty roubles, about two and a half by two inches in size. These were issued in large sheets which could be cut up as required: small change was in postage stamps of the Romanov Centenary issue, bearing the head of one of the Romanov Tsars, specially printed on thick, ungummed paper. These got so worn that they were almost illegible after much use. There was also the local Turkestan currency which was very much distrusted at first, but later came more and more into use. The smallest denomination was a fifty kopek note which was of a convenient size and texture for rolling a cigarette! The Turkestan money was not controlled. It is true that it was numbered, but I have many notes of one denomination bearing the same number and the number was put on purely to give false confidence.

As the cost of living went up so salaries were raised and notes of higher value printed. The printing was done in a very simple way on paper that contained no watermark. From the street you could see the machine printing large sheets of five hundred rouble notes at a very quick rate. Without understanding a great deal about inflation one wondered where it would all end.

In any case small change had practically no purchasing value. A box of matches, for instance, cost thirty roubles, that is three thousand one kopek notes! At this rate a single match cost about forty of these notes. One *inch* of calico cost one thousand of these notes, one walnut twenty and one grape seventeen. Other prices in June 1919 were:

Potatoes	10 roubles per lb.
Tallow candles	10 roubles each
Eggs	9 roubles each
Milk	3 to 4 roubles a small glass
A reel of cotton	200 roubles
Ordinary pins	30 roubles for 10
A pound of tea	1200 roubles
Flour	700 roubles per pood (36 lbs)

A bowl of *pilau* in a native tea-shop was the cheapest and best food that could be got and supplemented the food supplied by the co-operative stores on the ration cards. This cost twenty-five roubles a bowl. A rouble before the war was two shillings.

Tea was drunk to an enormous extent in Turkestan by the whole population, both Russian and Sart. During my stay in Tashkent it was almost impossible to get any and 'fruit tea' was made. This was of apple. The apple skin and pulp were cut up small and roasted and looked a little like tea, but, naturally, tasted like the juice of stewed apples. Sometimes a little real tea would be mixed with this by those lucky enough to have any.

I bought some and gave it to people to whom I was indebted for help and kindness and who would not accept money.

We did not inquire too much into the meat given on the ration ticket. Never, of course, was it prime beef or any other kind, but whether it was horse or camel did not seem to matter!

Very occasionally we got fish — rather coarse, possibly something 'scrounged' from the fuel ration for the railway engine! I remember one occasion when someone came in and told my hostess as a great secret that a Jew at some house near by had some delicious fresh fish. She rushed off only to discover that the man had had some fish the day before but it had all been divided among his friends.

Andreyev's sister used to make quite a drinkable beverage, which we called coffee, from roasted and ground wheat flavoured with the kernels of apricots prepared in the same way.

All tailors and shoemakers were employed by the Government. They would do private work as a great favour and for large sums and then only if you supplied light, i.e. candles or paraffin oil — both almost impossible to obtain in place of the usual twist of cotton wool in a saucer of cotton oil. I had a suit made of good rough Kirghiz camel-hair cloth under the above conditions. I paid nine hundred roubles for the material and five hundred and twenty-five roubles for the work and I cannot remember how much for the lighting!

In these circumstances the Government worked out detailed requirements for every conceivable article, which they published. Here we learnt that women were expected to use three handkerchiefs each a year — men none!

All the money in the banks had been nationalized. Theoretically people with small deposits below five thousand roubles (five hundred pounds at the pre-war rate) were allowed to draw out small sums for living expenses. People with deposits of over five thousand roubles were considered *bourjoui* and the money was all confiscated. At first insurances up to ten thousand roubles were allowed to stand, but later these were also cancelled.

One thing struck me as peculiar and that was that most people had large sums of money in imperial notes in their houses. This was, of course, carefully concealed, but I do not think that under circumstances of this kind we in Great Britain would find ourselves with such large sums of money in the house. Perhaps there was some kind of innate fear of disturbances from which we in our country are exempt. A large amount of silver from the currency is absorbed every year in India for this reason. In 1916 a rich landlord in the north of India had six hundred pounds in gold dug up and stolen from his hiding-place. I told him that he should have lent the money to the Government for the war. He replied that he had subscribed largely to war loans but added 'a man must bury something'.

One day when I was having a cup of tea with some friends in their small garden the terrier, much to the embarrassment of his master, brought him a packet of Nikolai money which he had just dug up; the possession of this, if known to the authorities, meant imprisonment and probably a death sentence as a 'speculator'!

In their search for money the Government exacted what were called 'contributions'. These were sums of money from five to ten thousand roubles which people who were believed to have money were called upon to pay. The method of exaction was to arrest a number of such people and put them together in a room in the gaol. They were then called out one by one, and shots were heard by those remaining. Usually these people were not shot: the whole thing was a play to persuade people to disclose hidden money. Three people were, however, actually shot by the sadist Tolkachov who was temporarily sent away as a punishment! There is one horrid story of this brute. He was shooting a man with whom he had been friendly and the man asked him to shoot him clean with one shot. Tolkachov took six.

The names of many streets in Tashkent were changed to those of heroes of the revolution. We had 'Lenin', 'Karl Marx',

'Engel', 'Communist' and such names. There was a fine bronze statue of General Kauffmann in the square. He had commanded the Russian Army that had captured Tashkent in 1865. The general was supported by two soldiers, one sounding a bugle, the other planting a flag. There were also tablets giving the dates of his victories and the dates of the occupation of the principal towns of Turkestan. This was considered an eyesore, so for May-Day the statue was screened in greenery and red flags and pictures of Lenin, Karl Marx and the Bolshevik 'Martyrs' shot by Ossipov in January.

CHAPTER XIV

SPRING ACTIVITIES

On March 27th a special train was sent from Tashkent to Moscow with any foreigners who wished to leave the country.

I was sorry to lose several friends, though I had not seen much of them lately. The greatest loss was that of Tredwell who had been in constant touch with me and whose support and encouragement had been of great value and comfort, and whose help, if I had been captured, might have been invaluable.

The life of an accredited consul in Soviet Russia had not been a bed of roses. Tredwell had been arrested on October 15th, 1918, along with myself and other subjects of the Allies. He had been kept five hours, after which at Tsirul's instigation, Kolesov and Damagatsky had both come and ordered his immediate release and apologized.

He was again arrested on October 26th and marched through the streets to the Cheka office to be questioned. He was then kept under strict arrest for five months. For the first two he was kept continuously in his quarters, but after this he was taken out and allowed to walk in the streets for exercise with a guard on each side of him. I myself once saw him being exercised in this way, but though we passed each other shoulder to shoulder no glance of recognition passed between us.

At the time of the 'January Events' he was again taken out and threatened with being shot. His guards made a feeble protest but ceased to interfere when threatened with hand grenades. His abductors told him that he would not require an overcoat as the place where he was going would be warm enough! There was also no need to trouble about food.

He was told that he was to be shot at six in the morning. Shortly before that hour he heard the tramp of feet outside; the door of his cell was opened. He thought this was the end, but it was Tsirul with some of his militia who took him out by force from his gaolers and escorted him back to his own quarters, where they guarded him until the immediate danger was past. A truly fearful experience.

Only once did I have an opportunity of speaking to him, and that was the day before he left. I went to the back door of his house at dusk and he slipped out and we had about twenty seconds' conversation in the street; he then had to hurry back before his two guards noticed his absence.

His journey home was not uneventful. He joined forces with Captain Brun and some of the Swedish Mission who had been helping prisoners of war. He and a Swede cooked for the party over a small brazier. He had much useful information on the situation in Turkestan, and this he managed to send out via Siberia in case the worst should happen to him in passing through Russia. Had things gone differently in Russia, his information and reports would have been of the greatest use to the commerce of his great country.

On reaching Moscow he was still kept for twenty-four hours under close arrest at the railway station. He was then released but was shadowed by the Cheka and had difficulty in shaking off these people while he delivered messages from his friends in Tashkent to their friends and relatives in Moscow who had been without news of them for eighteen months.

Apart from his help to me in Tashkent I learnt later that on reaching America he asked for permission to go to Persia whence he hoped to be able to communicate with me and to help me to get out of the country. The friendship formed under unpleasant conditions in Tashkent has lasted.

Captain Brun of the Royal Danish Artillery had done wonders under the most difficult conditions in mitigating the hardships of the Austrian prisoners. He had also been arrested and threatened with death. Once they attempted to nationalize the house in which he was living where he flew the Danish flag. With great coolness he defied the authorities, invited them to come on with their machine guns and all the paraphernalia of war while he took photos to send out to the world. An account of his life and work in Tashkent will be found in his book *Troublous Times*. In this he mentions that he once recognized me in the street, but did not dare to speak; so my disguise was not as good as I had hoped. Before the war he had been attached to the 16th Lancers at the Curragh and had many friends in England. His opposite number, Mr. Kleberg, the Swede in charge of German prisoners of war, had been shot by the Bolsheviks, so Captain Brun's diplomatic immunity might easily have been violated, and his firmness and courage in the interests of the Austrian prisoners entailed great risk to himself.

Tredwell carried messages from me. Events, even life itself, were so uncertain that I also sent a message through Captain Brun. Possibly Tredwell might be lost and Brun get through. One had always to be thinking along these lines. In this message I mentioned especially the names of Sir Arthur Hirtzel and Mr. (now Sir John) Shuckburgh. My object was to convince them that the message was really from me. No one else could have known that these were the two men in the India Office with whom I had had extensive dealings. This plan was successful. The message reached the India Office from Stockholm and my object was understood and a reassuring message was sent to my mother, whose anxiety during all this time was very great.

The remainder of the Swedish Mission also left, as did Captain Bolterno, the Rumanian officer. Miss Houston was given an opportunity to depart but decided to stick to her charges, the family of three children to whom she was governess. It required great courage to take this decision.

In the middle of April I managed to get fresh quarters. This was a relief from the discomfort of sleeping in a different house each night and then never in a bed. One of my hosts treated me most royally in this matter. His house-proud wife made me a wonderful bed on the floor with soft mattresses and clean sheets every time I went there. At other places I did the best I could with rugs and blankets on chairs or a sofa.

One of my kind helpers had a peculiarity. She knew Paris well and loved to talk about it. Speaking to me she always translated place names into English. 'Peace Street'; 'Elysian Fields' and 'Concord Place' all seemed strange to my ears, and once 'Fat Liver Pie' gave me a moment's doubt.

My new host was an old man, Yakovliev, who lived with his sister in the basement of a house. He was a clerk in some government department. I did not feel it fair on people to let them keep me without saying who I was and clearly letting them understand the risk they were taking. On this occasion, however, a very kind friend, Madame Danielova, who had found me the quarters, begged me not to. The sister was a great gossip and the brother only slightly less so, and Madame Danielova was convinced it was better to keep them in ignorance. It was not pleasant to have to deceive people like this.

The Yakovliev house was not ideal for me. They had harboured Ivanov, my proposed courier, who had been arrested when trying to leave the town. The Cheka had means of extracting information from people who got into their hands and they might make Ivanov or his wife say where they had been living. This would have meant the arrest of Yakovliev and also of me if I had been found there. However, many risks of this sort had to be taken.

To the two Yakovlievs I was a Rumanian-Austrian prisoner of war who had joined Ossipov in January and was being hunted by the Bolsheviks. They were always bringing me interesting news and rumours of events in Rumania in which I had to take an interest. More awkward at first were the questions I was asked about Rumania. If we had a melon on the table I was asked if such things grew in Rumania. If we had fish for dinner I was asked about fish in Rumania. In the end I derived some amusement from inventing detailed answers to such questions, knowing full well that what I said would be soon forgotten and if I said the contrary the next day it would not be noticed. For instance: there are two kinds of fish commonly eaten in Rumania, one very good but expensive, the other very salt and nasty and really not as eatable as the rather unpleasant salt fish we get in Turkestan from the Aral Sea! Melons in Rumania are much smaller than those of Turkestan and not quite so good and cost a good deal more. I had to discuss bread, meat, different kinds of fruit, etc., in this way and rather enjoyed it.

After my departure the Yakovlievs must have learnt who their lodger really was and must have been surprised at the glib way he was able to give them details about Rumania, and I hope they forgave me for all my deceptions, especially when speaking of the whereabouts of Colonel Bailey! Vambery, who visited Central Asia in disguise in 1863, felt this same difficulty and describes his unhappiness at having to deceive people who had become his close friends.

Besides Miss Houston, who was very much suspected and watched, I had two firm and trustworthy friends in Tashkent whose houses were not suspected, Andreyev and Madame Danielova. Once when going to the latter's house I passed in the street Noyev's very clever child, Jenia, who without looking at me or showing any sign of recognition, her lips hardly moving muttered 'Pas y aller', as I passed her. I learnt later that at that moment a search was being made by the *Sledstvennaya* commission. Madame Danielova had got one of the cryptic telephone messages through to the Noyevs to ask them to warn me, and the plan had succeeded owing to the skill and carefulness and above all, the bravery of my friends. At this house I once found a Swiss governess, Mademoiselle Lina Favre, having an angry conversation with one of the members of the *Sledstvennaya* commission whom I recognized as one of the six men who had actually arrested and questioned me some months before. He took no notice of me at all but I slipped away as unobtrusively as I could.

I was once having my hair cut when another of the six members of the Cheka who had arrested me took the next chair! I never enjoy having my hair cut at any time, but I think this was about as uncomfortable a time as I have ever had in a barber's chair. There was nothing to be done but to submit silently. I daresay the danger was not very great but the feeling was unpleasant, to say the least of it.

One day at Madame Danielova's I met a member of the German secret service, named Schwarz. I was introduced, clicked my heels, shook hands, giving my name at the same time and made a rapid exit. Later, I avoided this house as Madame Danielova's circle of acquaintances was too large and varied for my liking!

Schwarz once told Miss Houston that the Germans in Afghanistan had been forced under threat of death to fight with the Afghans against us. I wondered whether this was true. I thought it quite possible that as Schwarz himself and other Germans in Turkestan and Afghanistan might eventually be forced to travel through India to get home they would naturally conceal any hostile acts they or other compatriots might have committed against us.

Madame Danielova had a great friend Tsvetkov, a clever, cultured man and a poet. He was arrested and tried for the part he had played in the 'January Events'. One day when I went to see her I found her in a very unhappy and depressed state. She had just had a secret letter from him to say that he had been found guilty and condemned to be shot and asking her to send him some poison. She told me that she could not bring herself to do this. Something might turn up to save him, and if she had sent the poison asked for, she would feel as though she had murdered him. A few days later she went to the prison and asked to see him and was told he had that minute been shot. The man who told her this said that several of the komissars were sitting in chairs smoking cigarettes and laughing and joking when the execution took place before them. One of the komissars was an acquaintance of Madame Danielova — I have said she had a varied circle of friends. Not knowing that she was Tsvetkov's friend he told her that he had ordered his instant execution when it was proposed to have a fresh trial as some more evidence had been produced in his favour. He said that a fresh trial would have given a great deal of trouble. When he witnessed her horror at his callousness, he said that the proposed evidence would have involved a number of other people and would have led to a fresh batch of executions.

Once a week I used to go to the Noyevs for a bath, a meal and the news. I also used to see my servant Haider and my dog Zep. Zep had been given to me by His Highness the Maharaj Rana of Dholpur. Both parents were pedigree dogs, but Zep had been an accident. His father was an Irish terrier and his mother a smooth-haired fox terrier. He was like a well-bred fox terrier with the colour of his father.

I later learnt that for the first three months of my disappearance the Bolshevik police had put spies on the dog to see if I ever saw him. They had been taken off before I actually did talk to my dog again. Once, however, I saw the dog walking in the street and rapidly made off in the opposite direction lest he should come up to me. The Noyevs' house was dangerous for me as I had been so much there in the early days; later, Voskin, one of the 'big men' from Moscow, was quartered there and we considered that this would make it much safer. Who could imagine that the most wanted man in the town would be having his bath in the next room to him!

Curfew hour was eight p.m. up to March when it was extended to eleven and later again curtailed to ten. It was important to know this. For an ordinary individual to be found a few minutes later in the streets merely meant a night in the lock-up and a fine of three thousand roubles; but in my case the danger was that any inquiry or the examination of my prisoner of war passport might have led to discovery. Remember, I was going about as a Rumanian and did not know one word of the language.

On Easter Eve the authorities extended the curfew time to three in the morning. The Russians keep Easter as the most important religious occasion — much more important than Christmas. I went to the cathedral with Andreyev. The crowd was enormous. A procession headed by the bishop went round the cathedral carrying religious emblems. They then entered followed by the most fervent crowd. As the clock struck midnight everyone in the church kissed those near them saying *Kristos Voskress* (Christ is risen). The reply was *Vo istinu voskress* (He is indeed risen). The bishop then went to the steps of the altar while the whole congregation (except I myself who always avoided conspicuous positions) filed past receiving an embrace and a kiss from the bishop, dressed in his jewelled robes. It was a moving ceremony and showed that the anti-God activities had not gone very deep into the minds of the populace. The shocking and revolting posters condemning religion as the opium given to the people by which means the *bourjoui* kept the proletariat in subjection had up to this time had little effect.

The bishop had for seven years been Orthodox Bishop of San Francisco. Many of the Indians of Alaska had been converted to Orthodox Christianity by the Russians when they were in possession. When the country was sold to the United States in 1867 the Russian Church retained this religious connection. Even in the days when I was free I had never seen the bishop.

People I visited were apt to get into the bad books of the authorities. The bishop was later shot by the Bolsheviks. This caused great resentment and distress. The bishop was a very fine high-souled man with great influence for good. My host Yakovliev's sister could not be comforted and was continually praying before his photograph.

At Easter my humble abode in the basement was a hive of activity. The best cooking stove was there and the people from the upper parts of the house came to use it. My hostess did not sleep for two nights. Numbers of eggs were cooked and painted various colours, and what luxuries could be found in the way of food were produced. I contributed a pound of real 'caravan' tea, i.e. tea which had come overland from China and which had not crossed salt water.

The first of May, a very hot, sunny day, was a great Bolshevik Festival. By this time most buildings of any size had been requisitioned by the Government for some purpose or other. All these were hung with red flags. The newspapers were being printed on red paper — very trying to the eyes — and these were also used to give the required tint to the town. All school children were taken out in procession carrying red paper flags, the girls with wreaths of faded poppies. I saw one comic but pathetic sight — a poor little girl lost and in tears carrying a red flag in her hand and a wreath of poppies in her hair. The Sart schools were especially well organized, the boys all dressed alike and marching in step. There were processions of the different trade unions carrying banners, some written in Jewish characters and some in Arabic. The Russian slogans on the banners were 'Long Live the Proletariat', 'Down with the Bourgeoisie', etc. Most of the crowd were wearing a red favour of some sort and one little girl seeing I was wearing none offered me a poppy, which I wore. I estimated that there were four thousand five hundred people in the procession, of whom about a quarter were women. At least an eighth were Sarts. There were several bands which played revolutionary music. Soldiers were not much in evidence. They were presumably doing more important work elsewhere. There were about two hundred infantry and three hundred cavalry and, conspicuous by their smart appearance, the German detachment. The three chief revolutionary songs were the 'International', the 'Workman's Marseillaise' and the 'Hymn of Freedom'. These were sung in the procession and the crowd joined in. This singing was well organized. Among the crowd were people who led the singing and who, as the band struck up the tune, distributed pamphlets with the words. I can never forget the comic sight of the bandmaster of the leading band — a small man with fierce red whiskers and huge spectacles who smoked cigarettes as he marched at the head of the procession. It was difficult at times to realize that this was forced. Nine-tenths of the parents of the children in these processions had nothing but bitter feelings against the authors of these demonstrations. I know that many of the teachers leading these processions felt the same. With all this clever organization, however, it was very easy to get a feeling of enthusiasm, at least for the occasion.

There were still great hopes of British intervention and the stories of people who came from Transcaspia were very comforting. One of the most encouraging signs was the attempt of a man to cash a cheque on the Tashkent branch of an English bank! Of course, no such thing existed; but if the British were actually drawing cheques on the Tashkent bank it was felt that they *must* be in earnest! There were strong rumours of a big turning movement through Termez and south-east Bokhara to cut off the Bolshevik forces from Tashkent. This seemed to me to be impossible and unnecessary. It only required a little determination and there would have been no need to leave the railway line. The maintenance of a force away from the railway would have been most difficult, if not impossible.

On May 5th, a special telegram was published announcing a great victory on the Askhabad Front. This was purely imaginary and was not even referred to in the newspapers next day, but there was a reason. Reinforcements were showing some reluctance to leave Tashkent for the Front and this was a means of encouraging them. As soon as the train had left there was no further need to carry on this farce.

Bokhara had been in the position something like that of an Indian State, i.e. with a good deal of internal independence but no relations with foreign countries. The railway with a few yards on either side, and a small area round each station were Russian territory. Bokhara itself is ten miles from the railway and the nearest station was Kagan, where there was a small Russian town. In the summer of 1919 there had been constant rumours of war with Bokhara. The Bokharan representative in Tashkent lived in a house in the 'Square' and spent the whole day sitting in the window dressed in his bright silken clothes, gazing out and doing absolutely nothing. Whenever

I was told that war had actually broken out, I used to stroll past his house and if I saw him sitting there I knew it was merely another Tashkent rumour. I had not visited him, being anxious to avoid casting suspicion on him. Captain Brun had, however, been to see him and had received a spirited protest from Damagatsky who pointed out that Bokhara's foreign relations were still conducted by the Russian Soviet Government.

A man named Videnski, who had been a kind of political officer for Bokhara in the imperial days, was a great friend of the Amir's. He was living at Kagan and had been treacherously seized with the help of Bravin, his old friend and colleague. The Amir was anxious to have him released and this led to some amusing negotiations. The Bolsheviks promised to release him if the Amir would order the British not to enter Bokharan territory. The Amir replied that he had already done so. This sarcastic reply enraged the Bolsheviks. They told him that he must resist with his army. The Amir replied that he was neutral. The Bolshevists were using the railway through his territory for their troops and the British might also do so if they could.

CHAPTER XV

SUMMER DIFFICULTIES

WITH the early summer life became almost pleasant in Tashkent. The food situation was relieved by the appearance of fruit in the kiosks on the street corners. Turkestan is a great country for fruit. Before the war special trains took this to Central Europe and some of it may have found its way to London. This fruit arrived some weeks before the Southern European fruit. In the beginning of May strawberries and cherries appeared in the streets. There was an enormous but rather tasteless strawberry called a 'Victoria'. I have never seen any of such an enormous size. The apples of the previous year were still to be had when the fresh crop came on sale. Apart from having fresh apples all the year round, we had good dried fruit. The hot sun made preservation easy. The fruit was merely cut into slices and laid in the sun in the autumn and this gave a supply for the whole winter and spring. In this way pears, apples, cherries, peaches, nectarines, etc., as well as raisins, were dried by each household for its own use.

Nightingales could be frequently heard singing in Tashkent and Yakovliev, who spent a night in a *dacha* in the spring, told me that no one could sleep for the din they made. When I was out in the country in July they had stopped singing.

One of the most beautiful and conspicuous birds in India is the Paradise Flycatcher. It is a little larger than a wagtail. In India the cock bird when fully plumaged is a wonderful glossy black, or rather a very dark green and snow white, with a pair of white streaming tail feathers fifteen inches long, which give this beautiful bird the appearance of a comet dancing in space. The hen is black and chestnut but — and here is a curious thing — the cock bird in India for its first three or four years is like the hen, black and chestnut but with long chestnut tail feathers, whilst in Turkestan and also in Indo-China the cock bird is never white but all its life has the plumage, chestnut and black, of the Indian bird in its earlier years. What can be the reason for this?

As an example of the difficulties of getting into communication with the outside world I will give an account of one of my efforts. A trustworthy friend told me that the barbers' union were sending a man to Bokhara, where there was still a free market, to buy various necessities: razors, soap and, above all, drugs of which there was a serious shortage. This messenger was a Czech and could be relied upon to take a message for me. After some time he returned. He had had the greatest difficulty in getting from the railway station at Kagan to Bokhara. He had to wait until a friend of his was on sentry-go, and he could not return from the city for three days when the same sentry was again on duty. He reported that no Russian could show his face in Bokhara and that for him the position had been very dangerous. He had delivered his message and brought me back the following receipt: 'Received the lock referred to, but as we have no key it has been sent to the workshop; when it is received back it will be sent or I myself will bring it.'

My messages were to be sent to two British colonels named Enders and Timme who were said to be at Kerki. I never found out further about this. No officers of names resembling these had been in Meshed and no officers at all had been in Kerki. The messenger did not know who I was and told me that as he was starting he was asked if he would take with him a British officer who was hiding in Tashkent. He had refused as it would have been too dangerous. I never knew who had interested themselves in my affairs. I came to the conclusion that it was someone (possibly a Bolshevik agent) trying to get into Bokhara in my name.

When our war with Afghanistan commenced the Press burst out with a flood of anti-British articles with a Pan-Islamic flavour and on June 4th an Afghan envoy, General Mohammed Wali Khan, arrived with a large staff and an escort of soldiers in scarlet tunics. The Bolshevik Government made a great deal of him. The station was decorated, he was given a guard of honour and fireworks were let off. A gala performance was given at the theatre which was decorated with rugs and carpets requisitioned from the bourgeoisie. Incidentally none of these decorations were ever returned. The envoy published several interviews in the Press.

His account of the causes of the Afghan war was rather naive. The Rowlatt Bill had been passed by which Mohammedans were forbidden to pray in their mosques and Hindus in their temples. The people of India had appealed to Afghanistan through their newspapers (in spite of the tyrannous Press laws!) for help against this inhuman law. Disturbances had broken out near the Afghan frontier and the Afghans had moved troops to strengthen their frontier posts. Eight aeroplanes from India had attacked these Afghan troops and five of these planes had been destroyed. Afghanistan had then been forced to declare war.

The General had come to Turkestan to offer help in men and to ask for help in arms, especially artillery. (Of course the Turkestan Government had no arms to spare.) He said he was going to the Peace Conference, and then to visit the capitals of the world to announce to them Afghanistan's independence.

News of the war — all Afghan successes, of course — was about three weeks old. Those who know the Mohmand frontier will be interested to hear that one Mr. Haji Sahib Turangzaiski (a Mohmand firebrand with whom I once had dealings) had occupied the English town of Shabkadar. Peshawar was surrounded by the Mussulman army. Relations with India were friendly!

The General carried an Afghan order for the Amir of Bokhara. It is also believed that at the request of the Amir military instructors and men to make cartridges were sent from Afghanistan to Bokhara. This must, of course, have been directed against Soviet Russia. This mission, after visiting various European capitals, reached London in August 1921.

During this time I was living with the Yakovlievs in their basement. There was a certain amount of shooting in the streets at night, said to be the police firing on robbers. I once saw the militia firing down a street when they shot a deserter, but not until he had killed two of them and wounded several. One day the *Sledstvennaya* commission actually arrested a man in one of the rooms of the house in which I was, but they did not trouble about the humble people in the basement. Once I heard that the commission were searching for a man in my street who was not a prisoner of war but who held a prisoner-of-war's passport. Could this be me? It was quite possible. Madame Danielova, who had friends in the street, went at once to make inquiries. She learnt that the wanted man was a pock-marked Russian whose photograph they had, so I did not disturb myself.

In the summer Colonel Ivanov, who had been accepted by Damagatsky the foreign komissar as a suitable courier to take my messages to Kashgar, was put up for trial for participation in the 'January Events'. He had a pretty good alibi, up to a point, as he had been in gaol! He was supposed to have been in close and secret communication with me and the opportunity was taken at his trial to question him about me. Miss Houston was also called up and cross-examined. When had she last seen me? Did I say good-bye to her when I left? Did I say where I was going? She answered all these and many other questions. Then suddenly: 'Why are you keeping his dog?' Wrong information by the spies. She was doing nothing of the sort, the dog was with other people but often went to the house as the Noyev children were very fond of him and fed and petted him. There was really only one dangerous connection between Miss Houston and Colonel Ivanov: when Lukashov came back from Kashgar with letters for me he had asked Ivanov where I could be found. Ivanov had told him to ask Miss Houston (she herself did not know where I was but had to pass Lukashov on to Mateveev.) This connection between the two did not come out at Ivanov's trial: he was given three years' imprisonment; as he expected to be shot, he was quite satisfied. His wife was given a year's imprisonment 'for failing to denounce her husband'.

One day, my host, Yakovliev, told me that the English Colonel Bailey was hiding in the village of Khumsan near Brich Mulla, and that his courier, Ivanov, had been arrested and imprisoned and was being starved in prison. Of course Yakovliev had no idea who I was. I said that I knew a friend of Ivanov's and would see if he would do anything for him. A few days later I gave him money to get Ivanov special comforts, saying it had come from Ivanov's friend. Ivanov's 'hard labour' was the making of straw hats, and for this he had to go out about once a fortnight and cut the right kind of grass. Once my host said that his guard was going to bring him in to dinner! I hardly knew Ivanov but thought it best not to give him a chance of recognizing me so I 'lunched out', i.e. bought some *liposhkas* and fruit which I ate walking about in the street. A *liposhka* is a round, flat loaf, rather like an Indian *chupatti*. Then again one day without any warning Ivanov and his Sart guard came in for a meal. We all sat down together.

At the same time the wife of Colonel Kornilov, also a very much wanted man, came in. It was an embarrassed and confusing meal, the two Yakovlievs, Madame Kornilova, Colonel Ivanov, his Sart guard and myself. I was not sure whether Ivanov had recognized me and unless he did so no one present knew who I was. I wished to have a word with him in private to tell him that my host did not know who I really was, but I did not have an opportunity and now I think that Ivanov himself had no idea at all. Madame Kornilova and Ivanov knew each other, but were afraid to give any sign of recognition owing to the presence of the guard. The latter was, I believe, quite 'safe'; he had been a rich man but had had everything confiscated by the Bolsheviks and had been forced to join the Red Militia as an alternative to starvation. He himself said he was glad of the good meal provided by my hostess.

One day a strange Sart speaking perfect Russian came to our midday meal and something made me suspect that this must be Kornilov in disguise. After he had left I asked Yakovliev and he said I was right but that no one must know. After this he came several times and his wife who was going about quite freely in her own name also came. This seemed to me to be most dangerous. The police had only to shadow her to catch him. Later he came to the house to live and shared my tiny room with me. It seemed to me most risky for the two most wanted men in Tashkent to live in the same room. I could not well ask my host to be more careful so I decided to move my quarters. This, as usual, took some time to arrange. After a few days Kornilov left and went to live in a *dacha*, a small native house, in a garden on the outskirts of the town. The Russians in Tashkent and also those in Kashgar used to go away for a change in the summer and took some native house in a pretty garden as a summer holiday home. The Yakovlievs and I used to go on Sundays and spend the day with the Kornilovs at this *dacha*. On July 3rd I heard that Kornilov had been arrested. A small boy had told the police that a suspicious man who sometimes wore native clothes was living in this *dacha*. The police at once went there and took him. Our visits to him were, of course, known to his family and neighbours and I feared that the police might establish a connection between Yakovliev's house and Kornilov, so I left, much to the relief of Yakovliev.

I was sorry to leave people who had been very kind to me for nearly three months, who never knew who I was and whom I was never able to thank as I could have wished.

It was very foolhardy of Kornilov to live in this way and to receive frequent visits from his wife and children. Once I suggested this to Yakovliev. He replied that the Bolshevik police were too stupid to be able to trace Kornilov through his wife. He proved, unhappily, to be wrong and Kornilov was arrested, tried and convicted. It was reported that the Turkestan Government asked Moscow to permit them to reprieve him; the answer came that they might do so, but it was too late. He had already been shot.

In June I heard that Captain Capdeville, the French officer, was to make an effort to get out of the country. I arranged to see him and to give him a message. We had not seen much of each other before we went 'on the run' and were both of us disguised. Consequently the question of mutual recognition had to be overcome. It was dangerous to make definite appointments to meet in the street. The police were always suspicious of people loitering about, and if one person were a few minutes late for an appointment this would make it dangerous for the other.

The arrangement was that we were to start at a definite street corner at a definite time and walk round the block, I keeping the houses on my right and he on his left. We were each to carry a newspaper rolled — not folded. My messages were rolled up inside my newspaper. Punctually I arrived at the spot and started to walk round the block. Presently I met a most curious sight. A man with the queerest mutton chop whiskers the like of which I had never seen before in Tashkent, or anywhere else. He was carrying a rolled-up newspaper. We stopped and conversed for a few minutes. I pointed out something in my newspaper to him and in this way we changed papers. He left me with the remark uttered in an excited and loud voice that the situation was *incroyable*. He was later caught on the way to Kashgar, as I will relate. I always felt that perhaps his extraordinary and conspicuous whiskers had got him into trouble.

Madame Danielova had a large house. It was requisitioned but she was allowed to keep one room. She had several talks in English with Abdul Ghani, the interpreter of the Afghan Mission, who was astonished to learn that her house and furniture had been confiscated without any compensation, and that she did not know from day to day when she might not be turned out altogether. The Bolsheviks had to conceal many of their ideas and much of their programme from their Afghan allies.

I used to visit my few friends in the town for a change and talk and a meal. It was in some ways a risky thing to do as I had left my various quarters on account of dangerous suspicions which had been aroused. Therefore I only went by appointment and used to walk up to a certain point by a fixed known road so that (as happened on one occasion) I could be stopped if necessary. Actually entering the house I used to go round by different ways so that people would not recognize me as a regular visitor. At first I felt very self-conscious meeting people I had known previously but later felt more confidence in my disguise. Several times I passed Damagatsky in the street but always avoided looking at him. I also at one time passed Mrs. Gelodo, the landlady of my house in the Moskovskaya, almost daily. She never knew me.

Once when I was visiting the Pavlovs, I found there a boy of sixteen belonging to another family living in the house. He had been with Ossipov but had been left behind somewhere as he had frostbite. A few days later he and a friend of his aged nineteen were found and arrested and the elder boy sentenced to be shot, the younger, owing to his youth, was sentenced to ten years' imprisonment, but was later released. Later the elder boy was reprieved; the first time the Bolsheviks had done such a thing. The fact that the boy was living in the house made it very suspect and it was as well that I had already left it. I think this boy had been purposely released as a decoy for his counter-revolutionary friends. However that may be, two fresh spies were quartered in the house and I seldom visited it again.

On June 14th the Afghan Mission, under General Mohammed Wali Khan, left for Moscow, leaving behind a Consul-General who carried on the chief business of the mission — anti-British propaganda. The same day Bravin left for Kabul on being appointed first Soviet Ambassador to Afghanistan. Neither party got to their destination. The Afghan Mission to Moscow got as far as Emba, where they heard that Port Alexandrovsk, on the Caspian, whence they had hoped to sail, was occupied by anti-Bolshevik forces. They must have been surprised to learn that these anti-Bolshevik forces they were up against were the Royal Navy which had captured the port on May 28th. The Afghan party returned to Tashkent and left again later. Bravin's party went up the Oxus by boat but were forced to return owing to the action of some enterprising White Guards. A man who had been on Bravin's boat told me how it all happened.

The Oxus flows through Bokhara territory and Bravin had asked the Amir for an escort. After a good deal of trouble this was promised, but at the last moment the soldiers themselves refused to go, and Bravin had to go without one. The steamer was towing a barge on which was an old gun and ammunition. At one place near Kerki the steamer had to pass under a cliff and from this they were suddenly fired on with a loss of two killed and eighteen wounded. There was great confusion and to add to this the barge caught fire and shells on board began to explode. My informant, who was a Russian, said that Bravin and all his party lost their heads and behaved badly. The only man who behaved well was the old Turkoman captain of the steamer, who, quite coolly, turned it round and then went and put out the fire on the barge! The Government made serious complaint of this incident to the Bokhara Government on whose territory it had occurred, but no settlement was ever arrived at. Bravin made another attempt to reach Kabul and was this time successful. He travelled via Merv, Khushk and Herat, thus avoiding Bokharan territory, where he had been so scurvily used. In his reports he complained of surveillance everywhere in Afghanistan. He described his reception in Kabul as 'pompous but without cordiality', and his audience with King Amanulla as 'without interest'.

He advised his Government to take advantage of the weakness of Afghanistan after the war with us, and to demand the cession of certain frontier posts and districts which were of strategic advantage to Russia. He did not long survive his arrival at Kabul where he was soon assassinated. He was succeeded by one Suritz who later came to some prominence as Ambassador in Ankara. He had special orders to forward the policy of uniting the East under the leadership of Russia against the West, where the treacherous proletariat would have nothing to do with their would-be Bolshevik liberators.

CHAPTER XVI

BACK TO THE MOUNTAINS

PRIVATE teaching such as that given by a governess was not allowed, being, as we all know, the worst form of *bourjoui* activity which eventually leads to exploitation, imperialism, speculation and various other dreadful wickednesses. Private teaching, therefore, was forbidden. Many (especially Czech) prisoners of war were earning a little money by teaching music and foreign languages — among these Chuka, whose passport I had once held. A drive against this undemocratic activity was carried out in September 1919. The teacher was called a speculator and the employer a *bourjoui*. If you want either to learn or to teach, you should go to a school open to all. Teaching had to be on special lines; for instance in the teaching of history no mention could be made of kings. At the same time education was very keenly advocated and pushed forward. The streets were placarded with notices: 'Education will be the saving of the Revolution', 'Get yourself educated', etc. etc.

Miss Houston was at this time forced to teach in a Soviet school. In addition she had been made to teach Madame Bravin English. This lady was very vindictive and hated us. She once showed Miss Houston some rifles, saying that they were being sent to Turkomans to attack our troops in the rear.

After the departure of Tredwell, Voskin, one of the men sent by the Government from Moscow, took the rooms he had vacated at the Noyevs, where Miss Houston was still living as governess to the children. Voskin was not a very pleasant lodger. He was always giving secret information of Soviet successes and defeats of the British troops in Transcaspia, with fantastic numbers of killed. We never believed any of this, but constant reiteration certainly made many Russians convinced of the superiority of the Soviet forces.

I once arranged to be in an unlighted room in the house when Voskin was brought up to the door under the lights in the next room so that I could have a good look at him.

In spite of domestic troubles inseparable from the conditions prevailing in Tashkent, the Noyevs had managed to keep together some sort of a household. The presence of Tredwell as a lodger helped them and later the presence of Voskin. However, they only had three rooms left for the family of wife, three children and governess. One day the cook refused to work, so he got an Austrian prisoner who was engaged to replace her. The old cook, however, got a *mandat* for the kitchen and refused to leave it!

Tashkent got very hot in July and all who could used to go out to *dachas* in the hills for a holiday. Miss Houston wished to do this so she applied to Voskin who was lodging in the same house to arrange for her permit (you could do nothing in the country without a paper of some kind signed by half a dozen people). Voskin had lost a photograph of himself and thought that Miss Houston had taken it. He told her that the position of the Government was very unstable and he did not want anyone, especially the British, to have his photo if he should disappear! She knew nothing about this. My Punjabi servant, Haider, had been with me in Persia and spoke the language fairly well. By this time he also spoke Russian to some extent. Posing as a Persian he was engaged by Voskin as his servant. Here was curious lack of co-operation in the Bolshevik Government, for the police knew quite well that he was not a Persian, but was my Indian servant, and it was risky and stupid of him to pretend to be anyone else. However, Voskin never realized who he really was. Haider had stolen the photo, thinking it might be of interest to me! I made him return it and it was found 'where it had fallen behind a chest of drawers'. Miss Houston was given her permit! She had to go before a medical board who were very rude to her when they learnt she was a British subject. They said no English should have any permits to go anywhere. She replied she was not

English but Irish. They then said that, in that case, she could have anything she wanted. This made her angry and she said that all Irish were by no means hostile to England. This infuriated the board who told her not to talk politics! Eventually with Voskin's aid she was given the permit.

At the beginning of July there was a recrudescence of violent articles in the Press. 'Seventy thousand workmen had been shot by the bourgeoisie in Finland.' 'Kolchak's bandits shoot and hang all Red Army prisoners they take.' 'Seas of Blood' and 'Saint Bartholomew's Nights' were advocated. 'The proletariat again draws the sword of Red Terror which they had sheathed after the Ossipov incident', etc. Many people were arrested. An order had been issued that everyone who had ever been arrested was to be arrested again for further inquiries.

Owing to the dangers occasioned by the arrest of Kornilov, I had to leave the Yakovlievs very suddenly. For a few days I carried on my old plan of sleeping a single night in different houses. This was, to say the least of it, uncomfortable. I had to start out in the morning, taking my very small bundle with me and leave it at the house I was to sleep in. I then walked about and perhaps visited one of the few friends I trusted entirely. Finding fresh quarters on this occasion was proving difficult and all plans made were failing to mature for one reason or another. In the end I decided to go out of town, partly to study the conditions in the country and to find out what chance there would be now of getting out to Ferghana, and partly to give my friends in Tashkent time to arrange for another safe and satisfactory lodging. As it turned out we never found such peaceful and suitable places as I had had with the Mateveevs, Andreyev and the Pavlovs, and for the rest of my time in Tashkent I flitted from house to house, usually staying only a single night in each place as I had had to do before, until, when I was safely enrolled in the counter-espionage department of the army, I was able to live openly with Manditch. An opportunity to leave the town occurred when a man we will call Alexandrov had some official business out in the direction of Brich Mulla where I had spent most of the winter. He and Petrov were to help me on the road.

For travel purposes I obtained a false paper in the name of Muntz. This name was so badly written that it might have been read as something else. There was a Czech prisoner of war officer called Merz, whom I had met before when returning from the mountains in January. I thought that it might be possible to be mistaken for him on paper if any awkward questions were asked, but I always felt that I could never stand up to any suspicions. My plan was to avoid any situation that might lead to inquiry. I was supposed to be a geologist and to be looking especially for iron ore. My only stock-in-trade was a small compass and a piece of *kara tash*, i.e. black stone. This was some kind of iron ore and attracted the needle of the compass, and when asked my business I said I was looking for stones like this for the Government. I walked out of the town down the Nikolskoe road. After going about three versts I stopped in a tea-shop as arranged and after an hour was picked up by Alexandrov, who drove a covered *arba*. This is the local native springless cart with huge wheels drawn by one horse. I timed this vehicle on a good road and it took twelve minutes to do one verst. We drove through the familiar village of Troitskoe and reached a village called Tarbus at about eight in the evening. Here I found Petrov, who was to be my companion also. We slept on the ground in the open after getting a very good *pilau* from the local chai-khana (tea-house).

The next morning Alexandrov and I left at 4.15 a.m. and passed through Iskander. It will be remembered that the komissar of Iskander was Ivan's relative, and as I passed I saw his wife in front of the house, but she did not notice me. I learnt that Edwards and his wife were also hiding in this village where he had the job (under a false name, of course) of reading a water gauge in the river at stated intervals for the Hydrometrical Department. The Edwards knew Alexandrov and I did not wish them to see him as we drove past. It would have meant one more person knowing where I was, and in the case of Edwards it was particularly undesirable as I had taken so much trouble and used him to spread the report that I had left the country for good.

In Iskander was a tall wooden tower built by the Grand Duke Nikolai Constantinovitch from which he could get fresh air and a view of the country.

The Grand Duke's morganatic family took the name of Iskander from this village. We went on to Khojakent via Chimbalik, a different road from the one I had used in the winter. The road was bad and at times we had to help our horse over the rough places by man-handling the huge heavy wheels of the *arba*.

Khojakent is a lovely village with a pretty green shaded by large chenar trees (an oriental plane tree) under which we slept. It reminded me of some of the villages in Kashmir. Petrov and some friends passed through in the evening and went on to the meteorological station at Yusuf Khana where I had stopped in January. Alexandrov and I spent a hot day under the chenar trees. In the evening a youth from one of the shooting parties which had visited us at the bee-farm in winter arrived. I naturally wished to avoid him. He spoke to me but it was dark and he never recognized me. It is quite possible that by this time the authorities knew who the supposed Austrian with the damaged leg had been and so it was important I should not be recognized. My friend, Merz, the Czech prisoner of war, also arrived from Yusuf Khana. He assured me that all the papers I had left with Edwards in January had been destroyed. They were rather compromising and I was glad to be sure of this.

From Khojakent a road goes up into the mountains to a place called Chimgan which was used as a hill station by the people of Tashkent. The Governor-General had had a house there. The Bolsheviks sent their sick workers and soldiers there for a change of climate. Chimgan was also the centre of the world supply of santonine, a valuable drug made of wormwood. This plant has now been found in other parts of Asia, especially the Indian frontier, and the Russian monopoly has been broken.

While we were at Khojakent the commander-in-chief of the Turkestan army, a man named Federmesser, passed through on his way back to Tashkent. He was travelling quite simply with no staff. He came up and spoke to us and asked what we were doing. I produced my compass and piece of iron ore; he was most interested and wished us luck as the Soviet Government were anxious to find more iron for munitions! He told us jokingly that he had visited the Aktobinsk front where Dutov's Cossacks were in the vicinity of the railway, and that as things were going so badly there he was off to Askhabad where things were going better!

The next day Alexandrov's business took him up the valley of a stream, the Kizil Su. I climbed the hills round here, the first time I had given my leg anything serious to do since my accident in December. It was lovely country: we saw quail and chukor and many butterflies on the flowers and fish in the streams. We stopped the night at the village of Khumsan. There was not even a tea-shop here so we slept in the village street, getting some food from a small shopkeeper. We then went up the Ugam Su where, passing through a pretty valley among walnut and fruit trees, we got to a considerable altitude. We then left the horses and climbed some two thousand feet to ten thousand feet, where in this latitude we were above tree level. On the turf were numbers of butterflies, including a very fine form of our clouded yellow and some Apollos. We then returned, had a rest at Khumsan and continuing down the valley were met by Merz and Petrov, and we all went together to spend the night at our bivouac under the chenars of Khojakent.

Alexandrov, having finished his work, returned to Tashkent the next morning and Petrov and I went off to visit the Pskem Valley. In Khojakent we paid eighty roubles a day for each horse and one hundred and twenty for a native mounted guide, getting special rates as people travelling on behalf of the Government. In Nanai village we sent for the Vice-President of the Ispolkom, a portmanteau word for *Ispolitelnaya Komitet* or Executive Committee. He was a very nice Tajik who did not attempt to understand the changes of government which had been forced on him. He behaved as the ordinary headman of the village and produced fresh horses for us. In order to conform to Soviet methods each village had been told to elect an *Ispolkom*. No sort of election took place but the *Aksakal* (or headman) was told by someone that he was no longer an *Aksakal* but was 'Comrade the President of the Executive Committee', and a notice board was affixed to his house, 'Headquarters of the Executive Committee'. Needless to say there was no committee and no one knew what it all meant. In any case it made no difference to Comrade the President or anyone else, and if it was a government order, it had better be obeyed without inquiring into the reason for this subtle and harmless change.

The Tajiks are a Persian-speaking race and I could understand a good deal of what they said but could not let this be known or my role of Austrian prisoner might have become suspect. At the farm of Besh Kalcha we slept on a platform under a vine, being provided with a delicious *pilau* by the kind inhabitants. On July 10th we continued up this valley; as we got deeper into the hills and further from the high road we came on people who knew nothing of the revolution. They even addressed us as *Tura* which means 'Sir', instead of the usual *Tovarish* (comrade), which the populace had been taught to use by their Bolshevik masters.

The next day, July 11th, I climbed a hill to about ten thousand feet from where I expected to get a view into the valley of the Kok Su and to see the bee-farm of my long winter's residence. I found, however, that I was only on a spur jutting into the Pskem Valley. I saw marmots, ram chukor (*Tetraogallus*), and tracks of ibex, and caught many interesting butterflies with a net issued by the Soviet authorities, a result of my visit to the Tashkent Museum some months earlier. We descended and rejoined our ponies and we returned, sleeping the night at Besh Kalcha where we were given a good meal of native bread and fresh butter.

We had a very hot ride down the valley the next day. We were glad of a drink of icy water at the spring of Kara Bulak. We passed a herd of 'wild' horses. I could not understand the alarm of my companion, Petrov, who called to me and galloped hard away to one side; I followed, and when we pulled up he explained to me that about here the people turn their horses loose to run wild and catch what they want for work. We had to get away from them and make a detour to avoid the stallions which are dangerous and attack strange horses which may pass, much to the danger of the rider.

We found Russian Bolsheviks at Nanai registering the inhabitants and animals for mobilization purposes. It seemed horrible to disturb the 'pathetic contentment' of these happy, hospitable people. The Imperial Russians had left them very much to themselves and they had been contented. They told me that no Russian had been to the head of the valley where we were for nine years. The Bolshevik officials did not question us. They were doing their job and we ours of searching for iron ore.

The Bolsheviks had requisitioned all the good ponies and I had to be content with an old beast, together with a broken saddle, only one stirrup and a bit made of string which the pony kept biting through. In the end I had to ride without any bit. We had a long ride into the night, taking a different road as we were afraid of a complicated ford over the Ugam River in the dark, and we had to go by a bridge. Several of the bridges in this part of the country had been destroyed by Ossipov to delay the pursuit when he had retired from Tashkent in the winter. These had not been remade.

We reached Khojakent by moonlight at about eleven p.m. and shortly after midnight reached the Yusuf Khana meteorological station. We woke up Merz and found the house more than full. The eleven inhabitants were Russian ex-officers on the run and Austrian officer prisoners. All these would have been sympathetic to me but I always tried to keep the number of people who knew me down to the minimum. Merz was the only one here who knew who I was. I was not at all pleased at having to take the unnecessary risk of meeting such people, but it was really too late to get anywhere and we were tired and hungry and Petrov was anxious to stop here. The height of the station was known exactly: eight hundred and ninety-two metres (2,926 feet), and I was able to check my aneroid with which I had been measuring heights on my mountain trip. The next morning I got up early and had a bathe in the stream and kept away from the house with its, to me, dangerous inhabitants. I had, however, to sit at breakfast with them and when I left I asked Petrov how things had gone and what they made of me. He said that as he was saying good-bye a Croat officer named Drapszinsky, said to him, 'and who is your English friend?'

In the evening Merz and I rode over to Brich Mulla where Miss Houston was staying with friends in a garden. Miss Houston's friend had a small native house into which they could go in rough weather, but as a rule on these holidays everyone lived and slept in the open using mosquito nets after dusk. I also slept in the open, as indeed I had done since leaving Tashkent; having no mosquito net I was awakened in the morning by the fall of a beautiful ripe apricot on to my head! It was altogether a healthy and idyllic life, but I only lived it for twenty-four hours.

Petrov was to stay here and I was to return to Tashkent, but the man with whom I was to travel went off suddenly somewhere else without me for no explained reason. I later learnt that it was fortunate I did not travel with him as he was stopped and his person and property minutely searched by police on the road. In his place a Kirghiz called Mulla Bai, who spoke Russian well, agreed to travel with me. I found it always advisable to have someone who knew the ways of the country to explain and talk to anyone who might make awkward inquiries. Mulla Bai had no idea who I really was.

In the evening I walked back to Yusuf Khana and spent the night with Merz. The others had left and there was only himself and his staff in charge of the meteorological work.

On July 15th I started off with Mulla Bai and three other Kirghiz and, crossing a bridge which had been partially destroyed by Ossipov in his retreat, we entered Khojakent, where eleven cartloads of people had just arrived from the hill station of Chimgan.

Travelling along the foot of the hills with a marsh and flooded ricefield on our right hand, we passed through Kizil-kent, Khush Kurgan, and Kara Bai, and reached Seskinata, where one of my companions owned a large two-storied house.

The inhabitants of this part of the country were all Kirghiz and their round *yurts* were pitched everywhere among the scattered houses on dry patches in the ricefields. Kirghiz women, unlike the Sarts, are not veiled. When they pass you on the road they fold their arms in front of their bodies and bow from the waist, casting their eyes down to the ground and greet you with the one word 'Amin'. On reaching his house at Seskinata our host's wife brought us tea and bread, and he lay down and played a kind of mandolin while she removed his boots and massaged his feet.

Late in the evening two soldiers of the Red Army, armed with rifles, arrived. I thought they were Russians but they turned out to be Mohammedan Tartars. My first thought was: 'Have they come for me? Has someone given me away or have I made some stupid careless mistake?' They were rather curious about me at first, but it was idle curiosity. I explained that I was a member of the 'Mountain Department', that I had been sent out to find iron ore, that I had found some (here I produced my bit of black stone and the compass), but the road to the place was so difficult that it would not be worth while to work the mine. My cart had broken down and these Kirghiz were taking me back to a place where I could pick up another cart, etc. etc. We became very friendly; they asked me where I lived in Tashkent and what pay I received. I was rather pleased with my Muntz papers which no one had troubled to ask for, and so I showed the papers to them and asked them if they had also permission to leave Tashkent and travel. They told me that they had made an excuse to be sent out to patrol the country as Tashkent was very hot and they wanted a change for a few days. We three slept together in the veranda — I in the middle with one of these men on each side. I felt sometimes as though I was being guarded.

On the 16th Mulla Bai and I left our other Kirghiz companions and our two nice soldiers and continued over the marsh and ricefields, and passing Kabardan rejoined the cart road, which we had left at Kara Bai the day before. We were now on the main road between Tashkent and Parkent. Crossing a bridge at Yangi Bazar we passed Shurum and reached Shinama where we rested, fed the horses and had a meal of tea and *liposhka*. Russians in Turkestan interlard their conversation with Sart words like this, much as some Europeans in India use Indian words. Here we also got the first melons of the year. Our meal for the two of us cost thirty roubles and was delicious. Turkestan is a great country for melons and the people are specialists. They claim a different flavour for the melons of each district — even of each village. Continuing, we crossed the Chirchik by a straggling bridge partly of wood and partly of iron which went from island to island and was over five hundred yards long, and reached Tashkent by the Kuilukskaia bazaar.

I did not know where I was to sleep the night but wherever it was I did not want Mulla Bai to know. One could not tell; some suspicions might have been aroused somewhere and the police might try to trace through him the Austrian geologist who had travelled with him. Mulla Bai thought I was something to do with the Yusuf Khana meteorological station, so I told him to go and wait outside the hydro-meteorological office where I would later meet him with his horse.

My idea was to spend the night at Andreyev's and then to find out whether Miss Houston had been able to arrange fresh quarters for me. I rode round to the house but was alarmed by what I saw. There were soldiers at both of the gates of the small garden who looked at me in a curious way that made me uncomfortable. I had large, bulging saddlebags. I was carrying everything including my blanket for the night on the horse. It would not be possible just to slip in quietly. I therefore rode past and went to the Yakovlievs. It was July 16th and about a fortnight since the arrest of Kornilov. Any suspicion on the Yakovliev household would, I calculated, have materialized by now. No one was at home. I had to go somewhere so I just went in and left my things there, took the horse to Mulla Bai, who was waiting at the meteorological office and then went to Andreyev's and the Noyevs' for the news. This was discouraging. Rumours of the withdrawal of the British troops were confirmed, and Askhabad had fallen to the Bolsheviks.

I also heard that the French officer Capdeville had been captured. It will be remembered that he was carrying letters for me to Kashgar. He was arrested when passing through Osh and brought back to the gaol in Tashkent. There was a French governess in Tashkent. This brave woman did what she could for Capdeville and asked to be allowed to see him in prison. The authorities refused. She then said she was his wife! On this an interview was allowed. The prisoners were behind bars and their visitors were kept some distance back by a rail. Between them walked the gaolers. All the prisoners and their friends were shouting at the tops of their voices, each trying to make him or herself heard through the din. Capdeville managed to tell his visitor that my papers had been burnt. I afterwards learnt that the soldiers who arrested him used my letters as cigarette papers. The paper was thin, clean and of a suitable thickness! What would have happened if my secret

ink had responded to heat, it is interesting to imagine! Poor
Capdeville was in an awful state of filth and misery. It was
difficult to do anything but some comforts were sent to him.

One day in July I saw a large scaffolding round the monument to General Kauffmann. They removed the General
himself but left the two soldiers, one playing a bugle and one
planting a flag. Later they realized that this left a queer,
ill-balanced and badly composed monument, so the soldiers
were also removed.

The only sculptor in Tashkent was an Austrian prisoner
named Gatch. He was asked to make a statue of a workman
carrying a flag, but the flag had to be red. Gatch, so the story
went, refused to have his statuary painted in this way. The
Bolsheviks on their part feared that people might think he was
carrying some other flag, so this had to be dropped. In the
end Gatch made a bust of Lenin, but the only material available
was so unstable that Lenin's ear fell off in the first shower of
rain. Besides this bust of Lenin he made a beautiful monument
of a dying camel to commemorate the thousands of Austrian
prisoners who perished in Turkestan. I saw this in the church-
yard shortly after it had been made. I believe that this also
fell to pieces owing to the bad material which was all the poor
sculptor could find.

About this time the Bolsheviks passed an order that people
who got married could buy four bottles of wine and a little
extra food to celebrate the event. Many people already married
in church took advantage of this, and, to get a little more food
and enjoyment, got married again in the civil registry office.

The grapes of Tashkent are very fine. In the season they
could be bought in native kiosks and stalls and cost twelve
roubles a pound. The Bolshevik authorities decided that this
was 'speculation' and ordered them to be sold for three roubles.
Having regard to what three roubles would purchase of other
goods, the retail vendors refused to sell. They actually offered
to give away what they had in their shops. Their intention was
to dry the whole crop and keep the raisins until free trade was

again permitted. Suddenly there were no grapes to be had at all. This was a serious matter for the Tashkent citizen who in summer eats grapes all day long, whatever he is doing, and he was obliged to revert to his other habit of eating sunflower seeds.

Very scant news was published of the Afghan War. This was encouraging to me. Later it was felt that something should be done to encourage the public whose sympathies had been worked up on the Afghan side. So the capture of Peshawar, Tonk, and Thal was reported and the desertion of Indian regiments to the 'Mohammedan Liberators'.

It was announced that the Afghans had captured Baluchistan and thus acquired a seaport.

These items of news may be of interest to those who saw the war from another angle.

An Afghan communique on May 17th: 'Our brave army operating against the English was divided into three columns, right, left and centre. Owing to the arrival of strong English reinforcements our centre retired. Our right and left then attacked and our centre also advanced and completely defeated the English army.'

Here is another item of news from the paper dated August 31st: 'In Afghanistan the offensive is developing favourably and one thousand five hundred sepoys have been captured with their equipment and ammunition. On being captured the prisoners burn with desire to fight against the English. On the Western Front one hundred cavalry and forty infantry surrendered with all their arms and equipment and joined our ranks.'

Troubles were also reported from London and it was stated that police had fired on crowds of demobilized soldiers. I disbelieved all this, but many Russians did not, and they sympathized with me in the defeat and difficulties of my country.

In July some consternation was caused in government circles by orders from Moscow insisting that the Government of Turkestan should contain a number of natives in proportion to the population. This meant ninety-five per cent and an end of the Bolshevik Government. This order had been given previously but had been ignored by the local officers, who knew that a native government at this time would have made an end of anything to do with Bolshevism. The native population wanted religious freedom, peace, order, trade and, above all, a decent government.

CHAPTER XVII

TASHKENT AFFAIRS

In the late summer of 1919 I realized that there was no chance of the regime being ended by the advance of the small British force in Transcaspia. The messages I had sent off had on the whole not fared very well and it was high time that I returned. Travelling was very difficult. The authorities were still trying to arrest people who had taken part in Ossipov's movement in January. I decided to get into touch again with Manditch and see if he could help me.

I approached a trustworthy Polish-Austrian prisoner of war and asked him if he could see Manditch and find out his attitude towards me and the prospects of getting him to help me. This he did and reported to me that Manditch was now a genuine Bolshevik. He had casually mentioned my name and Manditch had said that he was surprised that I had not come to him and trusted him when I must have been in grave difficulty and danger. Although the report was not favourable I decided that I must take the risk and see him. I had only known him as a Bolshevik counter-espionage agent and although he had been useful to me I did not entirely trust him at that time. In any case, my plan had always been to let as few people as possible into the secret even of my existence.

An interview was arranged at which, after explaining the reasons for my not asking for his assistance earlier, doubts and suspicions were brushed aside. I now learned many things.

On my first disappearance in October the authorities thought I had been murdered by the Germans. The war was still going on and Tredwell and I had been pressing the Government to keep control of the prisoners of war whom the Germans, led by Zimmermann, were trying to organize. The Germans, therefore, might be expected to be glad to see the last of me. I also learnt that a small thing had helped to confirm the Bolsheviks in the belief that I had been murdered. On leaving my house I had decided to start my new life with a new toothbrush and I left my old one behind. The Bolsheviks said: 'This is not the type of man who would have run off without his toothbrush so he cannot have left voluntarily. He must have been murdered by the Germans.'

Later when no further news of me was received they believed I had run away. Orders were sent everywhere to look out for me and the roads towards Ferghana were especially guarded. A special man who had been spying on me for some time was sent to Andijhan as it was thought probable that I would make for Kashgar whence I had come. This man was still there. The town of Tashkent was searched and every house I had ever been into was suspected. One spy had seen me enter No. 58 Zhukovskaya. The house was searched and a man who might have been my double was found!

One of the maids who was serving in the Regina Hotel when I stayed there was a Cheka agent. She had been made to follow me in the street to learn to recognize me by my walk. A man may easily disguise his face — the usual means of recognition — but it is harder to disguise his walk — at least so I was now told, though I knew nothing of this. Perhaps the damage to my leg accidentally helped me in this matter. This woman guaranteed to recognize me in any disguise and was one of the special agents put on to look for me.

During the fighting in winter three Indian soldiers of the 28th Cavalry had been captured. They were a credit to the regiment and army to which they belonged. They behaved with great coolness and bravery. Subjected to threats and cajolery they maintained a firmness in their loyalty. They were put through a course of Bolshevik propaganda and promised freedom if they would spread the doctrine in India. They maintained that they were contented in their homes, were well governed and preferred to be as they were to living under the conditions they saw around them in Turkestan. I was, of course, unable to see them but friends of mine did so and reported to me. The Bolsheviks could hardly believe that any 'oppressed' Indians could have such ideas. One of them was an N.C.O. named Lall Khan, and on my return to India I reported to their commanding officer, and they were, I believe, suitably rewarded. Their captors were especially impressed by the good state of their uniforms and equipment which was, they said, better than anything in the Russian army. They were in the hospital and I could see no way of helping them to escape.

During August 1919 requisitions and searches were continued with renewed vigour. I heard of several incidents.

One lady I knew slightly had a piano in her house. It was considered very *bourjoui* to keep a piano privately. Pianos were requisitioned and sent to a school of music where the children of the proletariat were taught by state teachers. To save her piano this lady and her husband became Afghan subjects. The authorities did not dare to touch the property of an Afghan; they were hoping for an alliance with Afghanistan against the imperialists. The property of others was taken ruthlessly. These people were subsequently allowed to go to Afghanistan and finally reached India. When there in 1920 I heard from them and wished to help them. On arrival in India they had been questioned about their journey to Afghanistan. I asked to see the report they had made and found that they had concealed many important and interesting details of this journey about which I knew. I consequently refused to help them. There were so many people in a similar position who had loyally put all possible information at our disposal that I did not feel that any special measures should be taken for people who had deliberately withheld information from some motives of their own.

Another man who had his piano nationalized lost his temper and broke up the piano with an axe. He was taken to gaol and shot.

A friend of mine witnessed a scene between a working-class woman and the Quartering Commission. The woman, who was beautifully dressed in silks, was telling the head of the commission that his office was useless and no one took any notice of his orders. It turned out that she had got herself billeted on a lady's house and that she and her family had the whole house with the exception of one room which had been left to the lady, the original owner. The working-class complainant had now got a *mandat* for this last room. The lady refused to go, so three soldiers were sent to eject her. When they arrived the lady said that they had already shot her husband and son and taken her house and all her property, and that she had been left only one room for herself and her small daughter. Rather than leave this she would ask the soldiers to shoot her and her daughter. The soldiers refused to enforce the order and the woman with the *mandat* had come round to complain!

With all these confiscations and requisitions many people were trying to sell their furniture or other property to Sarts in the old town, who would have means of concealing it. This was stopped by an order prohibiting the sale or even the removal of furniture from a house; so that when a house was requisitioned the furniture was requisitioned with it and the miserable owner would in the end get a *mandat* for some other quarters which might be insufficiently or unsuitably furnished or perhaps not furnished at all.

During August I visited the Mateveevs every morning where I gave the little girl a French lesson, then I went to Andreyev's for my dinner which was handed in through the window. Then I frequently went to spend the afternoon at the Pavlovs and slept the night in one of these or in one of a couple of other houses.

At the end of August I heard that the Cheka had information that I was in Tashkent and were making renewed efforts to find me, and were specially watching Noyev's house and 'two others'. As I did not know which were these two others I avoided Andreyev's and Pavlov's and one or two other houses, and lay low at Simeonov's. He it was who had made the miraculous escape from the mass executions in January. The reason for this renewal of activity was that messages had been received from the mission which the Bolsheviks had sent to Meshed as related in chapter five.

It will be remembered that Kalashnikov had been released and on joining the Mensheviks had been shot by them. The other two, Afanasiev and Babushkin, had been arrested and held as hostages for the safety of Tredwell and myself. They had written a letter to the authorities in Tashkent to say that I was in Ferghana and asking them to take me and exchange me for them. They reported that I was in communication with Noyev (which was true), and also with two others, one whom I believe I had only once met, and one Savietski, whom I had never met. This led to a secret meeting of the *Kraikom*, a portmanteau word for the local Turkestan Committee of the Communist Party, when they ordered a renewed search for me. Voskin, one of the men sent from Moscow to run the Turkestan Government on the right lines, was now chief of the local Cheka and he showed the letter from Afanasiev and Babushkin to Noyev and asked him where I was. When I received this information I knew that the houses I used to stay in were not the suspected ones. I carried on as before, staying one night in each of my friends' houses — only avoiding Noyev's.

One day at the end of August I received a message by telephone to be at a certain house at a certain hour to hear important news. The source of the information was reliable and I went. Here I met a man named Chernov who had been in Kokhand, of course forced to work in some way for the Government. A friend told him that I was hiding in Tashkent and the Cheka were anxious to find me and that as he had met me (before my arrest, of course) and knew English he might be able to find me. He had come to Tashkent to warn me of this fresh interest of the Cheka in my movements. He told me that some months before he had managed to get out of the Foreign Office letters which had arrived for me by post. These he had given to his wife to keep, hoping for an opportunity to deliver them to me. His wife had, however, burnt them when the house was about to be searched.

All this made me not less anxious to get out of the country and I was considering the possibilities of trying some scheme to this end with the help of Manditch. He was well in the confidence of the authorities and we came to the conclusion that a bold plan would succeed. If I could with his help get into the secret service of the Bolsheviks, no one would ever suspect me. It was not easy to do, but if I did succeed I might arrange to be sent somewhere whence I could make my escape. A detachment of the Red Army was being sent to take over the military posts on the Pamirs. This detachment had had to fight its way there, and the road behind it was closed by robbers after they had got through, and so a plan for me to be sent as a secret agent to them, whence an escape into China would have been possible, had to be given up. I had an interest in this detachment, however, as one of them carried a message to the father of the girl in the photograph mentioned on page 20. The photograph was sent with the message to guarantee the authenticity of the sender.

At the beginning of September I was at the Pavlovs when I heard that Krasnov, who, I have explained, had been wounded in the January fighting and was concealed in the house, knew a man named Bobrov who had a letter for me from Meshed. I was naturally afraid of a trap. One had been laid like this before at the time of my disappearance. I saw Krasnov who guaranteed Bobrov, but I did not entirely trust Krasnov himself. He had had a fearful time; badly wounded; instead of being cared for and given every possible kindness and comfort he was hunted and had to hide with the fearful feeling that if found he would at once be shot. He had been shot in the leg and the broken bones had never had a chance to join. Just when rest was essential he had had to be moved elsewhere to save his life. Had it been known that a wounded man was in hiding it would have been taken as certain by the authorities that he was an ex-White Guard, so his very presence as a human being had to be concealed — whereas I myself could be seen as long as I pretended to be someone else. The poor man could only just hobble a few yards, even now in September, eight months after he had been wounded. Some of the 'Whites' were tired of being hunted, and a man might decide to purchase his life and perhaps freedom by giving me up. I did not know Krasnov very well. I decided to take the risk, and in this case my doubts were quite unjustified.

I sent a message to Bobrov to say that I would meet him alone at a certain place on Sunday evening. On Friday, September 5th, I went to the Pavlovs to get an answer confirming the time and place of our meeting. I was excited at the prospect of receiving my first news from my countrymen outside Soviet Russia. Here I saw Krasnov who said that he was to see Bobrov that evening and would fix up a meeting between us.

I spent that Sunday night at Simeonov's. When it was quite dark Simeonov asked me if I would leave some books at a house for him as for some reason he did not want the people of the house to see him. We went out together. There was a bright moon. After going a short distance we passed some people sitting at a doorway in deep shadow. Someone called: 'Georgi Petrovitch!' I took no notice. This was my name on my Lazar passport which I was carrying, but people who knew who I was called me Feodor Feodorovitch, which is my true Russian name. Simeonov's name was Georgi Pavlovitch. He called again and then a young man ran after us. He asked if I was Georgi Petrovitch. I said 'No'. He then apologized and went away. Simeonov, who of course knew nothing about the letter which I was expecting, said he recognized the man as one Bobrov. I asked Simeonov the name of the street we were in. When he told me I knew that it was the very street in which the Bobrov who had the letter lived, so I stopped and Bobrov, who had only walked back a few yards, returned. I then said: 'Have you a letter?'

'Krasnov is in my doorway and recognized you, let us go and talk,' he replied. So we went back. He then told me that when he left Bahram Ali in March Colonel Tod had given him a letter for me. Another copy of the letter had been sent to Tashkent by a Turkoman. These messengers seem to have taken no steps to find me. Bobrov gave his letter to a lady who was supposed to know me, but I had never even heard of her. She still had the letter as far as he knew and he would try to find her and get it back for me. He never found the lady and I never got the message.

I was glad thus to have seen Bobrov for the first time alone, without warning, as I still thought he might be an agent of the Bolsheviks trying to catch me and on a chance meeting like this could not have people at hand to arrest me.

I then took Simeonov's books to the house he told me of. I knocked and two women came to the window and asked what I wanted.

I said: 'I have two books from Georgi Pavlovitch.'

They said: 'Put them on the doorstep and go right away.' This I did. Such was life in Tashkent in 1919!

About this time a friend of the Pavlovs arrived in Tashkent. He was a komissar from Kokhand and a dangerous man. He paid frequent visits to their house and I found it advisable not to go there any more. Also Simeonov's landlord had noticed me and guessed that I was keeping out of the way for some reason. He asked Simeonov not to have me in the house as he thought it was being suspected. There had been frequent searches in the houses of that street and he thought that the authorities suspected something. This left me with only two houses to spend the night in, Manditch's and Alexandrov's. It was an unsatisfactory arrangement as to spend every other night in a house did not fit in with the extra-cup-of-tea and I-overstayed-my-time excuse.

At Manditch's I sometimes met men of the counter-espionage department. This was not pleasant but it all helped to establish my identity as an Austrian prisoner friend of Manditch, which might be useful if I eventually entered the service. One day in the street I passed a man, Ivanov — not the Colonel Ivanov who was to have been my courier, but a prominent man in the counter-espionage. I was rather nervous of meeting this man.

He was unpleasant and suspicious. After going a few yards I looked back and saw that he was also looking back at me. I went on to see the Mateveevs. The next day Manditch told me that Ivanov had followed me and had reported that I had entered not the Mateveevs' house, but the next one — the house of a much-wanted man who was also on the run. This was a pity. It showed me that in spite of my friendship for Manditch, one of their trusted agents, the counter-espionage people were not sure of me and these suspicions were unjustly and unfortunately increased by Ivanov having mistaken the house I had entered. I was, however, glad that no report had been made that I had entered the Mateveevs' house.

The day before the armistice which ended the Afghan war was reported in the Tashkent newspapers, the *Komunist* had announced the usual Afghan victories. Fifteen hundred sepoys had been taken prisoner who had at once expressed a burning desire to fight against the English. This did not fit in with the announcement of the armistice and the evacuation of Afghanistan by British troops, especially as the only news published had been the occupation of India by Afghan troops. In the face of a stream of realistic messages to this effect I had never, of course, lost faith and had told all my friends, sometimes in a heated argument, that the Bolshevik and Afghan version of affairs was impossible.

The *Komunist* interviewed the Afghan Consul-General to ask him to reconcile these facts. The Consul-General stated that he had had no news for some time but his latest was that there 'was an armistice to gain time necessary for gathering the harvest and supplementing and re-grouping our armies and the strengthening of our position in the enemy's territory we have occupied. The English have offered to pay five million sterling a year and the Afghans have sent envoys to India to offer peace on this condition, and also on condition of the grant of full freedom to India, Baluchistan, Persia and Afghanistan and the return of all territory taken from Afghanistan in previous wars. The envoys are to consider no concessions from the above terms and, if the terms are not immediately accepted, they are to return at once'. The Consul-General declared in the name of his government that even if the English agree to these terms, which is most unlikely, 'and peace is attained, the Afghan Government realizes that peace cannot last long, because on the first opportunity the English will try to recover what they have lost. Friendship with Soviet Russia was the only way of guarding themselves from the rapacious appetite of England'.

One night I was walking 'home' to the Alexandrovs' when I saw a crowd of about a hundred men and women surrounded by guards at a militia post. I avoided them and saw another small party being escorted by militia. I found out later that people were stopped all over the town that evening and asked for their certificates to show where they were employed. Those who had not their certificates with them were detained until they produced them. Those who were not employed at all were considered *bourjoui* and sent off to Perovsk, on the railway two hundred miles east of the Aral Sea, where they had to perform various forms of forced labour. Apart from my having no certificate of employment my papers would not have borne close scrutiny and it was most lucky that I had not been caught in this round-up. I very soon provided myself with the necessary certificate. On the same day they arrested all people in the public park who were not members of trade unions. There was a large Red placard over the entrance of the 'Workmen's Club' and the authorities did not see why others should use it. Inside was a cinema and a theatre where good concerts were performed.

Several things in the 'English Government Gazette', *The Times*, annoyed the local Press. It was reported that Winston Churchill had made a speech in which he said that by September fourteen states would be united against the Bolsheviks. The local papers were amused. No fourteen would ever work together, and in any case a few pamphlets dropped on the armies would make them refuse to move against their fellow workmen and probably persuade them to kill their officers and join the Bolsheviks. *The Times* had also stated that Petrograd could not now be taken till the spring. The reply was 'International Imperialism will not see May roses next spring'.

In September two thousand five hundred soldiers from Siberia appeared in Tashkent. They were said to be deserters from Kolchak's army who had murdered their officers and gone over to the Bolsheviks. Many were in British uniforms and belts with the Royal arms on their buttons. Others were in Chinese clothes. It was at first a homely sight to see these uniforms, but a closer view showed a great difference in the wearers and all in favour of our men. I was exasperated to see these undisciplined and unsoldierly loafers in the streets in our uniforms. The appearance of these men was not improved by the uniform having been given out anyhow with little regard to the size of the wearer. The papers were full of jokes about Tommy from Tomsk, etc. It was annoying to see that we had presented the ragged Red Army with this excellent equipment.

Important Bolsheviks were buried in a large mound in Federation Park (late Alexander Park) to a pretty funeral march which was at one time a tango tune in the West. I attended a demonstration here on September 14th, as one of the crowd. It was very easy to make a Bolshevik speech. You mumbled something inaudible except to those nearest and then roared out 'Long Live Red Turkestan'. On this the band played a few bars of the 'International' and everyone clapped. You then did the same thing again and shouted 'Down with the Bourgeoisie' or 'International Capital' or 'International Robbers' or whatever came into your head. The band then chipped in with some revolutionary chorus. I extracted the following from a speech which I heard and which was afterwards printed in the newspaper. It shows the type of lying propaganda which was fed to the public, and which by constant reiteration and lack of education among the listeners was in the end believed: 'Workmen, Peasants and Soldiers of the Red Army. Remember the regulations for elections in the freest countries such as France, America and England. The elections in these are fixed for weekdays and the workmen are forbidden to leave their work so that they may be prevented from giving their votes.'

At this meeting a militiaman who was controlling the crowd caught my eye and walked straight up to me. My first thought was that he was a man searching for me and had recognized me. He, however, came wreathed in pleasant smiles and said: 'How do you do, *Tovarish*?' I then recognized him as one of my friends with whom I had spent the night in the Kirghiz village a couple of months before. We had a long friendly talk while the crowd did not seem to suffer from the lack of control. I afterwards saw him and his companion several times in the streets but usually managed to avoid them, though they were the nicest and most friendly couple you could hope to meet anywhere.

One day Manditch and I went to the Afghan consulate in Tashkent. I thought it might be interesting to talk to someone there if it were possible to arrange it. As we approached it I proposed to take a photo, but Manditch hurriedly stopped me. Among the men sitting on the bench at the gate was one of the Cheka's most dangerous and efficient spies. We were walking away and considering whether anything could be done when a man came up to us, greeted Manditch as '*Tovarish*', the only Russian word he knew, and turned to me and said in Persian, 'Do you speak Persian?' I pretended not to understand. Then another man came out from the consulate and addressed us in Russian. It turned out that Manditch had been to Bokhara in June to get information for the counter-espionage department. On his return he had travelled in the train with the man who had first greeted him who believed him to be the 'Komissar of Samarkand'. Manditch believed him to be an Afghan, but he was really an Indian revolutionary from Peshawar named Mohammad Mian with an alias of Moulvi Hamal.

With his Russian-speaking companion he invited us into the consulate and passing several Afghan soldiers we were conducted into an inner room where lying sick on a bed was an old man to whom we were introduced. I believe this was a Mohmand from the Peshawar border named Saif-Ur-Rahman, but it was not easy to be sure when every man had several aliases and every reason at times to conceal his real name.

Our Russian-speaking friend had left the room and the others discussed us. I understood all they said, but, of course, they had no idea of this. Manditch's Indian revolutionary friend of the railway journey said that he (Manditch) was a komissar from New Bokhara or Samarkand and that he had never seen me before and knew nothing about me. They then called to a servant to get an interpreter and a youngish Afghan came in who asked us both in English whether we spoke English. I said that Manditch did not but that I understood a little, but could not really speak. We then all sat down to tea and were joined by an old man introduced as the 'Head Mulla of all Afghanistan', while the Indian from Peshawar who had met us in the street was the 'Head Mulla of all India'.

Our tea party consisted of four besides Manditch and myself. The old Mohmand on the bed, the two alleged head Mullas of India and Afghanistan and the English-speaking interpreter. We spent an hour here talking to them. I acted as interpreter, putting Manditch forward as the important person. I spoke very little English and that slowly and badly, and then translated into German to Manditch. I had never had to do this before and found it very difficult. More so than it sounds. The interpreter spoke to the Indian in Hindustani and to the Afghan in Persian. I understood all they said and this complicated things for me further. I sometimes found myself on the point of referring to something which had not been given to me in English.

Naturally the conversation turned to abuse of my own country, and presently the interpreter went to get the 'English Official Book', where they would show me official insults to Afghanistan. I wondered what was coming. The book turned out to be *Whitaker's Almanack* for 1919 where it was stated that Afghanistan was a buffer state whose foreign relations were conducted by Great Britain. Could any freedom-loving nation sit down under an insult like that?

In order to carry on with the idea that I knew very little English I pretended to be puzzled by the expression 'buffer state', and said to Manditch that I did not quite understand what this meant. Manditch at once said 'Ach! Buffer Staat, Buffer Staat'. The English and German being so close together in these words I had, of course, no excuse for not being able to translate at once. Had our friends been very sharp they might have noticed this lapse of mine and caught me out.

The Afghans had won the war, and peace had been made on the Afghan terms, i.e. complete freedom of Afghanistan and large concessions for Indians.

The Afghans intended to rest awhile on their laurels, strengthen themselves, and then again make war on the British in India and drive them out. Peshawar had never been actually captured as stated in the Russian papers, but had been closely besieged until the armistice. The Province of Waziristan had been captured. The Bokharans being the people with 'dark brains' had remained neutral, but after the Afghan victory Afghanistan had become the centre of the Mohammedan faith and all Mohammedans looked to King Amanullah to lead them, and Bokhara was now contemplating an alliance.

At one time the old gentleman on the bed became suspicious of me and said to the interpreter: 'Who is this?' They all turned to the Indian and asked him. He said: 'I have never seen him before. He was walking in the street with the komissar.' The interpreter than asked me who I was. I replied: 'Austrian.' The old man knew what this word meant and leaning over shook me by the hand saying: 'We have both bled on the field of battle against the tyrants!'

The interpreter told me that he had once travelled on the Pamirs with Sven Hedin. He had learnt English in Kabul University. 'Do they teach German there?' I asked. 'No, not at present, but they are about to begin.'

'That's right,' I said.

'Yes,' he said. 'Germans and Austrians are the true friends of Islam and had shed their blood in one battle with Moslems against the enemy.'

The Indian told me that he could not return to his own country as the British would kill him, but he would live in other places until India was free.

We parted friends and they invited us to come again. It was interesting to get an idea of the nonsensical propaganda that was being circulated, but one dangerous peculiarity of that beastly weapon, propaganda, is that especially among insufficiently educated people any nonsense goes down.

On September 20th Edwards and his wife left Tashkent in an attempt to get out of the country. I had given them the necessary money but did not see them as I had led them to believe that I had already left. Their false passports were in different names and so they got married again in the Soviet manner and thus got a fresh and genuine passport. They went to Semirechia and eventually Vyerni. From this place it was their intention either to make south-east to China or north-east to Siberia, and it had been arranged that if they telegraphed 'Olga ill' they would be making for Siberia and if the message was 'Olga well' they would be making for China. The telegram came in due course 'Olga ill'. No news was ever received of them again and efforts made subsequently to find out how they perished were unsuccessful. They were a brave couple but rash and indiscreet. I always felt that if they had given themselves up no serious harm would have come to them, but in a matter of life and death of this kind a man must judge for himself. Mr. Smales, the other English teacher, was not interfered with beyond spending a few days in gaol from time to time. I had often seen him in the street, but he had never recognized me. When I was making arrangements to leave Tashkent I again saw him by chance. I stopped him and spoke to him in Russian. He replied: 'You know me?' I then spoke in English, much to his surprise as he had quite failed to recognize me. I told him that I was leaving the country and asked if he was getting on all right and whether he required any assistance. He said that he had succeeded in keeping clear of all complications and was still teaching, his services having been commandeered for the Soviet schools. I believe he died in Tashkent some years later.

In September there was quite a flutter in Government circles. Kobozev was one of the men sent from Moscow to put the Turkestan Government on lines more in conformity with the policy at the centre. He was president of the *Kraikom*. Several young politically-minded Mohammedans joined him, not so much because they approved of the programme, as because there was no other party whose programme in any way approached their idea of independence for the ninety-five per cent Mohammedan majority.

Kozakov, the President of the Republic, however, understood Turkestan well enough to know that, were these orders from Moscow carried out, Turkestan would cut itself off from the Federation of Soviet Republics and become independent on anything but Bolshevik lines. Already the few Mohammedans who attended party meetings were, according to published 'complaints', former merchants who led the others with complete disregard of the party programme. It should be remembered that a former merchant was a speculator and as such to be liquidated as soon as possible.

Kobozev accused Kozakov of disregarding orders from Moscow, especially his neglect to maintain the correct proportion of Mohammedans. Another accusation was that Kozakov had not helped the Afghans in their war with us and that his conduct of this affair had been grossly inefficient.

The Tashkent politicians got so excited that the great Kobozev from the 'Centre' thought it advisable to disappear, and Kozakov had all roads watched to try to catch him. Kozakov at the same time made a lengthy defence in the Press in which he said that he was afraid to give arms to the Afghans as he could not be sure that the arms would not be used against the Bolsheviks themselves.

This suspicion of the reliability and loyalty of the Afghans was supposed to have upset them and a peevish letter signed 'Afghanets' appeared in the newspaper, but many people thought that the author of the letter was Kobozev himself.

'When England was giving hundreds of guns to Kolchak and Denikin to fight against the Soviet would she not also have given some to Afghanistan for the same purpose? Yes, certainly English arms and gold were offered by British imperialism but were refused and the hand of friendship was offered to the workmen and peasants of Soviet Russia.'

Kozakov managed to wriggle out of this dilemma. He replied that he was misrepresented in the newspapers. But there was, he said, also this real danger. When Bravin was going to Afghanistan he carried arms for the Afghan Government. He was attacked on the way and those arms might easily have failed to reach their destination and been captured by the enemies of the Soviet. England was employing robber bands to prevent arms from reaching Afghanistan.

In the end Kozakov was arrested and orders received from Moscow that he was to be deprived of all powers and tried for making unnecessary trouble! All such matters were thrashed out in public in the local Press, each party getting hold of a newspaper to push their views.

CHAPTER XVIII

TO KAGAN

WITH the aid of Manditch I was making arrangements to enter the Bolshevik counter-espionage service. This was a branch of the general staff and called in Russian 'War Control' (*Voinye Kontrol*).

This had been a branch of the Cheka but had just been separated. Its duty was to deal with foreign agents and spies in Turkestan, and to collect information from Persia, Afghanistan, Bokhara and China. It had nothing to do with counter-revolutionaries, hoarders, speculators, sabotagists and 'hooligans' and such-like enemies of the proletariat. These miscreants were left to be dealt with by the Cheka.

I had been posing as an Austrian prisoner of war of Rumanian nationality. This was dangerous as I could not speak a word of the language. This did not matter in ordinary life as much as one would imagine. I was accepted as an 'Austrian' and Russians seldom asked whether I was German, Rumanian, Magyar, Czech, Pole, Italian, or to which of the dozen nationalities I belonged to. At the same time there was always the risk that I might find myself with Rumanian prisoners and someone might mention that I also was a Rumanian. By taking care and avoiding prisoners of war in general the misfortune never happened.

The head of the counter-espionage department was a man named Dunkov. He was a most dangerous type. An educated and comparatively wealthy man before the revolution, he had given all up for what he believed to be a better method of living, and with this had come a fanaticism which led him to hunt out people suspected of opposite views and have them executed! He would enlist no one into the counter-espionage without a personal interview. This all seemed very difficult, but risks had to be taken and if the thing succeeded I would be in an unassailable position as a member of the Bolshevik Military Secret Service.

These difficulties gave us a good deal of thought. The solution was a suggestion by Manditch that I should be an Albanian. Perhaps I did not look like an Albanian and certainly could not speak one word of the language, but as far as we knew no one in Tashkent except Manditch had even seen an Albanian or heard one talk! No story could be expected to bear close and clever inquiry, but it might be useful to have a mother tongue which no one could check. I had to have a story to explain myself, and this was what we concocted:

At the beginning of the war large numbers of Serbs deserted from the Austrian army to the Russians—I have recounted above how Manditch himself had done so. These deserters were formed into a 'Serbian Volunteer Corps' which fought in the Russian army. Some officers and N.C.O.s had been sent from the Serbian army to Russia to help to organize this force. My story was that I was an Albanian soldier clerk in the Serbian army, by name Joseph Kastamuni. As a child I had spent a short time in America and knew some English. At the end of 1915 I had been sent from the Serbian army to Russia to help with the organization of the Serbian Volunteer Corps. Manditch had the rubber stamp of the 5th Regiment of the Serbian Volunteer Corps. He also had some blank papers which the colonel had signed when the corps had been broken up. With these we manufactured a passport on the model of one we possessed. It must be remembered that I expected to face a pretty close questioning in an interview with Dunkov, the head of the War Control Department. Andreyev was keeping for me my large 4A Kodak. With this we took a series of photos of myself in Austrian and Serbian uniform. One would be required for the passport. There were no Serbian uniforms in Tashkent, but from the photo on our model passport we found that the Serbian uniform could be sufficiently well copied for a photograph by cutting the shoulder straps off the Austrian uniform and turning the kepi back to front, as in our model photo the Serbian cap had no peak. In our model there was a badge of some kind in front of the cap. This we fudged by sticking on a piece of white paper over which was a piece of brown paper. We had no paste so these were temporarily fixed for the purpose of the photo with the only sticky thing at hand, a kind of apricot preserve! These photos were developed and printed by Andreyev and one of them was cut out about the size of the one in our model and pasted on the paper, which, as I have said already, bore the signature of the colonel. The precious genuine rubber stamp was used partly over this photo as the embossed stamp is used on a British passport. I was not the only person to leave Russia as one of these Serbian soldiers. I believe that Kerensky did the same thing. Our next business was to invent a story to account for my movements since I left the 5th Regiment and to account for my presence in Turkestan. This had to be supported by visas on the passport.

This was the story: I had been given permanent sick leave in Odessa on February 14th, 1918. I then went to Viatka where I worked for a couple of months. I then went to Archangel where the British Fleet were evacuating the Serbian Volunteer Corps. Here I was forced to serve in a railway regiment as a clerk. On August 1st, 1918, I was given two months' sick leave and on November 4th, owing to ill health, was given my permanent discharge as unfit to serve any more, and given permission to live anywhere in Russia. I then wandered about doing what work I could and had visas for Chita in Siberia on April 4th and Omsk on April 23rd, 1919. I then travelled through Semipalatinsk to Semirechia, the province of Turkestan adjoining Siberia. These visas were all forged with imaginary signatures. In one place we copied the genuine signature of the colonel of the 5th Regiment who had signed the blank paper. We used our only genuine rubber stamp rather freely and the others were borrowed stamps which had been so carelessly applied that they were illegible. I showed this document to Simeonov who had been in the Russian imperial police. He said it would not have deceived him for a moment, but was good enough for the casual glance of a Soviet policeman or small government official. As a matter of fact, after all this trouble the passport was never shown. This was perhaps fortunate. The genuine papers that I received as a member of the counter-espionage service were all that was necessary. How by chance we managed to scotch detailed inquiries by the redoubtable Dunkov will be explained.

The special reason for enlisting me in the secret service was the following: The Government were perturbed by persistent rumours that British officers were in Bokhara drilling and organizing the Bokharan army. Details were most circumstantial. The British officers were kept concealed in the barracks and a most careful cordon of sentries prevented anyone from entering. The officers never came out or showed themselves. A number of secret agents had been sent to find out about this. None returned. The Bokharan secret service was too good and we were told that fifteen of these agents had been caught and strangled! Dunkov was having great difficulty in finding a sixteenth; Manditch told him that his friend, Kastamuni, would try. Dunkov told Manditch to bring me to his office for the interview.

Bokhara city is ten miles from the main Transcaspian railway. The station is Kagan. Russian territory in Bokhara consisted of a strip a few yards wide on each side of the line and a small area round the stations. Owing to traffic with Bokhara city the station at Kagan was more important than others and there was a small Russian town here. The plan from the point of view of the Bolshevik counter-espionage, was that while I undertook the dangerous duty of the sixteenth spy to enter Bokhara, Manditch was to remain in Kagan to help and support me and to receive my reports. Actually, once we got into Bokhara we intended to have nothing further to do with the Bolsheviks, but to arrange some means of escaping into Persia or possibly Afghanistan.

This is how we proposed to arrange affairs in Bokhara. Simeonov was a friend of Mir Baba, the Bokharan consul in

Tashkent. He told Mir Baba that an Austrian friend of his named Kastamuni wished to go to Bokhara to buy some things which could not be got in Tashkent and which he would sell at some profit. Mir Baba at first refused to do anything, but in the end, out of friendship for Simeonov, and on his guarantee that Kastamuni was not a Bolshevik, he gave a letter of recommendation. My Bolshevik superiors knew nothing of this.

Manditch told me that the interview with Dunkov would be difficult and dangerous. I would have to walk down a long room where all the hottest Soviet spies were working at their desks. Some of these men had been specially on the lookout for me for months. I would then have to carry out a difficult and detailed conversation with Dunkov, who might be suspicious. I told him that this was not good enough. My story could not bear that amount of scrutiny. We therefore made the following clumsy plan which we hoped was slightly better: Manditch had with my assistance obtained some good German wine. He invited Dunkov to help him to drink it. I was supposed to be giving lessons in English somewhere in the town. I was expected to join the party at five p.m. after a lesson. Actually, I was to mistake the hour and arrive at six, by which time it was hoped the wine would have mellowed Dunkov to a friendly and unsuspicious frame of mind.

Preparations were getting on well. Manditch was to be married to a charming Polish lady whom he had met in Tashkent. They were Roman Catholics and the marriage had been arranged to take place in a few days' time. We three hoped to start as soon after that as possible.

The day before our proposed interview with Dunkov I was walking in the street with Manditch. Three men were walking a few yards ahead of us. Manditch told me that the centre oı the three was Dunkov himself. I said to Manditch that I did not like the complicated plan we had made for the interview. It seemed to me that something might easily go wrong. The wine might not have the effect we hoped; Dunkov might bring someone else; he might tell us to go to his office, etc. It seemed to me that here he was, quite off his guard in the street, and if we could get our interview over, we might manage to avoid any further contacts, and Dunkov would have carried out his fixed principle of an actual personal interview with all his agents. I therefore told Manditch that we would overtake the party and he was to introduce me. This we did. The first thing that Dunkov did was to notice Manditch's boots! Boots were wellnigh unobtainable in Tashkent and I had given Manditch a pair that Miss Houston had cleverly rescued from my house after my disappearance. They had been kept hidden by one of my friends in case they were wanted. 'Where did you get those splendid boots? Such things are not to be seen these days in Tashkent, look at mine.' We all laughed and Dunkov seemed in a good humour. Manditch, always ready with an apt reply, said that he had got them from an Austrian prisoner who had died last year and that he had kept them aside till wanted.

Dunkov and I then walked ahead while Manditch followed with the other two men. Dunkov said to me: 'We are very anxious to get definite news of affairs in Bokhara as soon as possible. You must go at once and see what truth there is in these stories of British officers. Our information is so detailed that we are sure there is something going on. Time is of great importance and you must start at once. In fact, there is a train going to-morrow and I will have your documents made out immediately so that you can catch it.'

This put me in a difficulty. I could not go without Manditch. His experienced assistance was essential for the journey and in dealing with the authorities at Kagan, whom he knew well from the days when he had himself been to Bokhara as a secret agent. This was Sunday. Manditch was being married on Wednesday. I could not possibly go till Thursday at the earliest, and here I was being ordered by the head of my department to go on Monday. There could be no question about it. I had to choke him off from this unseemly haste and refuse in some way to leave before Thursday. There could be

no excuse on account of preparations. People like me owned
no property — a small bundle was all I could possess and that
could be got together in a few minutes.

I did not know whether Dunkov knew of Manditch's proposed marriage. Marriages in church were not popular with
Bolshevik officials and it was quite possible that Manditch had
not mentioned it. It also could not be considered essential that
Manditch should come with me to Kagan. I could not use
the argument that he would not be ready. I had to think of
something that would prevent Dunkov from hustling us like
this. I said:

'Comrade, I am not a Communist.' He stopped and stared
at me as though I was mad and said: 'Not a Communist.
You mean you are not a Party Member?'

'No,' I said. 'I am certainly not that. I am a friend of
Manditch, who asked me as a great favour to him to go and
find out these things in Bokhara. I never realized that I was
coming under military discipline again, being ordered off here
and there at a moment's notice. I would rather have nothing
to do with it at all.' I have never seen a man change his tone
so suddenly. It must be remembered that after the fate of his
last fifteen agents he was having great difficulty in getting
anyone to go to Bokhara at all and now he was in danger of
losing me! He said:

'Never mind, you go whenever you like and send the news
back as early as possible. I will have your documents prepared
and when you want to take your train just let them know in the
office. Only please get off soon!' With this we parted in the
most friendly way.

A day or two later we received our papers: an open permit
to travel, to be shown to all and sundry, and a second paper
marked *Sekretno* (secret), to be shown to Cheka agents and
such people. Just at the last moment another matter arose.

Manditch had a Serbian friend, named Baltschisch, who had
joined the Bolshevik service and who was head of the counter-
espionage department at Askhabad, on the Persian frontier.

Baltschisch had often discussed with Manditch the problem of escaping from the country and returning to Serbia. Manditch had made it a condition with me that if he helped me to leave Turkestan I would see him and his wife back to Serbia. To this he now wished to add Baltschisch. I said that if Baltschisch could join us in Bokhara I would agree to take him as well.

As we were making our final preparations to leave Tashkent the authorities received a telegram from Askhabad to say that Baltschisch with his wife and child had tried to escape to Persia. They had started over the mountains on donkeys but had been caught and brought back to Askhabad. Here Baltschisch flourished a revolver, invited all to 'come on' and said he was not a Communist but an Anarchist! He was considered one of their best and most useful men and they didn't want to lose him, so Manditch was ordered to go and settle this affair in Askhabad, then to return to Kagan and send me into Bokhara.

It might have been easier for us to get away from Askhabad than from Bokhara, the distance to Meshed was much less; we would arrive at Askhabad with unassailable credentials, but I thought that I ought to see what the position was in Bokhara and we might possibly go to Askhabad later. This action of Baltschisch caused the authorities to be a little suspicious of all Serbians. Possibly others had ideas of getting away? What about Manditch himself? We sent some telegrams to Askhabad to gain time and, in the end, our orders to go to Askhabad were cancelled. We had not, however, seen the end of the *affaire Baltschisch*.

It will, perhaps, be remembered that when I went to the meteorological station of Yusuf Khana in July, an officer prisoner of war had said to my companion, Petrov, 'And who is your English friend?' This was a Croat astronomer named Drapszinsky. I heard that he was about to attempt to escape in the usual way, i.e. to be posted to the meteorological station of Sarakhs, on the Persian frontier and just walk over the border into Persia. I thought it a good opportunity to inform the

British Mission at Meshed of my intended movements, and I met him by appointment in the street and gave him messages which were safely delivered.

We were always thinking of possible events which might give us away and bring our plans to nothing. We had heard that all trains were stopped in the desert outside Tashkent and searched. If this happened we were determined to join the search party. No questions about us would then arise and we would have collected more evidence that we were actually Bolshevik agents in case anything went wrong on the way or at Kagan. Suppose Drapszinsky were on our train, carrying my messages and suddenly saw me with the Cheka search party, his first thought would have been that I was really a Bolshevik agent who had planted the letters on him! Would this make some sort of a scene and give us away? This nightmare was not fulfilled but it shows the state of our minds that we were always thinking of possibilities of this kind and preparing for them.

I said good-bye to all my kind friends in Tashkent: to Miss Houston who had so bravely helped me in every way; to the Noyevs, two of whose children are now in England, naturalized and both doing well; to Andreyev, who has a farm in France; to Petrov, who worked for some years in India and is now in Chile; and the Pavlovs and Simeonov, Alexandrov, Madame Danielova, all of whom remained in Tashkent.

A year later I received a letter from the father of Merz, the Czech officer prisoner who had helped me, to say that his son was a prisoner in a hulk on the Neva. Eventually he was released or escaped and returned to his own country.

I had a suit of clothes made of a hard, coarse but lasting native woollen cloth in the collarless fashion favoured by komissars, such as was worn by Soviet officials, and wore a red star with hammer and sickle, the badge of the Red Army, in my hat.

We were to take a train on the night of October 13th, but the departure of the train was put off for a day. Trains ran with great irregularity. There were no railway tickets but travellers obtained a *mandat* and were supposed to be on some kind of government duty or with special permission for some purpose useful to the country. About eight o'clock in the evening of October 14th, Manditch, his bride and I went to the station and installed ourselves in the corner of a goods wagon. There were no passenger coaches.

I was able to take very little out of Tashkent but managed to bring some papers and a small cigarette box containing the butterflies and seeds I had collected in the mountains, and a small camera.

There was a great crowd and confusion at the station and we had difficulty in getting through. Manditch, however, cleverly made friends with a soldier on duty at a gate and told him he was an old Communist and showed him his certificate of membership of the Communist Party. The soldier was only too glad to help, but refused a tip of a hundred roubles, saying he could not take it from such genuine Communists. 'If you had been *bourjoui* it would have been different.'

We were told that the train would start at ten — then at twelve — then at two. It actually left at seven-fifteen on the morning of the fifteenth. Our wagon was full and we three had just room to sit on the floor. Others were travelling in great discomfort and some danger on the roof. At four-fifteen we reached Chernayevo, where the Orenburg-Tashkent line joins the Transcaspian railway — 142 versts or 90 miles in nine hours and ten minutes. Here we had to leave our carriage as it had developed a hot axle. The railway officials said that there would be another train in a few days and we must wait for that! This was a ridiculous proposal, for all trains from Tashkent were crowded like our own with people sitting on the roofs of the carriages. There was and never would be any room on any other train for us. We had to go on this one. There was a branch of the Cheka at the station and we went to the office; I remained outside and Manditch entered and showed them our papers, including the 'secret' document signed by Dunkov, saying we were members of the War Control Department of the General Staff. We did not know who was going to be turned out of the train, but we were certainly the most essential passengers. This view was accepted, and a Cheka man was sent to see us into the train, who emptied a wagon for us. I told him that not only must we get on the train but that the Bokharan counter-espionage people were on the lookout for us and we must be very careful who was in the wagon with us.

We three installed ourselves in the wagon and the Cheka man pointed out different people and asked whether we would mind having them in with us. In this way we were able to choose our companions. We got some teachers and some actors. One of these teachers, a woman, was one of the most unpleasant type of political agitator. She spent most of the time talking of the enormities of the *bourjoui* and of the unpleasant way she would treat any she met, adding that each sleeper of the railway was laid in the blood of a workman!

Near Chernayevo were many ruined villages, traces of the 'Jizak Event' which has been referred to above.

At one place the railway passed through a rocky gorge where in the fourteenth century Tamerlane's successor, Ulug Beg, had carved an inscription recording his passing that way. When the Imperial Russians built the railway they erected a monument and tablet near by to record their arrival. The Bolsheviks had removed it and only traces remained, but Ulug Beg's inscription was allowed to stand.

We reached Samarkand before daylight on the morning of October 17th. We were told that the train would go on at nine-thirty. The town was six versts from the railway station. There was not much time, and as the train was not run to a timetable but just started when the railway officials were ready, there was always a faint danger that it might start before the hour given out. Still I had to see Samarkand. Mrs. Manditch and I started off. Manditch himself, who had been here several times before, was left to look after our simple luggage and was to take it out of the train if by any chance it started before our return. After going some distance we picked up a *droshky* (or horse carriage) and in this drove to see the sights.

The world-famous Registan, surrounded by magnificent mosques and colleges, looked neglected. Among the ruins of broken blue tiles, which were being removed by souvenir hunters, wire supports to one of the large minarets showed that the Soviet authorities were not entirely neglecting their duty of preserving these unique beauties erected when Tamerlane made this city his capital in the fourteenth century.

We visited the mausoleum of Bibi Khanum, Tamerlane's queen, where I took a photo of Mrs. Manditch standing by the enormous carved marble Koran stand on which a large copy of the sacred book was placed to be read from the window of an upper story.

We were shown over the Shah Zinda, the tomb of the living king — a Moslem saint buried in the most beautiful surroundings of dome and minaret. The gem of all, however, was the blue-tiled tomb of Tamerlane himself. The shape of the dome is unlike any of the Mogul tombs of India and is said to be designed from a melon. The arrangement inside is on the lines of the tombs at Delhi and Agra; the tombstones — that of Tamerlane, a large piece of dark jade — are directly over the actual bodies which are in a crypt below. We were taken underground to this, our only light being a candle.

I had no time for close study and this is hardly the place for a description of these wonderful buildings dating from the early fifteenth century.

In Samarkand I bought the best and largest grapes I had ever seen, nearly as large as walnuts. I also bought two round baskets of enormous raisins which were subsequently a great luxury on our desert journey. We returned to the railway station about ten o'clock but the train did not start till five in the afternoon, and we might have made a leisurely tour of all the wonderful sights instead of hurrying through Tamerlane's capital.

Manditch here met several Serbians, all of whom asked him to help them to leave the country. We could do nothing about it. We did not know under what conditions we would eventually get away. From one of them I bought a cigarette case which he had carved with views of Samarkand mosques.

At Samarkand a party of six Afghans joined the train. They called themselves a mission. All carriages were full and wherever they went they were refused admission with considerable abuse both by Russians and natives. I was surprised to see the dreaded Cheka begging the people to take these passengers. 'Remember they are our allies who have been fighting against the Imperialists,' one man said. Our own carriage had a little room; we had been able to manage this at Chernayevo by pointing out to the Cheka the danger of our having Bokharan spies in with us. I therefore offered to take the Afghans into our carriage, rather to the annoyance of the other passengers. This precious mission turned out to consist of three soldiers taking a letter from General Mohammad Wali Khan to the Governor of Mazar-i-Sherif, and three petty traders who I afterwards saw squatting in Bokhara bazaar selling tea!

These Afghans spoke Pushtu among themselves and I understood a good deal of what they said. I asked in my innocence whether they were speaking Persian. They said no but the Afghan language, and gave me the names of the different things in Pushtu. The travelling theatrical company amused us with little turns, while the Afghans amused me still more with their stories of their victorious war. They had captured Peshawar, Attock, Lahore and Delhi, but not Calcutta or Bombay. Altogether, I think, we managed to pass the long, tedious railway journey better than the other passengers.

At one place in the desert away from any station the train stopped for some reason, as in fact it often did. There was a weary, armed Jewish soldier waiting at the side of the line, who tried to get into our wagon. We told him it was full but he 'threw his weight about', saying that he was a soldier back from the Front and could do what he liked. Manditch at once jumped up and said: 'Do you know who I am? I am a representative of the General Staff.' On this the soldier changed his tune and slunk off and got in elsewhere. He must have been one of the few Jews in the lower ranks of the army.

At various small stations Russian women sold hot water from samovars as well as food of various kinds to the passengers. In fact food on the railway journey was more plentiful and better than in Tashkent.

We reached Kagan, also known as New Bokhara, at half-past eight on the morning of October 18th. Here there was a small building called 'The Russian Hotel'. It was only available for Soviet officials and was full up when we arrived.

We spent the day bivouacked on a small piece of open ground. Presently Manditch, who had been to the hotel to establish contact with the authorities, came back to us and said that a room was now available. An agent of the Cheka who was staying there nominally in some other capacity had had too much to drink the night before and had given out that he *was* a Cheka agent. He was therefore removed by his colleagues and we got his room. It was just as he left it, with pictures on the walls of Karl Marx, Lenin and others.

Just across the passage was a room occupied by Mahendra Pratap. This man was a fanatical Indian revolutionary. During the war he obtained a passport to visit Switzerland and with this had gone to Germany. Here he became the centre of a group of disloyal Indians. He had been one of the prime movers in the 'Silk Letter' case. These letters written on silk were from the German Chancellor, Bethmann-Holweg, to the rulers of the principal Indian States, inviting them to rise and turn the British out. Needless to say the Indian rulers at once handed them over to the British authorities. This movement was organized by Mahendra Pratap who wrote a translation in Hindi to go with each letter. He had formed in Berlin the 'Provisional Government of India' of which he had constituted himself President with Barkatulla, who was also in Tashkent as foreign minister. Barkatulla it was who had thrown my Punjabi servant, Haider, into prison.

When in Germany Mahendra Pratap had an audience of the Kaiser himself, successfully passing himself off as an Indian Prince of great influence. He was given a personal letter by the Kaiser for the Amir of Afghanistan. On his way from Berlin to Kabul, he passed through Constantinople where he saw the Sultan and also Enver Pasha. At Kabul he was received by the Amir Habibullah who told him that he could not accede to the Kaiser's request to join the Germans in the war against us, giving as an excuse that his country nowhere touched the frontiers of Turkey or Germany.

Mahendra Pratap returned with this reply to Germany, passing through Russia in 1918 where he interviewed Trotsky. He was in Berlin in 1919 when the Afghan War broke out and lost no time in hurrying back to the east where he saw an opportunity of doing the maximum amount of harm to the British. The Germans supplied him with an aeroplane to cross the frontier into Russia. On his way through Russia he interviewed Lenin several times. He adopted various aliases as it suited him. If he wished to pose as a Christian he called himself 'M. Peter'; if a Moslem, he considered 'Mohammed Pir' suitable.

He was, to put it mildly, an eccentric; his chief mania a hatred of the British Government. He once propounded a scheme for the reorganization of the world with the scarcely novel idea of peace based on justice. In this scheme the whole of Asia was to be a self-governing country under the name of Buddha!

In the end he became such a nuisance that in his wanderings from California to Japan, via the Old World, no country would have anything to do with him. Once in Japan he posed as the representative of Afghanistan. He was arrested and deported. The whole incident reflected so little credit on his adopted country that on his return to Kabul he was very coolly received. Subsequently Mahendra Pratap's property in

India was confiscated, but not to the Government, as would have been done in many countries. It was placed in trust to be given to his son, then a minor, on attaining his majority. He must again have returned to Japan, for on the defeat of Japan in 1945, we demanded that the Japanese should hand Mahendra Pratap, who was styling himself 'President of the Aryan Army', over to us.

Manditch had been told that he was to take charge of the counter-espionage organization in Kagan. Of course, he had no intention of doing so, his only plan was to get into Bokhara with me, where we would be out of reach of the Soviet authorities. Still, this appointment placed us in an unassailable position among the Bolsheviks of Kagan.

By now I had gained confidence in my new position as a member of the Soviet army and felt myself completely safe from detection and arrest. In Tashkent I had been able to send for documents from the General Staff archives and books from their library. Among these I got a copy of Lord Ronaldshay's book, *Sport and Politics under an Eastern Sky*, from which I tore out the map to help me on my journey from Bokhara to Meshed.

It was lucky that I was not travelling on my Rumanian passport as there were some Rumanians serving in the Cheka actually in the hotel.

Manditch visited the head of the War Control Department, which it was proposed he should take over. Here he was handed an extraordinary telegram from the Chief of the General Staff in Tashkent: 'Please communicate all information you have regarding' [here the telegram goes off into cipher] 'Anglo-Indian Service Colonel Bailey.' Just before we left Tashkent, Manditch had heard that a wireless message about me had been received from India and that the authorities had made some inquiries and had learnt that I had been in Ferghana and had gone to Northern Afghanistan. It is also possible that some of my friends who knew I was going to Bokhara, thinking I was safely away, had talked. We concocted

a reply to the following effect. From secret agents we knew
that Bailey had been in Ferghana in December of last year.
In January during Ossipov's rebellion he had been in the
old town of Tashkent. In September three Europeans in
native dress, one of whom agreed with the 'verbal photograph'
of Bailey, left Pattar Kessar on the Northern Afghan frontier
for Shirabad (a town in Eastern Bokhara). From there it was
believed that he was either returning to Ferghana or going to
the Pamirs. All was known to Finkelstein.

Finkelstein was one of the komissars who had been shot by
Ossipov in January. His wife carried on Communist propaganda, especially among the Sart women and children. I
thought that the mention of this man might lead the authorities along a troublesome and barren line of inquiry. The whole
thing was intended to direct attention to another part of the
country. We never knew whether our telegram had this result.

'Verbal photograph' was a favourite secret service cliché
supplied by Manditch, which would add to the apparent
genuineness of the report!

In the hotel the Bolshevik agents looked on me as a very
brave man, who, for the Soviet cause, was about to meet an
unpleasant death in Bokhara. Remember, I was the sixteenth
spy to be sent there. I avoided these people as much as
possible. They asked Manditch how I proposed to get into
Bokhara, a walled city with every gate guarded and all
who entered, especially Europeans, thoroughly searched
and questioned. He said that that was entirely my affair and
he did not know himself. One man asked me about this and
I broke off the conversation saying I could not tell anyone
my plans.

Actually, I had to take the letter I had obtained from Mir
Baba, the Bokharan consul in Tashkent, to the Bokharan
consul in Kagan and get from him a permit to enter the town.
I went to his house. A well-dressed Bokharan, in a large white
turban, was sitting in the archway looking on to the street. As
I approached a sort of secretary came up and asked me what I

wanted. I said I had a letter for the *Bi* (the Bokharan word for Bey). He pointed to the Bokharan in the archway. I approached him with my letter, on which the secretary pulled me rudely back, told me to stand back, take off my hat and wait while he presented my letter. This I did. After reading Mir Baba's note, he gave an order and presently a note was brought to him which he sealed. This was given to me and was my permit to enter the city.

This being done I returned to the Manditches and, with them, went to a Bokharan eating house where we had a good meal of *shashlik* and *pilau*. This was a treat after our rather light rations on the railway which, though better than anything obtainable in Tashkent, was inferior to the food to be found in *bourjoui*-ridden Bokhara. After this we went to our room in the hotel. I passed Mahendra Pratap who was sitting on a bench in the small garden. I had previously seen a photograph of him wearing glasses. This man was reading without glasses, and I told Manditch that it could not be the man. We then noticed that, although he was not wearing glasses, they were laid on the bench beside him, and we confirmed that it really was the Indian revolutionary. That he was considered a man of importance was evidenced by the continual succession of messages and visitors he received. Several times that afternoon he received a message brought by Afghan cavalry soldiers in uniform. These men were much smarter and better turned out than the soldiers I subsequently saw on several occasions both at Kabul and at Torkham, the Afghan frontier post in the Khyber.

I wished to have a talk with Mahendra Pratap and intended, when he was alone, to go boldly to him. Living in this hotel I could be nothing but a genuine official of the Soviet Government and he would have no suspicions. When it was getting dark I went for a stroll in the garden to see whether Mahendra was alone. He was in the room talking to a young European. The window was a little bit open at the bottom and I heard through this that the language was German. I then returned to my room to await the departure of his German-speaking friend. I was sitting there alone when there was a knock at the door.

I said: 'Come in,' and who should come in but Mahendra himself, wearing his very strong glasses. He asked me in very bad Russian if I could give him an envelope.

I said: 'Yes, certainly.' Then added: 'Are you not the great Indian Prince?'

He replied: 'Yes, I am.'

'Then,' said I, 'you speak German.'

He was very relieved, for he knew practically no Russian and said: 'Yes, I speak German and English besides my own language.'

'I would like an opportunity of talking with you about the state of India,' I said.

'Gladly will I speak about that,' he replied, 'but just at the moment I have an important letter to send off, after which I am free.'

'I will wait for you and in the meantime will prepare a samovar and we can talk comfortably,' I said.

He then returned to his room and in a few minutes the Manditches returned. I told them that I was expecting a visit from 'Raja Pratap', as he was known here. We prepared our samovar and waited, and presently Mahendra Pratap came in and we sat down to a glass of tea.

He said that he spoke German very badly but knew English well. I said that I also knew some English, that Manditch knew none and we must speak in German. The interview was rather difficult as, gazing at the ceiling, he muttered what he wanted to say in English and thought out carefully and laboriously the German translation, and I found it hard sometimes not to rush in and say: 'I quite understand.'

He said that the one aim of his life had been to unite Hindus and Mussulmans against the English, and had wished to give all he possessed to found a college where members of these two religions could be taught together for this purpose, but the law prevented him from disposing of his property in this way and depriving his heirs. He had, however, given all he could. During the war he had tried to go to Germany via Kashgar. When near the Chinese-Afghan frontier he had received a letter (he said from Nazrulla Khan, brother of the late Amir of Afghanistan) to say that as China had joined the Allies he had better not go that way. He then wrote to General Kuropatkin, Governor-General of Turkestan, and asked for permission to enter Russian Turkestan which was refused, and he was only able to travel when, after the Russian revolution, Kuropatkin had been deposed.

He disagreed with the revolutionary policy of Lenin, as he had explained to the Bolshevik leader in several personal interviews; Lenin aimed at the 'Dictatorship of the Proletariat' and the extinction of the upper classes. Mahendra Pratap thought that the system by which an upper class was selfish, worked only for its own advantage and used the proletariat for its own ends, was wrong. But you must have an intelligent upper class and this should work for the benefit of the proletariat and not only for itself. This, I said, sounded to me idealistic and difficult to work in practice, though many of the upper classes in many countries were actually filled with and carried out these and similar ideas. He said that that might be so, but the movement was slow and much more should be done. The Amir of Bokhara was refusing to see him, pleading illness, and he intended to return to Afghanistan where he expected a fresh war with the British would break out soon. In that event he would try to get the Hindus of India to unite with the Mussulmans in a rebellion which would support the Afghan armies by causing internal trouble in India. If he saw no prospects of this he would go to China to study Buddhism and Confucianism. He could not return to his native land. I asked him about British rule in India. Was it really very bad? It was not very bad and most individual officers, among whom he used to have many friends, were honest. More honest on the whole than Indians. 'If you take ten British officials you will find only two or three will take bribes, but among ten Indians the number would be five or six. This is entirely due to their lower standard of "Kultur".' 'One thing puzzles me, Raja Pratap,' I said: 'During the war we nearly had the English beaten. It was a near thing for them. Had the millions of India risen they surely could have turned the scale and we would not have lost the war. What was the explanation that this vast oppressed population did nothing? On the contrary, I had heard that Indian troops had actually fought for England.' Remember that although no details were asked or given, he thought I was an Austrian who would only have fought on the Eastern Front. Mahendra Pratap finding me where I was could not have had the slightest suspicions of me. He was also, I think, impressed by the pictures of Karl Marx, Lenin and other revolutionaries on the walls of my room, left by the previous occupant, the Cheka agent.

'That is a question,' said Mahendra, 'that I am always being asked to explain, and the explanation is very simple. I will ask you a question: "Who were your allies in the war?"' 'Germans, Bulgarians and Turks,' I replied. 'That is the explanation. The task of governing India is a most difficult one. Although I hate English rule, and all foreign rule, I think the English are better at it than you Germans would be. I do not think the Germans have been very successful with their African colonies: moreover, you are sensible people and even had you been victorious you would never have taken over the government of India. What you would have done is this: Owing to your alliance with Turkey, the chief independent Mussulman State, you would have replaced the English Government by a Mussulman government, either Turks, Afghans or Northern Indians, and the position of two hundred and twenty million Hindus would have been far worse than at present.'

'That is a point that never struck me,' I replied. 'So I suppose the Indian troops who did fight for the English were entirely Hindu.' 'That was largely so,' he said. 'But there were also a few Mussulmans from the uncultured frontier tribes led away by British propaganda.'

This description of the immense efforts made by the loyal Mohammedan population, especially of the Punjab, was hard to swallow without protest. But what could an Austrian (or Albanian) be expected to know of such things and I assented to all he said as the truth.

The names of all those staying in the hotel were written on pieces of paper and pinned on the doors. Mahendra Pratap's name was the only one written in Latin characters; our own and all the others were in Russian characters. When I left the hotel I removed the paper from Mahendra Pratap's door and kept it as a souvenir.

Several years later, in 1924, I was political officer in Sikkim and had control of our relations with Tibet. One day with my post arrived a small, insignificant letter posted in Peshawar city without a stamp, addressed to

H.E. THE REPRESENTATIVE

OF TIBET

DELHI.

It had been forwarded to me unopened by the Delhi Foreign Office.

Not knowing who this could be intended for, I opened it and was surprised to find a letter from Mahendra Pratap from Kabul, saying that he wished to visit Tibet. The signature corresponded with the souvenir I had removed from the Kagan hotel door four years previously.

CHAPTER XIX

ON TO BOKHARA

My plan of action in Bokhara was as follows: I had secret letters from Noyev to two people in Bokhara, one was a Russian named Tisyachnikov, and the other to a rich Sart, Arif Khoja. I wished that only *one* person should know who I was, and that this secret should be kept so that I could continue to keep in touch with the counter-espionage and Cheka people of Kagan. I wished to establish contact with Tisyachnikov or Arif Khoja and through one of these to obtain an interview with the Amir. The Amir spoke French, having been in the Corps de Page, at the Tsar's Court. I was told that it was not impossible to attend at an audience and I thought that if I could manage this, a word in French to the Amir, which would not have been understood by anyone present, might have led to a more private interview. I hoped to start with Tisyachnikov and only use Arif Khoja as a second string if Tisyachnikov happened not to be there or for any reason could not help. The essential thing was that only *one* man should know about me. Apart from danger to myself, should the Bolsheviks learn who I really was, there was the safety of Noyev who had given me these most dangerous letters.

Manditch himself knew nothing of them. For his benefit I had small notes concealed in a matchbox and in the back of my watch. These were written with the left hand. I have retained one of these. It is to the following effect: 'To the Esteemed Arif Khoja — Trust this man and do whatever is possible for him. This is the request of Ivan Kozim who is well known to you.' Ivan Kozim was an imaginary person. The paper is signed on the back in invisible ink with Noyev's usual signature.

This whole plan was destined to fail miserably.

On the morning of October 19th Manditch and I hired a *tarantas* and drove the ten miles to Bokhara city. Mrs. Manditch remained in Kagan and we intended to return for her either later in the day or the next day. On arrival at the city gate we were stopped by the armed guard. An official came out and asked who we were. I produced the permit which I had obtained the day before from the Bokharan consul at Kagan. The official said that this only mentioned me in person and so we could not both enter on it.

I have said that Manditch knew his way about Bokhara city as he had been there before as a Bolshevik agent. We, therefore, agreed that he should go and find Tisyachnikov and tell him that I was waiting outside the gate and had a letter for him. If Tisyachnikov could not be found he was to try to find Arif Khoja. In the meantime, I remained at the gate for over an hour in a state of some anxiety. At length Manditch returned bearing bad news. He had found Tisyachnikov who was terrified at the whole affair and who refused to have anything to do with me. On this I again saw the official at the gate. I explained to him that I had a secret letter for Arif Khoja and took it out from the back of my watch. This impressed him and in the end he let us both through, but kept our things and sent a man with us. We went to the Passage Nazarov, a kind of bourse where people used to meet for business. Outside of this Tisyachnikov met me in the street. I told him who had given me my letter of recommendation. 'Show me the letter,' he said. I produced a blank sheet of paper and said that I had the developer in my pocket. 'Develop it here.' 'I cannot do that in the open street. You must let me go into some room and, above all, no one must know anything about it.' Insisting on Manditch remaining outside in the courtyard, he, most unwillingly, took me into a very large hall where there were two Jews and a Russian. The latter I will call Adamovitch. I told Tisyachnikov that my affairs were very secret and I wanted no one to know of them but himself. I could not develop the writing in this big hall in which were three other people. The poor man was terrified and refused to look at anything without his friend Adamovitch. I was obliged to submit and sat and developed the writing. They were amazed when the writing with the signatures they recognized came out. It turned out that Tisyachnikov knew Manditch as a Bolshevik agent and this was largely the cause of his fear and suspicions. He asked me how I came to be travelling with him if I was really a British officer. I said that I had known him for a year and that he was my agent. In the end he refused to have anything to do with me. I said: 'If that is definite I would like to see Arif Khoja to whom I also have a letter.' Tisyachnikov then went and brought Arif Khoja and on this the two Jews who had been hanging about in the offing came up. I told them that I could not disclose my affairs to so many people. They replied that if anyone could help it was these people and they were quite 'safe'. At this moment another man arrived. This was a Bokharan official, the Karshi Beg, whose business it was to question all strangers and to submit reports on them. All the above took a couple of hours, during which Manditch was waiting in the courtyard. Once I went out to him as I knew he must be anxious, told him what was happening and returned to the room. Suddenly from the room I heard someone loudly abusing Manditch in the courtyard and telling him to go back to Kagan. I hurried out and found a small Tartar, Haider Khoja Mirbadalev. As I arrived he was shouting at Manditch:

'You are a brave man but you won't get back this time.'

I said: 'He has come with me and I have business with Tisyachnikov.' Haider Khoja got very angry and said he would have Manditch arrested at once and went off to telephone. I hurried back into the hall and told Tisyachnikov to stop him telephoning. If Manditch were arrested it would complicate matters. Tisyachnikov ran out and brought Haider Khoja into the hall and took him aside and explained what had happened. Haider Khoja then calmed down and came up and examined the letters. Matters now became less heated but my secret was out to seven people. The fact was that at the sight of Manditch, a known Bolshevik agent, all these people had been terrified. Tisyachnikov produced a pistol and told me he had had me covered most of the time! What we two unarmed people could have done to them, I don't know. We were completely in their hands. I may say here that Haider Khoja later apologized handsomely for his loss of temper and rage on this occasion. I told him that it was all quite natural and to be expected under the circumstances. We were close friends from this moment until he died in Persia in 1938.

They questioned me about Tredwell and about myself; where had I been living all this time? They asked me if I knew Colonel Yusupov. I said that I did. Where and when had I met him. I said in Yusuf Khana in January. They said he was here in the town. I at once said: 'Why did you not confront us, when he would immediately have recognized me and vouched for me and my secret would not have been public property?' There was no answer to this beyond the fact that everyone lost their heads at the arrival of two fierce Bolsheviks. At last they were more or less satisfied and it was arranged that I should bring my things which had been left at the tea-shop outside the gate.

This nervousness on the part of Tisyachnikov and his friends ended any chance of secrecy, so our plan that Manditch should take over the post of chief of the Bolshevik counter-espionage in Kagan, while I remained in Bokhara as his agent, had to be abandoned, and also our intention to join the army in Transcaspia when our position was quite secure and recognized.

We had now to get Manditch and his wife into Bokhara as soon as possible, before the secret of our arrival, known to seven people, leaked out to Kagan. The Bokharan authorities would not give Manditch a permit to re-enter the city with his wife, but said that he was to go to the Bokharan General who was posted at the Kagan-Bokhara frontier just outside Kagan, who would telephone about him.

I went with Manditch to the city gate, sent him off to Kagan and picked up my luggage and drove into the city to the female hospital, a group of modern buildings in a walled courtyard. Here I met the Mohammedan Colonel Yusupov, whom I had known the previous January and who recognized me at once. I stayed in a room with him and two Jews, named Sheer and Galperan. I had my meals with Mirbadalev and his family.

The next morning I went as arranged to the city gate to meet Manditch and his wife. He did not turn up but my great anxiety was relieved when he arrived in the afternoon. It turned out that when he got to the Bokhara frontier post the General was away and no one would telephone and he was kept waiting a long time. The post was only a couple of hundred yards from the hotel and Manditch was afraid that if the Bolsheviks had noticed that he and his wife had taken all their things with them they might suspect that they were deserting and arrest them, and bring them back. However, as the man about to be appointed chief of the counter-espionage office, he was in a fairly safe position, and after considerable delay he was allowed to pass with his wife, and joined me in the hospital in the evening.

The Mirbadalev family consisted of Haider Khoja himself, his wife, a son Iskander, aged twenty-five, who had been educated in Germany, two daughters aged about fifteen and ten, and a young boy aged eight or nine.

Haider Khoja himself, a man of between fifty and sixty, had been a kind of assistant political officer for Bokhara under the Imperial Russian authorities. After the revolution he joined the Amir of Bokhara's service and he had signed the armistice on March 25th, 1918, with Kolesov on behalf of the Bokharan Government. This was, as he always told me, done at Kizil Tepe in a railway wagon numbered 82482! He was a well-read and well-educated man and was accustomed to visit the Riviera or the Crimea every winter. He spoke only Russian, Turki and a little Persian. His important work had earned for him, besides

Russian decorations, honours from Turkey, Persia and Bokhara. In 1888 he had shown Lord Curzon over Bokhara city.

His son, Iskander, had a curious story. He had been sent to school in Mecklenburg and was on the point of leaving when war broke out. At first he was interned as an enemy suspect, but when the Germans realized that he was a Mohammedan he was released and sent to a military school, and later to Turkey, where he entered the Turkish army. He never actually fought but was among the troops who garrisoned the Gallipoli Peninsula in 1918. After the war he found himself in Constantinople, where he collected sixty-nine Mohammedans from Turkestan who had been held up on their way to Mecca and had not been able to move during the whole war. There were people from Bokhara, Samarkand, Tashkent and other parts of Russian Turkestan, and also several from Kashgar and places in Chinese Turkestan. He went to the British Mission in Constantinople and explained the case and they promised to send them all off in due course. He later received instructions to bring the whole party to a place where arrangements would be made to take them back to Turkestan. He did this, and the whole party arrived hours before the time. They were patient people and expected a long wait especially as there was no sign of any arrangements having been made. A few minutes before the time an officer arrived with a list with every man's name and a place was allotted to each and punctually they started off.

The same thing happened when they boarded a steamer on the Caspian — in fact until they reached Krasnovodsk on the eastern shore. The expenses of the journey from Constantinople to Krasnovodsk had been paid for the whole party. He was very grateful for all that had been done and admired the perfect organization. He told me that the documents for this journey were signed 'Ryan' but he did not know who this was. 'With such organizing ability,' he said, 'I am not surprised you won the war.'

From Krasnovodsk on there were no arrangements at all, and this youth conducted the party through the deserts north of the railway. It was not possible for them to travel by rail. The railway was controlled by the Bolsheviks and these religious pilgrims would have been classed as counter-revolutionaries. The party finally reached Bokhara, whence they dispersed to their various homes.

A couple of days after my arrival Haider Khoja said to me: 'Do you know a man named Awal Nur?'

For a moment I could not remember, and then said: 'That is the name of one of the N.C.O.s I left in Kashgar more than a year ago.'

Haider Khoja said: 'That man is here.' I could hardly believe this. How was it possible for this man to turn up in Bokhara? Later the Karshi Beg arrived to question me more fully on behalf of the Bokhara authorities. He was one of the seven people whom I had been forced to meet when I first arrived in Bokhara and when I was having my difficult interview with Tisyachnikov and the others. The Karshi Beg now asked me full details of my contacts with Awal Nur. I explained how I had first met him with the small party of sepoys from the Guides at Srinagar in Kashmir in April 1918. How we travelled up to Gilgit, over the Mintaka pass and the Pamirs to Kashgar, and how I had left the party in Kashgar and come on to Tashkent. It felt quite strange to tell a true story again, and this story happened to be true, and so tallied exactly with the story told by Awal Nur in his interrogatory. I signed my statement.

The Karshi Beg then produced a letter for me from Awal Nur and told me that he and his companion were at the Amir's palace at Sittar Mahasar and would be sent to see me. Later in the evening I was sitting at the table talking with Haider Khoja and his family round the samovar when the two men dressed in splendid Bokharan clothes entered the room. They clicked their heels and gave me a military salute. I got up and shook hands with them. It was an emotional moment, this first meeting with my own people. I heard Haider Khoja say: 'There cannot be much wrong with British rule in India!'

I do not know whether my two soldiers or I were the more pleased at the meeting.

Awal Nur was a havildar (sergeant) in the infantry, who had been twice wounded in France and once in East Africa. The second was a cavalry soldier named Kerbeli (Kalbi) Mohammed. He was a very fine man, a Hazara from Western Afghanistan, whose family had moved to Meshed when he was a child and who had been brought up in that town. This fact was to prove useful to us later. He had been three times on pilgrimage to the holy shrine of Kerbela, hence his title of Kalbi. Persian was his native tongue. He had been in Meshed in 1912 when the Russians had fought there and when they put a shell into the golden dome of the most holy mosque of Imam Reza. He hated Russians for this and believed that the Revolution was a punishment for this sin. He had himself fought against them at that time.

My two soldiers were resplendent in Bokharan silk *khalats*. Each of them wore the large star of a Bokharan order in silver and blue enamel. I was still in my Russian clothes, in fact they were all I possessed; I also had a star, the red five-pointed star of the Bolshevik army — but I had removed it from my hat when I entered Bokhara; I also wore a beard and must have appeared mean compared to their splendour. They told me that on his return from Tashkent they had joined Blacker and accompanied him to Yarkand and then back to India. They had then gone with him to join the force in North-East Persia. From Bahram Ali, on the Transcaspian railway, they had been sent on special duty with a hundred camel-loads of supplies to Bokhara. They had to travel very fast and very carefully as they had been informed that the Bolsheviks were trying to intercept them. Travelling through the desert they eventually reached the Oxus River at Kavakli. Leaving their camels and companions on the right bank, they themselves crossed to make arrangements. That night three soldiers arrived from Petro-Alexandrovsk, a place on the Oxus near Khiva, with letters to the Bolshevik forces before Bahram Ali. These men had seen

Awal Nur and his companions and, doubtless, their caravan, and would take the information to the Bolsheviks. It was therefore essential to stop them — but how were they to do it? They decided to send a letter to a Bokharan officer who was on the road which these three messengers would take, asking him to arrest them. This the officers did and brought the three Russians back to Awal Nur who told him to take them to Bokhara for orders. At this the Bokharan officers became very frightened and said that as Awal Nur had ordered their arrest he must be responsible. This Awal Nur agreed to willingly and said he would explain all when he reached Bokhara. The Bokharans then went off with their three prisoners. Awal Nur later heard that to avoid any questions and difficulties, they shot the three men that night.

Awal Nur was in no way responsible for this denouement and seems to have acted very well in a difficult and responsible situation. In any case, he delivered his supplies in Bokhara, which was his chief duty. At the request of the Amir, Awal Nur and Kalbi Mohammed remained in Bokhara.

It was evidently the presence of these two men which had led to all the rumours of British officers in Bokhara to investigate which I had been specially sent by the Bolshevik counter-spionage department. Had these men not been there and given rise to these rumours it might have been much more difficult for me to enter the Bolshevik service, and my interview with Dunkov might not have gone off so well. Awal Nur told me that he was being continually asked about conditions in India. Was it true that the British Government had closed all mosques and forbidden Mohammedans to say their prayers? Was it true that all Indians on the railways were obliged to travel in open trucks while passenger carriages were reserved for the British? They gave true and very creditable accounts of the situation.

A day or two after our arrival we sent a letter from Manditch to the *Voinye Kontrol* office in Kagan to say that we were engaged in very dangerous work, had already obtained important information, and would not be able to communicate for a week or so and were urgently in need of money. Would they send forty thousand roubles at once. We received a reply which showed that, so far, there were no suspicions of us in the minds of the authorities in Kagan, though the money was not sent! At the same time we could not be quite sure that they had not found out all about us and were themselves playing a double game against us! Later, in London, I told this to Admiral Sir Reginald Hall, head of our Naval Intelligence service in the last war. He said that our letter to our chief in Kagan was so typical of the type of report sent in by secret agents that they must have been convinced of our genuineness!

CHAPTER XX

BOKHARA

BOKHARA SHERIF (The Noble) was a great centre of Moslem religion and scholarship. The mullahs of the mosques are chosen by the people much in the same way as ministers were chosen by competition-preaching in Scotland. It was not an uncommon thing to see mullahs, usually young men, preaching in a sing-song voice to their followers on the steps of the mosque in order to show what they could do. I once saw two rivals sitting some distance apart competing in their discourses, each surrounded by a crowd of admirers.

Life in the covered-in bazaars of Bokhara was going on much as before. Trade seemed brisk. There was one covered cross-road where the money changers sat with piles of coins and notes in various currencies. Soviet money was not accepted, but was changed at nine times its value against Imperial Russian (Nikolai) or Kerensky money. I was offered two hundred Nikolai roubles for a ten-rupee note and sixteen hundred for a hundred franc gold-piece. I bought a pound of Lipton's tea for a hundred and twenty roubles; cheap 'Scissors' cigarettes were ten roubles a packet of ten.

The buyer has to beware in Bokhara as well as elsewhere. I bought rather a nice knife with a beautiful damascened blade. Iskander at once rubbed the blade gently and all the damascene came away. It was put on with onion juice and was an old trick which would have taken in no one else. I had paid several times the real value.

Quinine cost nine roubles for one five-grain pill. Another powder falsely sold as quinine could be bought for less as I discovered to my cost. So serious was the shortage of quinine to combat malaria both in Turkestan generally, and in Bokhara specially, that when I eventually reached Meshed I was asked to co-operate in a scheme for buying an aeroplane in India and flying it to Turkestan loaded with quinine. The profits from one flight were estimated to cover the cost of the plane, flight and all.

The language of Bokhara was Turki, but the connection with Persia was so close that in counting money the Persian language was usually employed.

To us it was curious — even something of a shock — to live in a *bourjoui* country again. To live on the differences in values was, according to their ideas, the height of infamy.

The money changers we saw squatting in their shops with piles of banknotes in front of them would have had a rapid interview with an executioner in Tashkent.

At night I used to hear a curious regular tapping which got louder as someone approached, and was later lost in the distance as the man receded. Haider Khoja explained to me that this was made by the police who tapped two sticks together as they patrolled the streets to frighten thieves and malefactors and thus prevent them from committing crimes. Dr. Morrison, in *An Australian in China*, referring to the city of Chungking, says: 'At night the streets are deserted and dead, the stillness only disturbed by a distant watchman springing his bamboo rattle to keep himself awake and warn robbers of his approach.'

In Bokhara were twenty-five Hindu merchants from Shikarpur in Sind. I spoke to several of them in Russian. Of course they had no idea who I was. I asked if the British oppression in India was very dreadful. They replied that there was no oppression at all! This was good for Manditch who was really beginning to believe the fearful stories spread in Russian Turkestan.

There were also numbers of Jews in Bokhara, some of whom were very wealthy. In Bokhara the Mohammedans wore a brilliantly coloured robe called a *khalat*. This was held round the waist by a cloth sash. Both Hindus and Jews were forbidden to wear this sash. Instead they tied a single cord or piece of string round their waists to keep the front of the robe together.

I had heard that the object of this was to have an instrument handy with which to strangle the wearer if this were considered advisable! I was told in Bokhara that this was not the case. No Jew or Hindu might carry arms. The Mohammedans usually stuck a knife or pistol inside the sash. This was not possible with the piece of cord.

Jews were not allowed to ride or drive in the streets of the town. Arif Khoja, a very wealthy Jew, kept a carriage and motor car just outside the city gate, to which he had to go on foot. His clothes were of the best silk and his waist-cord made of white silk. The Jews wear high hats made of astrakhan. They have a curious fashion. It is considered beautiful to find the whorls in the lambskins in lines and not twisted haphazard as I think we prefer. The longer and more numerous these lines were the more expensive the hat. These straight lines were always made the centre of the front of the hat. Three or four lines the size of a child's fingers in the centre of a hat would be of the greatest value. The Mohammedans had not this queer fancy, but Haider Khoja had a small brown astrakhan hat (seen in the photo; he called it gold) for which, before the war, he had paid eight hundred roubles (£80).

Europeans in Bokhara, including Manditch and myself, threw a *khalat* loosely over their ordinary clothes when walking in the streets. Haider Khoja's wife and daughters, who wore European dress within the walls of the hospital courtyard, were obliged to be veiled when they walked out into the street.

One of the features of Bokhara are the baths; these are on the lines of a Turkish bath. You are laid on a slab and massaged, pommelled and thumped and every joint cracked. The last thing they do is to lift your head up and bend it forward till something inside goes. At one period you are turned over on your face and the man stands on your back, slowly letting his feet slide back to massage your back! I used to go frequently.

On one occasion after returning from my bath I was sitting in the October sunshine on the doorstep of our house when Colonel Yusupov came up. 'Feodor Feodorovitch,' he said, 'so you didn't go for your bath to-day.' 'Yes, I did,' I replied, 'I have just come back.' 'How dangerous to stay out in the open like this!' After a bath in Russia, which is a less frequent but more thorough operation than with us, you hurry home and shut yourself up for forty-eight hours if possible!

Colonel Yusupov told me how, after we had last met at Yusuf Khana in the winter, he had gone over the mountains to Ferghana. This was what I had intended to do myself. He told me it would have been quite impossible. He was a Mohammedan and Turki was his own language and even he had difficulty. From there he had worked his way through the mountains down the Zarafshan River into Bokharan territory.

We lived simply but very well, compared with Tashkent standards. We had several special Tartar dishes at table. One day we had some pony meat which was considered a great delicacy. It was, they said, a young pony specially fattened for the table; after overcoming one's natural revulsion to such a thing, one had to confess that it was very good! Then we had *kaimak*, a sort of Devonshire cream, which was delicious. The people of Turkestan go in a lot for different milk products. In Tashkent were milk bars — booths in the streets where various kinds of sour milk, cream, curds, etc., were sold. In the days before the revolution people in Russia used to do a regular cure of this diet. They used to live with the Kirghiz in their tents and eat and drink nothing but milk and milk products during their cure.

A delicious food in Bokhara is the *shashlik* and Manditch and I used frequently to go and have a few 'skewers' in the city. The *shashlik* is something like the Indian *kabab*. Half a dozen pieces of meat, fat and onions are fixed on to a flat skewer. Hundreds of these are prepared overnight and are neatly piled in the form of a large high cylinder at the back of the shop. In front of the shop is a tin trough about six feet long by six inches wide and as many deep. This is half filled with glowing charcoal which is kept alight by a fan in the man's hand. You order your skewers, usually five, and the man takes them off the cylindrical pile behind him, lays them across the top of the trough, the whole time fanning with his left hand. As one side is cooked the whole five are turned over. Finally, when both sides are done to a turn he takes them off, sprinkles them with a little pepper and salt and hands them to you. You sit down and break off pieces of a huge flat loaf of bread and eat the *shashliks* with your fingers, washing it down with weak tea. The shashlik-cook does a roaring trade and works continuously for several hours — reaching for fresh ones from behind — turning over those half cooked — handing one those finished — and all the time fanning and adding charcoal when necessary. Sometimes there are so many batches being cooked that you have to wait your turn till your own go on.

The Chief Minister of Bokhara was called the Khush Begi. The second most important was the Kaznachei or Finance Minister. The Khush Begi lived in the Ark, a fort in the middle of the town. Over the gateway of the Ark is a very conspicuous clock. This was made very many years ago in exchange for his life by an Italian who fell into the hands of the Bokharans. In those days the Bokharan fanatics killed all unbelievers. Two British officers, Stoddart and Connoly, were executed in 1842 after being kept in misery in a filthy dungeon.

The Kaznachei lived with the Amir at his palace of Sittar Mahasar, about three miles distant. For this reason the Kaznachei was really more powerful even than the Khush Begi as he had the ear of the Amir. Another very high officer was the Kazi Kalan, or Chief Justice. Several times I saw him riding in the street accompanied by a gorgeously dressed staff. He carried a small beautifully inlaid axe as a sign of office. When I passed such high officers in the street I stood aside, took off my hat and bowed as was customary.

I had been hoping to see the Amir himself, or at least some

responsible person. The two Indian N.C.O.s were living at the Amir's palace where they were in constant touch with the Kaznachei; they told me that I was to be sent for in a day or two and that quarters were being prepared for me, but nothing happened. I consequently wrote a letter to the Kaznachei saying that I had left Tashkent for Persia but had, at some risk and inconvenience, broken my journey in Bokhara as I wished to see the Amir before I joined the British in Persia. If the Bokharan authorities did not want to see me I would go on to Khiva and then to Persia. This letter Awal Nur personally gave to the Kaznachei, who remarked that the Khush Begi had misrepresented the matter and he would speak to the Amir. At the same time he asked if I wanted money. I sent a verbal reply that I was not a beggar and would only ask for assistance of any kind if treated properly. A day or two later the N.C.O.s said that there was a quarrel between the Amir and the Kaznachei and that the latter was not being given an audience! I had seen something of these irresponsible autocrats and they are apt to be a bit of a nuisance if any important business is on. In Tibet nothing in Lhasa could be done without the orders of the Dalai Lama and sometimes he was quite inaccessible for business for several days. I told the N.C.O.s that I would make arrangements to leave Bokhara with them without any further reference to the Bokharan authorities. This was passed on. The Amir had his difficulties, of course. He knew the weakness of his forces compared with those of the Bolsheviks. The fact was that he was accustomed to have a Russian Resident at hand to turn to in difficulties, and now being deprived of this he did not know what to do. The British were far off, the Bolsheviks at the city gate.

At this time a Bolshevik commercial mission arrived from Tashkent. They were feasted and entertained by the Amir, who was in reality frightened of them and was especially terrified lest they should hear that he was allowing me to remain in the city!

The Soviet Government were badly in need of many things,

and among these cotton oil, which could be supplied by Bokhara. The Bokhara merchants refused to accept Soviet money. They demanded either Imperial or Kerensky money. Besides notes of higher value properly numbered, the Kerensky Government had issued notes of the smaller values (twenty and forty roubles) in large sheets. These bore no number and were uncontrolled. You cut off what you required, as we do with a sheet of postage stamps. In the end an agreement was made that payment for the oil and other things should be made in Kerensky money. The amount in question was twenty-five million roubles and, of course, it was expected that this large sum should be paid in the thousand rouble controlled notes. Imagine the dismay when the money was delivered in several hundred thousand rolls of the uncontrolled smaller notes quite fresh from the printing press! Merchants could be seen in the streets with rolls of this so-called money under their arms. The result of this 'ramp' was that no one in the bazaar would accept this money. They insisted on Imperial money.

Two important people, Axelrud (later Soviet Ambassador to Bokhara) and Michaelevsky, came from Tashkent to see Haider Khoja and Galperan. They said they had come from Moscow where the Central Government had discovered that the Turkestan Government had not understood the principles of Communism, and that all the members of the Government were to be tried and punished. What they wanted were men of education, culture and experience, like Haider Khoja and Galperan, to help in the administration. Galperan showed them a recent Moscow newspaper describing a concentration camp where the *bourjoui* were interned. Axelrud said that only 'untrustworthy' people were interned! Galperan said with some heat that they would prefer to remain free where they were and would not return until all the 'bandits' had been shot or hanged!

The arrival of these men from the Central Government had some temporary effect in moderating the regime in Turkestan. An official at Kagan, Vitkevitch, in a speech which was reported, said: 'We did at first steal a little but then we did not know how to carry on an administration!'

In Bokhara I met the Mullah of the Shai Khan Taur Mosque in Tashkent. He had been imprisoned by the Bolsheviks, released during the 'January Events', and fled to Bokhara. He told me with some confirmatory detail how he had received a letter for me from the British at Meshed. There were, he said, two copies of this letter. One was given to a man who was surprised in the desert by a Bolshevik patrol and had escaped without his coat. The letter was sewn in the coat and the Mullah did not know whether the Bolsheviks had found it or not. The other had come to him and he had given it to a certain lady who said she knew me. I had never heard her name in my life and the message never reached me. In fact I had received no message from Meshed the whole year I had been in Tashkent.

All this time Manditch and I were hoping that we were maintaining our superior officers of the *Voinye Kontrol* in the belief that we were their agents working for them. We sent one or two news-reports in, and then we reported that Manditch was ill. Our immediate superior in Kagan was one Bugaiev. We received a message from him asking us to meet him on very important business. Manditch replied that he was too ill, that I would meet him at the nearest tea-house on the right, outside the Kagan gate of the city. If necessary I would bring Bugaiev in to see Manditch after dark. We knew he would not dare to agree with this suggestion as the Kagan *Voinye Kontrol* people were terrified of entering Bokhara where, as I have said, they had already lost so many secret agents. However, we arranged a place where Manditch could be on his sick bed if Bugaiev had the courage to come in.

The nearest tea-house on the right was chosen for special reasons. So many people in Bokhara knew about me that there was always the fear that the Bolsheviks at Kagan also knew and that this was merely a ruse to capture me. In the gateway was a guard of Bokharan soldiers. I arranged that

Haider Khoja's son, Iskander, should remain with the guard all the time that I was outside the gate. He was to see that the guard had their rifles loaded and would take energetic action if any attempt were made to kidnap me. I also had a pistol and calculated that I could easily make the ten yards to safety inside the city if necessary. Actually, at the time of starting, Iskander could not be found and this part of the plan for my safety was not carried out.

After I had been at the tea-house for half an hour two empty carriages for hire came out of the city gate. One of the drivers called something to me in Russian. I thought he was trying to pick me up as a fare to Kagan and I called out that I was not going. I thought no more about it; but a minute later the driver returned on foot. I would not have recognized him as one of the drivers but for the whip he carried. In any case, as he had driven out from the city I could not imagine that he was Bugaiev in disguise or in fact a messenger who I was expecting from the opposite direction. He said to me: 'Are you expecting a man to meet you from Kagan?'

'Yes,' I replied.

'Well, he is not coming.'

'Who is the man, and who sent you?'

'I will not give his name as I am not sure you are the man I was to meet.'

'Give me the first letter of his name and I will convince you that I am the person you are to meet.'

'I cannot read or write.'

'What does it sound like?'

'Bu, in fact, Bugaievsky sent me.'

He had not got the name quite right. He then took a letter from his pocket addressed to Manditch and gave it to me. All this time I had been very much on my guard, ready to shoot and bolt for the city gate if necessary. The man then said:

'Are you living with Mirbadalev?'

It was very important that no one should know where we were living and this question made me certain that the Kagan people knew who we really were and were only out to catch us. I replied:

'No.'

'Do you know him?'

'No.'

'In that case you are not the right person. Give me back the letter.' I said:

'I am not the man. The man this letter is addressed to is ill, and has sent me to get it and I will give it to him at once.'

At this moment Iskander himself, having just arrived, drove past and saw me talking to the cab-driver. He sensibly, I thought, made no sign of recognition. The cab-driver said, pointing at him with his whip:

'Do you know that man?'

'No,' I replied.

At that moment Iskander stopped his carriage and got out and walked towards us. I hurriedly got up, told the cab-driver I must go, and left him protesting and asking me to return the letter. As Iskander came up I hurriedly said, as I brushed past him:

'Don't speak.'

He sheered off but did not know what was happening; the man caught him up and said:

'Do you know that man?' pointing to me just entering the gate.

'Yes,' Iskander replied, 'he is an Austrian prisoner who works for my father.'

I had by now re-entered the city and Iskander overtook me in his carriage and we drove home.

I still have the letter I was given, dated November 9th:

> I have been called to Tashkent. It is necessary that you either communicate immediately, or you return to Kagan. On Tuesday I will be at the place appointed by you.
>
> Yours
>
> BUG . . .

It was all very confusing. From the fact that the messenger knew that I was living with Mirbadalev, a well-known anti-Bolshevik, I am sure that the Kagan people knew all about me and that this was merely a trap to catch both Manditch and myself. The Kagan Bolsheviks must have been very angry when they learnt who their agents really were, not to mention the state of mind of Dunkov and others at headquarters in Tashkent.

CHAPTER XXI

PLANS FOR DEPARTURE

SHORTLY after our arrival at Bokhara I sent off a messenger to Tashkent to tell my Punjabi servant, Haider, to join me. I sent him a Bokharan passport and detailed instructions regarding the journey. He was also to bring my dog Zep if possible; but I said that, as Zep had been an object of great interest to the Cheka, who had kept spies on him for the first three months after my disappearance, he was to send him by another man and pick him up when he left the train. They arrived in due course. They very sensibly did not come to Kagan but got out at Kizil Tepe station and drove into Bokhara from there, thus avoiding the more tiresome scrutiny of the Kagan Bolsheviks. They brought some important letters, but these Haider had wrapped round some saucepans and sent them by the Bokharan agent who had taken him his instructions and passports. This man took them direct to the Khush Begi who sat on them for three or four days before sending them on to me! In the train with Haider was a Persian named Hassan. He was a spy who had been specially looking for me in Tashkent, and we thought he might have been sent to Bokhara on the same errand.

During our stay in Bokhara about two hundred and fifty Rumanian prisoners of war arrived. The Austrian prisoners of Rumanian nationality had almost all refused to join the Bolsheviks in any way. I have said before that the Magyars joined the Red Army in large numbers. These Rumanians had had a fearful time. They had gone to Kokhand where Madamin Beg, the successor to Irgash, had helped them. They had walked from there to Bokhara always in fear of being caught by the Bolsheviks and forced into the army or some service. Actually one party was caught and taken to Shahr-I-Sabs and forced to work on munitions. Their wanderings had lasted three months and they had hoped to find peace and freedom in Bokhara.

With them were two N.C.O.s. One told me he had a family at home from whom he had not heard for six years. He had, in fact, been five years in Turkestan. Many of these poor Rumanians were ill, all were penniless and hunger drove many to beg in the streets. I pressed the Bokharan authorities through Haider Kkoja to help them. I suggested that the Government should give them work and pay them so that they could buy a little food, but nothing was done. Some of these men went to the Bolsheviks at Kagan in their desperation. I warned the Bokharans that if these men were all driven to join the Bolsheviks after all they had gone through they would be very bitter enemies of Bokhara if trouble arose. Most of them eventually were employed by the citizens of Bokhara. About a dozen were too ill to work. I took a doctor to see them and gave them enough money to keep them comfortably for six months. One of these told me that he was a piano tuner by profession. Was there a piano in Bokhara for him to put right? I found out that years before the Amir had had one but had got tired of it and had thrown it away! After the peace treaty these Austrians had become Rumanian subjects. I made a list of these men and later gave it to King Carol of Rumania.

Among these Rumanian prisoners was an old Serb. He told me he was sixty-seven and had been mobilized in the Austrian army in spite of his age as the Austrians wished to remove as many as possible of the Austrian Serbians for fear of a rebellion. He had had to abandon a prosperous farm on which he had ten horses and had received no home news for years.

The Bokharan army was unimpressive, though profusely decorated with medals and orders. Generals had men riding in front of them carrying white sticks. They sang a lot as they marched. One song was 'The Amir is our Father'. Another which they were fond of singing at Kagan says 'Our General is a brave man and does not fear the Bolsheviks' — much to the amusement of the Red Army soldiers at Kagan who looked at them across the frontier.

One morning I was told that a Sart had come to see me. I

took him to my room and asked if he spoke Russian. No, only Tajik (a kind of Persian) and he started to question me. We were not getting on well in this language and I said I could not answer any of his questions unless he told me who he was. He then said in excellent Russian that he was from the Bokharan Government. It turned out that he was the private secretary and interpreter to the Khush Begi. I thought it very stupid of the Bokharan authorities to behave like this. Mirbadalev was their trusted man and knew all about me. The interpreter wanted to know whether it was true that I was buying six horses, which meant, of course, that I was taking the 'Amir's guests', i.e. my two Indian N.C.O.s with me; was I short of money? etc. etc. I said that my arrangements were all in good working order, but I was waiting for a reply to a letter sent to Meshed and also to one sent to the Amir.

Later I found out the cause of this visit. The Kaznachei wishing to speak to the Amir about me and, not knowing how to bring the matter up (confound these unapproachable autocrats!) told him that his 'two guests', Awal Nur and Kalbi Mohammed, were leaving and that I had ordered them to buy six horses. He then gave the Amir my letter which the Amir read and put in his pocket. The Amir told the Khush Begi to find out when I was leaving. Hence the mysterious visit of his interpreter.

One day Manditch and I went for a stroll along the city wall and took some photographs. Photography was not allowed in Bokhara. Three soldiers rode up and asked what we were doing. I managed to hide the camera in a hole in the wall and said we were out for a walk. They took us with them for inquiry and on the way we met Iskander Mirbadalev whom they knew and who vouched for us. It would have been unfortunate if any unnecessary incident had arisen from this affair. We returned and got the camera the next day. On this occasion I put up a pheasant from a bed of reeds within the city walls. It is a curious thing that there are no sparrows in Bokhara city, though there are plenty in the surrounding country.

I had sent two apparently harmless messages to the meteoro-logical department, saying that according to their request I had ascertained that mercury was obtainable in Bokhara and giving the price. These were passed on to Petrov who passed them on to Miss Houston who knew how to deal with them.

As a result Haider brought letters from Miss Houston and others from Tashkent. They contained interesting news. After five months in prison the French officer Capdeville had been set at liberty but was very ill. His release had been arranged by the Persian consul from Askhabad who had a French wife. A Chinese consul had arrived in Tashkent. The three Indian prisoners of war of the 28th Cavalry had been released. More Indian revolutionaries had arrived in Tashkent with Barkatulla. Haider had actually been to a cinema with these men. They offered him four thousand roubles a month if he would join them in their work. I had told Haider to get all the information he could about these men, including their educational qualifica-tions. The latter were described as 'Middle-fail' — on the Indian principle that you describe yourself as having failed for the degree next above that which you have passed!

A few days later I received another messenger who brought me my larger camera and some seeds I had collected in the mountains both during my stay at the bee-farm and during my trip to the mountains in July. All these messengers were first taken to the Khush Begi who kept my things for several days before letting me have them.

Three days after my arrival at Bokhara I had sent a message to the British Mission at Meshed suggesting that I should stay in Bokhara and act as go-between with Tashkent. I learnt that one copy of the message had been destroyed by the messenger who had been arrested on the railway, but I hoped that another copy had got through. I had, however, received no reply to this and so decided that I should, anyhow, in the first instance go to Meshed myself.

I intended that my party should be small. Smallness allowed of quick watering at the deep wells in the desert. It consisted of my two Indian soldiers, my servant, Manditch and his wife and myself. Later four Russian officers, who had heard of my preparations, asked if they might join me. I agreed with some hesitation; they were armed men and might be useful in a tussle, though it was against the advice I had received regarding desert travel, to take so large a party. One of these was Capt. Iskander, a son of the Grand Duke Nikolai Constantinovitch. Another, a Mohammedan Russian officer, Azizov. He was a Turkoman from Khiva who had been decorated with the St. George's Cross for bravery in the war. He had been A.D.C. to General Kornilov and had been in the room with the General when a shell killed him. He had been born and bred in the desert, and was also armed and I hoped would be useful.

I heard later that along with other refugees he was, on arrival in India, interned at Belgaum; later he went to Siberia, and a man of his name became the leader of a band in Mongolia who were raiding into China, whether as robbers, rebels or patriots I do not know, nor can I be sure that this was my travelling companion.

I told all these men to get ready, doing everything with the greatest secrecy, and that at the last moment I would only give them one hour's notice before starting. I told the two Indian N.C.O.s to ask the Khush Begi to help me to obtain the necessary good horses and saddlery and asked further for five rifles, one for each of us, pointing out that it would have been illegal for me to buy them. We also wanted a good guide. The reply to the message was somewhat disconcerting. The Amir had been approached and had refused to allow the two soldiers to go. He said the Indian Army was so large that these two men would not be missed! A little firmness, coupled with not entirely simulated anger, overcame this difficulty.

Eventually I bought the necessary animals. Buying a horse in Bokhara, and in fact all over Central Asia, is an interesting ceremony. The horse market is held on special days. Would-be purchasers try out the animals amid remarks from the large crowds of onlookers. The two interested parties then sit down and hold hands under their long sleeves and by signs make and reject offers. A very low offer sometimes elicits a cry of agony from the vendor. When all is agreed the crowd, who have been watching the faces of the two actors, cheer and show every sign of delight . . . a horse has been sold!

Considering the circumstances in which these two Indian N.C.O.s had come here, I do not think that the Bokharan Government acted with too much generosity either in the matter of rifles or horses. The actual purchase price of the horses was not a great matter, but the buying of a horse was a most public affair. There were probably many people in Bokhara who were not above earning a little money by taking information of this sort to the Bolsheviks at Kagan who would then know that I was leaving and would (and actually did) lie in wait for me. As things were I could not help this and the only thing to do was to keep my route and actual date of departure secret. Finally, after the Bokharan Government had graciously given me the necessary permission, I bought the required animals at an average price of four thousand roubles.

The Khush Begi also sent three rifles, not the five I had asked for.

We now had to make other preparations for the long desert journey. Saddles were bought and all girths, straps, etc., carefully examined. Then, as to food. The Bokharans and Russians thoroughly understand what is required for a desert journey, and I had the benefit of the advice and experience of the four Russian officers who were to come with us. We prepared a quantity of *sukhari*. This consists of a very tough rusk. Anything that would crumble would be reduced to powder on the long journey. Bread was baked in a special manner. This was then cut into cubes about two or three inches in size and baked again. The result was a very hard rusk quite impervious to any rattling about on a pony for days on end, but also quite uneatable until soaked in water or tea. We also took tea, sugar and salt, but nothing else except that I myself had a heavy basket of the wonderful raisins which I had bought in Samarkand. In addition we each carried a leather bag on the saddle for water. For bedding I bought two large pieces of felt. One of these was laid on the ground and the other spread over, and between these we six — Mr. and Mrs. Manditch, the two Indian N.C.O.s, my servant, Haider, and I myself — slept.

In Tashkent I had bought some fine large Bokharan carpets and two small camel-bags of Turkoman carpet work, also a couple of Bokharan embroideries and two Kashmir shawls. The large carpets had to be left in Tashkent but I brought the other things with me, using them as bedding.

For the desert part of the journey I used the two embroideries as blankets. The Kashmir shawls were sewn into a small bundle to make a pillow and the camel-bags were carried under the saddles. All these things arrived safely, though somewhat the worse for the rough treatment they received. I always slept on one of the outside berths of our big felts and found the embroideries very useful in the intense cold which we experienced.

Bokhara is the great market for karakul, the local name for the astrakhan skin of commerce. I bought a few of these but in the end sold them again, realizing that an overloaded horse might cost a life and that it was essential to carry only food. We were advised to wear Turkoman clothing. This was not really a disguise, and we wore our ordinary clothes under a grey woollen Turkoman *khalat* or over-garment and the large black Turkoman sheep-skin hat. The idea was that if seen in the desert from a distance we would be taken for a party of Turkomans. I myself wore the valuable corduroy riding-breeches so gallantly preserved for me by Miss Houston more than a year before. This added greatly to my comfort.

Before leaving Bokhara I bought a few simple medicines and while I was doing this two young men walked into the chemist's shop who spoke Punjabi, a dialect of Hindustani I could understand. They were evidently Indian revolutionaries, though I did not speak to them or hear anything of interest.

Our plans were to travel to Burdalik on the Oxus, with ponies only, having fodder sent ahead by camel and dropped at various places. At Burdalik we intended to buy camels. They would have reduced our speed but it was the only way, we were told, of negotiating the belt of desert and steppe between the Oxus and the Murghab Rivers. I was told that the wells here were so deep that the rope to reach the water weighed two hundred pounds, a weight which could not be carried by a pony. A camel would be necessary for this reason alone. The belt of country along the Murghab was controlled by Bolsheviks, and we could not expect to receive any food or assistance there for our next crossing of the steppe westwards to the Persian frontier.

Finally, my small party of six, including Mrs. Manditch, was ready to the 'last gaiter button', except for the shortage of rifles, of which, owing to the meanness of the Bokharan authorities, we only had three. In addition I had the four Russian officers, each with a rifle, who had made their own arrangements for food, horses, etc. We were longing to get off, and the sooner the better, before news of our preparations and intentions could reach the Bolsheviks. To intercept a party in the desert is the simplest thing. The Bolsheviks only had to know our route and then send a small party to hold a well. A thirsty party *had* to get that water for their horses or die, and it was a simple matter to kill or capture them.

A day or two before we started I received a shock. A large party of Russians and others had also been given permission to go at the same time and by the same route. I did not like this at all. My party was small and compact. A large party took longer to water at the wells and this would cause delay and difficulty. However, I could not avoid it and I did not know any details of this party till we were well on the road. I then discovered that they consisted of seven, and were all unarmed.

My final preparations consisted in writing a letter to the Foreign Office to be sent in case I was caught, and in doing what I could for the poor Rumanian prisoners. I left money with Galperan to be paid to the sick at intervals.

CHAPTER XXII

IN THE DESERT

On December 17th we left our quarters in the female hospital, where I had so long been the guest of Haider Khoja Mirbadalev, and joined my two Indian soldiers and the Russians at a *dacha*, a hut where the Turkoman officer, Azizov, was living. Here the party was finally organized for the journey.

Awal Nur, the senior of the two Indian N.C.O.s, told me that on taking leave of the Kaznachei, in whose care he and Kalbi Mohammed had been, they had been given a present of ten thousand roubles each and that half a million had been sent to me through the leader of the party of seven who had been added to us so unexpectedly.

The next morning, December 18th, the actual day fixed for our departure, I sent Awal Nur to the Kaznachei to thank him for some bandoliers which he had sent and at the same time to return the twenty-thousand roubles with a message that our soldiers were well paid by our Government and did not accept money in this way. I also said that if the half million was even offered to me it would be refused, for the same reason. I had been badly treated by the Bokharan authorities and could not let the account be squared by a money payment. Awal Nur returned to say that the Kaznachei was furious and that he would give orders to stop the whole party. However, we heard no more of this.

After my arrival in Meshed I learned that the Khush Begi had not been told of my departure from Bokhara for eight days, and was angry with the Kaznachei for allowing me to go.

My two N.C.O.s had made many friends and were loaded down with presents of *khalats*. These they were obliged to throw away. It seems to be the custom here to present these robes made of bright-coloured Bokhara silk. I was given several and managed to take one, which I wore under my other clothes.

Our party now collected together. We were in all seventeen mounted men, one woman and three spare animals. It rained all day and was very unpleasant, but the rain ceased at dusk. Just as we were about to start we found that our guide had forgotten to get the password. We finally started at eight p.m., riding through muddy roads and being challenged by sentries on several occasions. On leaving the city our road led along the outside of the city wall. Here we had the misfortune to lose one of the spare pack ponies loaded with food and were delayed for ten minutes. We happened to be just under the wall of the Afghan consulate and great caution and silence were necessary. We recovered the pony and continued our journey and after some miles came to the railway just as the train for Askhabad passed. It looked fine in the dark as it dashed past us a few yards off, the engine glowing with its burning wood fire. By half-past one in the morning we had come eighteen versts and stayed in the village of Khumun. Here we ate a little food and drank some tea and passed our first night in the open between our felts.

We were off again shortly after eight the next morning when for the first time members of the party saw each other by daylight. All were, as I have said, dressed as Turkomans. As I rode up the line I was greeted in German by a man whom I did not recognize under his big Turkoman busby. I went up to him and saw that he was one of the Rumanian N.C.O.s whom I had seen several times in Bokhara. He was very surprised to know who I really was. He and another man were accompanying the Russian party to help with the horses.

For over an hour we travelled among fields and villages, when with some suddenness we found ourselves on the steppe. With a rest at midday, but no water as the well had become undrinkably salt, we travelled till dark when it began to rain. The track we were following was very faint and quite invisible in the rainy darkness and finally we lost it. This was disappointing as we had sent food for the ponies and for ourselves ahead to the well a few days previously, and these supplies entered importantly into the arrangements for our journey. When it was quite dark a fire showed up and I suggested that this was the well we had been making for and we had better go on to it. It appeared to me to be quite close — scarcely a mile away. My experienced guides laughed at me and said it was many versts away and we would have great difficulty in the dark. I disbelieved them and walked towards it, but after going nearly a mile it was no nearer, so I returned. It turned out to be about five miles away as we discovered the next morning.

After spending a wet and miserably cold night in the open, we were glad to get off as soon as it was light enough to see the track which we found a few yards away. I felt that I had been wise to order a halt the moment the road was lost, so that we had not wandered about in the dark, and that we were not now obliged to waste time finding the road itself in the half light.

In a little more than an hour we reached the well at Khushab. This means 'sweet water' and the name was not untrue. We rested, fed and dried ourselves in the warm sun. Our next well had, we were told, turned too salt to drink and so we filled our leather bottles with water here. The salinity of these wells varies from time to time — in my limited experience — always for the worse. The salts contained in the water have a medicinal effect. On this day we travelled about forty versts or twenty-six miles. We had expected to find fodder sent ahead from Bokhara on the road, but did not do so.

On December 21st we started off and after going six versts came to a well where our fodder from Bokhara had been taken by mistake. Here we rested and fed the animals and towards dusk, after crossing a belt of flat desert on which were numbers of sand-grouse, locally called *bolkuruk*, we found ourselves among ditches and cultivation again and at dusk we reached Burdalik, where we were entertained by the Bokharan Governor or Beg. He had a whole sheep cooked for us. A huge mud oven was filled with firewood; when burnt out the sheep was hung inside and the top covered over.

The Beg was very pleasant and helpful in every way to us, but we learnt that it would be unwise to get the wrong side of the law here. Among other sights of the town he showed me the 'lock-up' where the prisoners sat in a row with one leg in stocks and chained by the neck. The Beg hunted with hawks, and I was anxious to go out with him. I had kept hawks myself in India and had done some hawking in Persia, and it would have been interesting to note any difference in method. At the last moment, however, I found that all my companions intended to come also, and that a huge party was being organized. I wished to avoid undue publicity. If a story of this sort reached the Bolsheviks they might think our party of such importance as to warrant special steps for interception. I therefore called the party off, and the hawkers went out alone and brought back a brace of pheasants.

We had expected to travel with camels from here but the Beg told us that we could do the journey with ponies. This would be quicker and simpler and reduced the risk of interception. I therefore jumped at the idea and, to arrange this, I bought some more ponies.

Our party now consisted of thirty ponies, nine being spare to carry food. We also added four guides, making a total of twenty-one people. We were advised to take several guides for these reasons: a single man may lose the way and then lose his head; two or three can consult and may get things right in this way; then, the guides have eventually to return and a man would not be safe alone in the desert or steppe.

We left Burdalik on December 24th and travelled for some miles through cultivation among which were villages and farmhouses. All were fortified but did not have towers as on the North-West Frontier of India. The Turkomans of the Oxus Valley here seem to be in a process of change from a nomadic to a settled life. Among the villages were many *yurts*, and the huts made of reeds and mud were very faithful copies of the *yurt* in which this people had been born and bred for generations.

The Beg made a point of our being his guests and treated us with the greatest hospitality; when we left, however, we were presented with a little bill of five thousand roubles for our entertainment! Still we had received much help and the essential guides and food for our onward journey for which I was quite ready to pay. I also wished to give the Beg a personal present for all he had done — without his efficient help we could never have continued our journey. The only thing I had which I could spare was a pocket aneroid, on which were engraved my initials. It is possible that this aneroid eventually found its way to Kabul bazaar and started the following rumour which I cull from a London newspaper of February 16th, 1920:

'A circumstantial story reached India a few months ago from Kabul. The story was that a certain man in the bazaar, who had arrived from Tashkent, was going about saying that it was he who had helped Bailey to escape from the Bolsheviks, but that later on, a quarrel arising between the two, he had killed Bailey and had looted him of his possessions, including a watch with the initials F.M.B. on the cover. This watch, it was stated, was for sale at the bazaar.'

On the fall of Bokhara the Beg of Burdalik was murdered by the Bolsheviks and presumably his property was looted, and this aneroid found its way to Kabul where it was believed to be a watch with my initials on it.

A couple of miles before reaching the Oxus we left cultivation and crossed reedy flats on which were wild geese and duck. We reached the banks of the Oxus in the afternoon, too late for the whole party to cross before dark. News could not get across the river as long as we remained on this bank and controlled all the boats, and I thought it better to cross the next day. This would give a little less time for news of us to get ahead to our enemies. We slept in the open and found it very cold and windy on the river bank.

On Christmas morning it took us three hours and forty

minutes to cross the whole party in three journeys of the large ferry boat. We had some difficulty with the new ponies who objected to carrying our loads, and our first hour's journey from the river through tall grass took us less than a mile.

In Turkestan ponies are not castrated and the stallions are apt to give trouble and scream and fight if loose at night. They had to be tied to stout *saxaul* bushes or on long pegs driven deep into the sand. In the end we had to throw away a sort of portmanteau of Mrs. Manditch's which we had brought so far with some difficulty. It was too large and clumsy for these half-broken animals.

We had by now had some experience of this waterless steppe travel and I decided that a great deal of time was wasted by camping at wells. You might reach your well at three in the afternoon and not be able to reach the next before dark and thus waste several precious hours of daylight. So from now on we disregarded wells as stopping places but just watered whenever we reached a well and then went on till dark, when we bivouacked wherever we happened to be. Sometimes of course, by good luck, at a well. From the Oxus we had several days of uneventful travel.

Manditch spoke German, Russian and Serbian but knew no English. For his long journey through India and on by sea he decided it would be useful to acquire this language, so I gave him lessons. We came to the future tenses: 'I will', 'you will', 'he, she or it will', 'we will', 'they will'. In Russian and most other languages the 'will' alters with the person and even, in some cases, with the sex of the subject. Manditch protested 'You said I will', but you also said 'you will' and 'he will'. Is there not something wrong? I said 'No. The language is as simple as that'. 'I could learn a language like that in a few days', he replied, and he did! I think that people whose mother tongue is one of the minor languages are usually brought up bilingually, knowing, besides their own, one of the important languages of the world. Such people pick up a third or fourth language comparatively easily.

The steppe through which we were travelling was rough, rather like a stormy sea, the waves of which had been frozen solid. In most parts it was covered with a small bush called by the Russians *saxaul* which provides excellent fuel, and we were never in any difficulty on this account. In some places the rain-water had been collected by damming up a small watercourse. This was called a *kak*. The water in such places was muddy but with no taste of salt, and we were always glad to collect a little dirty water from such places. One of the reasons which persuaded me to give up the original plan of travelling slowly with camels and to risk the journey with ponies, was that we were told that we would find people at the wells who would sell us a little food for man and horse. We found absolutely no one, and our poor ponies, on whom eventually our lives depended, had no grass at all for four days and only very little grain and salt water. The weather was dry, cold, windy and dusty. The wells about here were very salt and sometimes our ponies refused to drink, although they must have been terribly thirsty.

These long, waterless marches were hard on Zep. In my travels in Arabistan and over the Pamirs to Turkestan he had learnt to jump from the ground on to my knee on a horse when he was tired. This alarmed the horse until he got used to it. Zep coming alongside and asking for a lift caused much amusement to my companions, none of whom had much use for dogs.

There were numbers of jerboas all over the steppe — rats with long hind legs and long tails. There were also tortoise-shells lying about everywhere but these animals were hibernating and we did not see a single live one. The desert is impassable in summer owing to the heat and lack of water. They told me also that it swarmed with virulent scorpions which were sure to sting a man sleeping, as one had to do, on the ground.

The Turkomans have a curious, and to our minds, dangerous and senseless custom, for which there must of course be some reason. After watering a horse in the desert they gallop him round and round for a few minutes, whipping him to make him go as fast as he can. They say that unless they do this the water harms the horse. I did not do it to my horse and he came to no harm. The Turkomans and, for that matter, Tibetans and others who depend on horses more than we now do, treat their horses in a way of which we would disapprove. I once showed a Baktiari from the mountains of south-west Persia a photo of a yearling sold for nine thousand guineas. The price flabberghasted him and he asked me what that horse could do. I said he could go for a short distance, say a couple of miles, faster than most horses carrying a light weight. He would earn money in stakes and would be used for breeding. All this seemed quite useless to him. He would rather have his own horse which had carried him one hundred and seventy miles in two days with a good deal of weight. That was what a horse was wanted for.

When we were travelling through the steppe we were told of a Turkoman, believed to be in the neighbourhood, who was wanted for murder. I said that it ought not to be difficult to catch him as they only had to watch the wells where he must come for water. Not at all: his horse had been trained to eat mutton fat! If this were done the animal could go for several weeks without water!

About midday, on December 28th, Manditch broke down. He had been in pain from trouble in his back for some days without mentioning it. He now said he could go no further. We were, I calculated, one hundred and sixty versts from the Oxus and one hundred and twenty from the Murghab. Just about the worst spot in the desert for such a thing to happen, though the Murghab Valley under Bolshevik control was not likely to be a haven of rest for us. I told him he must come on, we would travel more slowly and do all we could to help him. He said we were to go on and he would remain behind and die alone. Then his wife wept. Some members of the party said: 'Leave him, we must go on, we have no food or water and will all die if we delay.' I said that this would not do. Then one of the guides had an idea. One of the pack ponies was an ambler and might be a more restful ride. We unloaded the pony, put Manditch's saddle on him and Manditch then mounted. He was delighted, said this was an entirely different matter and that he could ride on for ever on such a horse!

Soon after this we came on some deserted huts. The walls were made of *saxaul* twigs; to our delight they were stopped with grass to keep out wind. We tore this out and gave it to our famished animals. It was very little among so many but they ate it ravenously. If we had any delays such as watering at a well, or, in this case the delay over Manditch, we usually made it up by travelling a few miles after dark if we could see the path. This day we lost the track at dusk and had to stop.

The next morning our guides confessed that they were completely lost. I calculated that we were about eighty versts or fifty miles from the Murghab River. This valley, or rather the belt of cultivation along the river, was controlled and guarded by the Bolsheviks; our guides knew the people of one village where they hoped to get assistance and supplies. If we rode on a compass bearing it was doubtful if the horses could survive this long journey with no water. They were exhaused by their long marches with little food and their last drink had been at midday the day before. The chance of running across a well was so slender that it could be ruled out. Even if all these difficulties could be overcome, a large, exhausted, thirsty party rushing for the river, probably without proper precautions, would have been an easy prey for our Bolshevik enemies. The situation was certainly grave. Then one of the Turkomans with us said he *might* find a well, but not on our direct route. We let him lead us. After travelling for three hours in rather a hopeless way, he said he still had hopes, but he thought the well must be about three hours' journey on. At the end of the three hours he estimated that it was a further two, but he was by no means sure we would find it at all! In any case, he said that unless we found people at the well we would not be able to get at the water as it was too deep. In my inexperience I did not fear this. With all the ropes and straps of thirty horses we would get that water somehow. In the back of my mind was, however, the fear that it might take so long to water our large party that those first served would be ready for more before the last had finished!

Just after we had been promised two hours' further travel we suddenly came on a well with a hut and a flock of sheep. We were saved and our relief can be imagined. The place was called Yur Chilik. It was indeed lucky that we found people here or we would all have died of thirst. The well proved to be seven hundred and fifty feet deep, measured by pacing the length of the rope, and we would have had no hope of reaching the water. The rope itself would have been too heavy for a pony to carry. The well was cemented round the edge and gave a curious echo. The water was lifted in a large leather bag, the rope being drawn over a pulley by two camels. Each bag of water took the camels nine minutes. The task of getting a small bucket up by hand and giving water to thirty horses would have been quite hopeless. The water of this and our next deep well was wonderfully clear and with no trace of salt. We had been drinking only salt and muddy water since leaving Bokhara, except for the time at Burdalik.

What patience and confidence must have been shown to dig to this enormous depth in the desert. What must have been the feelings of a man who had gone down more than seven hundred feet without a trace of water! I think perhaps that at certain spots they had to find water or the desert would have been uncrossable and that they just dug until they found it. I was told that wells in the desert north-east of Krasnovodsk, east of the Caspian Sea, were much deeper than these.

The people at the well told us that we would have to stop at a similar deep well before reaching the Murghab River. This well was about thirty-five versts or twenty-three miles away. We spent the afternoon and the next morning eating, resting, and looking after our ponies, they having had scant attention during the last few days in the steppe. We cooked large *shashliks* on the cleaning rods of our rifles, as Peter Fleming did on his journey across China. We ate these with delicious hot bread baked for us by the Turkomans. The loaf was rather like an Indian *chupatti* but two inches thick and two feet across.

We saw one man go off with a flock of three thousand sheep. He had three camels, a donkey and a dog. He expected to be away twenty days during which time he and the donkey and the dog would drink water carried by the camels, while the sheep and camels would get none except perhaps a puddle of rain-water. They can go without water for twenty days. I wondered what a man all alone like that for twenty days would *think* about! He has no books and can't read. After twenty days this man would return to the well, give all the animals a good drink, and then go off again in the same way. The sheep were those from which astrakhan fur is obtained. This is not the skin of an unborn lamb but the lambs are killed as soon as possible after they are born. I often used to think that the lack of water and the very hard conditions under which they lived made their fleece curl and gave them their value! Haider Khoja told me that these sheep had been taken to the Caucasus and also to Canada, but in those places the lambs were born with no curl in their wool and were quite valueless.

The Turkomans keep large, fierce dogs with cropped ears as a defence, much as the Tibetans do with their thick-coated mastiffs. The Turkoman also keep a kind of greyhound with which they course gazelle. They can only catch the gazelle at certain times of year when the animals are in poor condition. They told me that when the gazelle are fat the dogs can overtake them but cannot get their teeth into them! Camels were forcibly fed here for some reason; balls of flour mixed with other things were pushed down their throats, a most unpleasant and apparently, for the man, a dangerous process.

We left our hospitable well at one o'clock on the afternoon of December 30th. At one place we found tufts of grass growing and stopped to pull them for our ponies to eat at night.

In the evening we reached a well similar to Yur Chilik, it was called Humli. This was six hundred feet deep and camels took seven and a half minutes to get a bag of delicious water.

On arrival we learned that four Russians had left that morning for Burdalik. We felt sure that they must have a message for us from Meshed and so sent a man off at once to see who they were and, if necessary, to call them back. We waited the next day for them.

I wished to get a specimen of a gazelle (*Gazella subgutturosa*) from this seldom visited locality. The information given me at Yur Chilik was that there were many near this well and, moreover, there was a sick one here. One very seldom sees sick wild animals. I went out and soon found that the sick one had died. I took the horns, and they are now in the Bombay Natural History Society's Museum. I went on to try to shoot one myself and soon saw three, but they were very wild and I did not get a shot. These gazelle were called *saigak* or *jeran* by the Turkomans.

The Russians arrived back in the afternoon. They turned out to be men that I had sent off from Bokhara on October 22nd and November 12th and bore a letter from General Malleson telling me to come to Meshed. One of these messengers had reached Meshed on November 16th and told me that the General had sent a letter to Bokhara for me on the next day, the 17th. On December 8th the Kaznachei asked Azizov, the Khiva Turkoman with me, whether he could read English, and a couple of days later he asked one of my Russian companions the same thing. They both replied that they could not but that there was a British officer in Bokhara who could do so. The Kaznachei said that that would not do. I am certain that these stupid Bokharan ministers held back letters for me, hoping to find out what was in them. This inability to trust their proved friends, as shown by the messages and gifts brought by my two Indian soldiers, and to avoid the temptation to intrigue, was none the less annoying for being expected. However, *de mortuis* ... these men, the Kaznachei, Khush Begi and all were shot by the Bolsheviks a few months later.

I heard very good accounts of the British force in Meshed and these four Russians were full of admiration for the clothes and food provided for the Indian troops there. They themselves had been clothed and equipped and provided in every way for the journey to Bokhara on what they considered a lavish scale.

That night it snowed and was very cold under our felt. The morning of New Year's Day 1920 broke cold and windy, with snow falling. Things looked so umpromising that we halted for the day.

During the next night the weather cleared, but was still very cold, with about five inches of snow lying, and we made rather a later start than usual.

CHAPTER XXIII

ACROSS THE MURGHAB

THE next morning after going about twenty miles we saw a great distance off a single horseman travelling very fast. This was the first human being we had seen in the steppe with the exception of the people at the last two wells. We did not think much more about it. Soon after this we came in sight of a well at which we saw people. They appeared to be preparing to defend themselves as we saw rifles in their hands. My Russian companions wanted to attack them at once — a nice mess there would have been, trying with our seven rifles to turn men out of houses, with no cover for ourselves and no hope, for a wounded man, of ever getting away, and with the alternative of surrender or death from thirst if we failed to capture the place.

I took one Turkoman with me to within shouting distance of the well and said that we meant no harm but must get water. We then found an old man who had evidently strayed from the well, collecting fuel and we explained things to him and told him that, if necessary, we would fight but would much rather not. We did not tell him how poorly we were armed and he must have been sure that every man carried a rifle. He went to his companions where we saw him explaining things to the people at the well who then signalled to us to come on. This we did cautiously. We found two rooms at the well and were glad of the shelter. The party at the well consisted of two notorious robbers, three or four of their friends, and a queer, suspicious fellow, a Persian by his dress. All armed, they were quite sufficient to keep us from the water, had they fought. We made an agreement with them that we would take one room and they the other and that we would not interfere with each other in any way.

Presently Kalbi Mohammed, my Hazaran soldier, said to me, indicating the Persian: 'I know that man, his name is Said Mohammed but he is also known as Eshan and he is a well-known bad character of Meshed.' This was a most extraordinary coincidence and, as it turned out, fortunate for us.

I called aside the chief Turkoman robber and asked who this man was. He said: 'I never saw him before. He arrived only a few minutes before you did and told us you were about to attack the well. He is a Persian.'

'In that case,' I said, 'I would not be breaking my word to you if I took charge of him.'

'No,' he replied, 'you can do what you like with him.'

On this I went up to the man and told him that I intended to take charge of him for the night. He protested but could do nothing, and we searched and disarmed him and tied him up. We took it in turns to do sentry-go and watch our prisoner and our fellow guests at the well. They did the same to us. We drew lots for times of duty and mine came in the early morning up to sunrise, which I spent watching their sentry while he watched me!

In the morning I explained to the Persian that we must take him with us. When he saw we meant business he was quite willing. All the same, we tied his legs under the horse and had his horse led by one of our men. What we feared, and what we were almost convinced of later, was that he was a spy sent by the Bolsheviks to bring in reports of just such a party as ours, so that a proper reception might be prepared for us at some well. The desperate situation of a party like ours can easily be understood, if on reaching a well we found it occupied by an enemy prepared for us. We would have no cover of any kind from their fire and we would have to get the water at once or perish.

On January 3rd we travelled about sixteen versts when we were near enough to the Murghab River for special caution. On the way we had passed three Turkomans with a flock of sheep. We also passed a well. Wells are naturally more

numerous in the neighbourhood of the river. We halted and
sent a man ahead to arrange for our crossing. I got on to a
hillock and could see the river and some houses. Our man
returned with food for us and our horses, and after feeding
them and eating something ourselves, we moved on at about
eight p.m. We were guided in the dark and at half past nine
reached the river bank. The river was about twenty yards
wide, with steep banks. We were near an iron factory chimney.
This was known as the 'machine' to our Turkomans. They told
us that it was an apparatus for lifting water and had been
installed by a rich Bai. We were near the village of Sari Yazi.
There was one boat in working order which was pulled back-
wards and forwards by a wire hawser. The boat was too small
to take a horse and the horses swam, two or three at a time,
being held and guided by men in the boat. The crossing took
us about an hour and a half. We were as quiet as possible as
there was danger from Bolsheviks who patrolled the railway
line, but we made sufficient noise to disturb a pheasant roosting
over our heads, who called noisily. The men who arranged the
crossing for us made a good thing out of it and I had to pay
twelve thousand roubles.

Three versts beyond the river we reached the Khushk-Merv
railway line. It was a bright moonlight night and by the light
of the moon I was able to read the number of the telegraph pole
where we actually crossed the railway, 167/12/12. We travelled
till two a.m. by which time we were again well into the desert,
and halted for the rest of the night. Before turning in, we
opened the bags of food which we had bought the previous
evening from the Turkomans, to find that we had been given
very short measure and that we only had sixteen *chupattis*
to last our twenty-five people for four days. I can only suppose
that the people who supplied us took advantage of the darkness
and of our inexcusable preoccupation with our dangers and
troubles from other directions to give us short weight. We
divided the sixteen *chupattis* equally and went to bed hungry.

The next morning we were off by half past eight, in a dense

and very cold fog. This lifted later and we saw, to our fear and disappointment, that although we had travelled a considerable distance since crossing the river, we were still close to it and could see the trees. It was always possible that the Bolsheviks might hear we had crossed and send men after us. I am sure that the duty of our Persian prisoner had been to warn them of the approach of any suspicious parties.

We passed several wells, at one of which we halted and made tea with melted snow, and felt very much the lack of food. We saw some gazelle and a hare, but could not get a shot. There were also sand-grouse about. It got very foggy again. I could see by the compass that we were not going straight, but our guide told us it was all right and that he knew where he was. Suddenly we came on the tracks of a large party and it took me a moment or two to realize that we had been going in a circle and were back on our own tracks again! The guide now confessed he was lost, so we followed our tracks back to the well where we had made tea. We left this again at six and by half past we were lost again, so we stopped. It was a cold, frosty night. We had travelled altogether twenty-six miles, of which six had been spent aimlessly wandering about. This was annoying, considering the danger we were in from our nearness to the Bolsheviks guarding the railway and our lack of food.

The next morning we left at eight and passed close by two wells which we had passed the day before. After fourteen versts we reached a group of five wells called Gokchu, under a prominent hillock. We could not reach the water as the well was too deep, so, after resting a little, we moved on and at six in the evening we reached a well with a hut called Gumbużli Tekke, where we found a man with one camel drawing water, who watered our ponies. This well was one hundred and thirty-five feet deep. By this time we had quite finished our own food and were eating the grain we had for the ponies which we parched or boiled. The man said his camp was near by and we persuaded him to let us have some food. We sent one of our guides with him to get it. We waited for an hour but he did not return, so we went after him in the dark and presently saw in front of us a fire. It is dangerous to approach people by surprise at night-time in this country. They are apt to shoot at once and see what it is all about afterwards; so we called to them. They replied, 'Go away or we will shoot'. Later our guide rejoined us with one of their men who told us that they were a party of robbers; this explains why they did not stay at the well, but camped one verst away, and sent one man to get their water. They were afraid of us and would certainly fire if we came any nearer to them. It was useless to fight; so we retired a little so that they should not see us by firelight and they promised to send us some food. As soon as we had gone a little way they called that they had nothing for us and we had better go away. It was all very tiresome and disappointing as we were very hungry; still we had had a good drink of water which we could not have had if we had not run across these unpleasant people.

We got back on to the track we had been following and after going for an hour we came on a well and hut called Krest. Here we lost the road in the dark, as the ground was all trodden over by sheep. We wasted an hour looking for it and then went and slept at the hut. We thought that we had finished our food, but here someone found a little flour. This my servant, Haider, was going to make into a *chupatti* for us, but Mrs. Manditch insisted on baking something else which entailed hunting for some soda which she had somewhere. All this took so long that I went to sleep without any food. Our hunger was telling on our tempers. I know I was annoyed with her.

In the morning, just as we were starting, a Turkoman rode up. He was going from Penjdeh to Sarakhs and had had supper with the robbers. They were very nervous of him and thought that he was our man sent to spy out their strength, and he told us that as soon as they had driven us off the night before, they had packed up themselves and moved quickly away, fearing that we would attack them during the night.

Our Persian prisoner had by now quite settled down to his position, though we relaxed no precaution. He knew something of the country — more indeed than our guides did. The food situation was serious and I thought I might with luck shoot something. The Russian idea of shooting was to go out in a crowd and all blaze together at anything they saw, till it was out of sight. Our prisoner seemed to be acquainted with the ways of the desert fauna; altogether we were getting on so well that I took him out with me to try to get some meat. We saw several flocks of sand-grouse which were apparently eating the patches of snow. I saw some foxes and about thirty gazelle. I got to within about one hundred and fifty yards of the latter and had an unsuccessful shot. I was using an old Bokharan three-line rifle, which had not been well cared for in the Bokharan army. It was disappointing, but all was well when later in the morning we came on a Turkoman camp where we bought bread and mutton, and stayed over four hours to cook and eat. In the evening we reached a well called Gumbezli, where we had hoped and expected to find people who would give us water and food. There was no one there however, and we had difficulty and delay in getting the water up from a sixty-foot well. It took us three hours to give each of our thirty horses one bucket of water. We had only one bucket in the party. A second bucket would have reduced the time as it could have been let down into the well while a pony was drinking. I had a row with one of the Russians for giving his horse two buckets. If we had all done this we would never have got on. Had we found some nice Turkomans with a camel or two we could have watered from the trough in a few minutes. There were so few places worth a name in the desert that it seemed unnecessary to have two close together with such similar names as Gumbuzli Tekke and Gumbezli.

CHAPTER XXIV

FRONTIER SKIRMISH

WE were now nearing the Persian frontier. Wells and inhabitants had been comparatively frequent. We left Gumbezli well at about nine in the evening and travelled along the direct and fairly well marked track leading to Sarakhs, the town on the Persian frontier. We could not travel directly there. A Russian town with a Bolshevik garrison stood on this side of the river which formed the frontier here. So after going for some way along this track, we left it and steered due west by the stars. We once passed a shepherd's camp and hailed the people, asking them to let us have some grain for our horses. They were terrified of us and said they had none, that there was a well half an hour's journey off in the direction we were taking, and that if we did not go at once they would shoot. We never found this well and I doubt whether it existed. This was serious, as we were getting desperate; we had given the very last of our grain to our ponies and had been hoping to buy some in this slightly more populous region. Soon after this we crossed a track of real desert twenty versts wide, on which nothing grew. The people called it Kerk, but whether this was a name for this peculiar type of land or the name of the locality I did not find out. We could not halt on this as there was no fuel and it was terribly cold. There was a moon shortly after midnight. By its light we saw that we crossed a well-worn track cutting across our direction. Our guides knew this and said it led to Sarakhs. At two-forty a.m. we came on *saxaul* bushes again and halted, lit fires, warmed ourselves and slept. The Russians spent a long time preparing tea, time which I think would have been better spent in sleep. We had travelled sixty-four versts this day — about forty-two miles.

When day dawned we saw a range of snow-covered mountains in front of us due west; between us and the mountains was a regular shaped conical hill. The mountains were in Persia. The feelings of all of us at the sight of a free land, even in the distance, is hard to describe.

We had travelled for fifteen versts in this direction when we came to a small hollow in the steppe. From the ridge of this we could see below, less than a mile away, the river which formed the Persian frontier. We had all, perhaps rather carelessly, ridden up to this ridge. In fact we did not know we were so close to the frontier. We hurriedly withdrew into the hollow and I went forward and lay in the *saxaul* bushes with my field glasses to see what I could.

On the other side of the river was what appeared in the distance to be a graveyard, but it was actually the Persian village of Naurozabad with very regular queer-shaped houses in rows. It was impossible to guess the size of the river, but I could see a belt of green rushes very wide on this side, and narrower on the Persian side of the river. What disquieted me more was that a mile away, on a hill overlooking the river, were some people who got up and walked off. Who were they? Had they seen us?

My first inclination was to ride on at once before any possible enemy could make preparations, but our guides could not say what the river was like and whether it was fordable. We could see what looked like a ford but no bridge.

To risk an attack on such a party with such meagre armament, while trying to find a ford or means of crossing a river of unknown size, seemed to be courting disaster. I knew that the river was wide and unfordable a few miles downstream at Sarakhs. I therefore considered it necessary to reconnoitre the crossing and so hid the party in the hollow and put out two Russians as sentries to lie concealed in the *saxaul* and to look out for any people moving in the river valley and specially to see that we were not surprised. Supposing the people I had seen were Bolshevik sentries who had supports somewhere, they might easily have rushed us. It was also possible that someone of the many people we had seen in the last few days had taken news of the approach of our party. All was uncertain and demanded caution. At the same time I told my two Indian soldiers, whom I could trust and who had been trained in such things, to ride to the left of the conical hill, go down to the river and come back the other side. They were to report above all as to how the river could be crossed. I went back to the rest of the party in the hollow and we loosened girths and did what we could for our tired and hungry animals. After about an hour I was surprised by Awal Nur and Kalbi Mohammed riding in among us. One of my Russian sentries should of course have seen them coming and have warned us, but he had come back to talk to his friends. I was very angry with him for letting us all down like this. The consequences of this lapse were very nearly serious as it turned out. The two soldiers reported that they had seen no one and that the river appeared only to be fordable at a well-marked ford straight below us, that is to the right of the conical hill. It took us a few minutes to get the girths tightened and to move off. These precious minutes would not have been wasted had my sentry not deserted his post. We all mounted and started off to do our last miles in Soviet territory. All were excited and wanted to gallop down hill and get into a land of freedom. I checked this however. Some of the party were very bad riders and I could easily imagine the confusion and difficulty of a manœuvre of that kind. 'No,' I said, 'we will go at our usual jog trot or amble.'

As a precaution I sent Kalbi Mohammed ahead to ride about two hundred yards in front as a scout. He galloped out and we started at the same time to jog steadily down the valley. The belt of reeds must have been four or five hundred yards wide on this, the Russian side, of the river, and when he reached this, Kalbi Mohammed called something out and waved his hand but continued down the valley towards the river. I could not understand what he meant, so telling the others to keep steadily on, I galloped out myself to overtake him.

I actually caught him up on the river bank and our two tired and thirsty ponies plunged into the water up to their girths for the long-wanted drink. The river was here about eight yards wide and four feet deep. Kalbi Mohammed told me that as he rode down to the river he had seen some people hiding in the reeds on his right hand. At that instant a shot rang out followed by many more. Kalbi Mohammed and I were actually in the river and the rest of the party were two or three hundred yards behind, trotting towards us. A fear I had in mind was that the Persians of the village of Naurozabad, which was about one thousand yards from the river, might think we were attacking them and resist us. I therefore took Kalbi Mohammed's rifle from him and told him to ride on as hard as he could to the Persian village and stop them chipping in. I waited for my party, who by this time were at full gallop, to reach me. I then saw that Mrs. Manditch, who was a very weak rider, was alone about twenty yards behind with her hat off and her hair down. She had no control over her pony, who had taken it into his head to stop at a pool among the reeds to drink! I suppose that in less than a minute the party were all plunging down the steep bank into the river, trying to prevent their thirsty ponies from drinking, and riding over the flat Persian bank to a long wall a few yards from the river which would give protection. As they dashed past me, Awal Nur's saddlebags fell off into the river. He jumped off to rescue them and I helped him to put them back. This took only a few moments and when I looked up I saw that Mrs. Manditch's pony was plunging riderless down the bank, and that she was lying on the ground while Captain Iskander, the son of the Grand Duke, was riding back towards her. All this time a few shots were dropping among us. The Grand Duke's son reached Mrs. Manditch, and spoke to her. I feared she must be seriously injured. I was on the point of going to see if I could help when a shot hit the ground kicking up the dust a couple of feet from her; on this she jumped up and tried to mount behind her rescuer, but she could not do so, so ran towards where I was in the river, holding on to the officer's stirrup. When they arrived at the steep river bank, a couple of yards from where I was, Captain Iskander got his pony down the bank and the lady was easily able to mount, and she crossed and joined the others.

It was all very theatrical, with everyone in Turkoman clothes, and reminded me of some scene from a film. Firing from both sides was going on all the time. This brave action of Iskander's would have been recognized by some award for gallantry under other circumstances.

The two other Russian officers, as soon as they crossed the river and were on the flat bank, on the Persian side, opened fire from their saddles. Their ponies were twisting about and trying to join the others who were already behind the wall; there was, of course, no prospect of their hitting any mark.

The Bolsheviks were no better; they were hiding in the tall grass about four hundred yards off, bobbing up to fire a hurried standing shot, and bobbing down again, their large Turkoman hats making conspicuous marks. The only man who was behaving like a trained soldier was Awal Nur, who was lying down taking steady shots. I had remained in the river ready to go out and help the Grand Duke's son and Mrs. Manditch if necessary, but they came to no harm and as soon as they had crossed the river, I turned my pony and dismounted and got Awal Nur to hold it and took a few shots myself, especially at a man who had left the reeds, and was hurrying across the open. My shots made him think better of it and he ran back. As soon as the whole of our party were across we and the Bolsheviks mutually decided not to fire lest we should violate Persian neutrality! They came out of the reeds and the two Russian officers and Awal Nur and I joined the others behind the wall.

There was great excitement and Mrs. Manditch was very distressed as she had lost her saddlebags containing trifles (her *kleinigkeiten*, she called them). I then learnt what had happened behind the rush of galloping ponies and the dust screen as they all made for the river. Mrs. Manditch had at last persuaded her pony that it was no time for a drink and galloped to overtake the others. She fell off and at the same time her saddlebags fell off a few yards away. She refused to go without the saddlebags and the Grand Duke's son was arguing with her about this when a Bolshevik bullet, one of the few that came anywhere near any of us, hit the ground quite close to them. This decided her to leave the precious bags behind and she tried, as I had seen, to get up behind him.

I was naturally annoyed with Mrs. Manditch for having risked her own and other lives for her trifles. She then told me that the bags did not contain *kleinigkeiten*, but jewellery. I said it was very foolish to put small valuables in the saddlebags. Such things could have been carried on her person. The truth then came out. During our two months in Bokhara Mrs. Manditch had been employed in making herself dresses of beautiful Bokharan silks. The results of her labours, seven lovely dresses, were all in the missing bags! This made me still more annoyed, as I had said we were not to load our ponies down with useless things, but only food and absolute necessaries were to be taken. The ponies had to carry us about six hundred miles with very little food and water and our lives depended on them.

We left our shelter and went up towards the Persian village. The people had rushed out with rifles in their hands, firmly believing that Bolsheviks were attacking them. It was lucky that Kalbi Mohammed had been able to assure them. They were still very excited and one armed man rushed up to me and said: 'Do you know that this is Persia?'

'Yes,' I said, 'a pleasant land which I have been hoping to reach for a long time. I am a British officer on my way to Meshed.' He then became quite friendly. We were all taken up to the village and a Persian N.C.O. came in and asked who I was and what it was all about! He said the Khan and the officer commanding the detachment of troops were both away. I explained things briefly and then, by this time feeling very sorry for Mrs. Manditch in her loss, I asked him if he could do anything to get the bags back. We went out on to the roof and through my field glasses I saw the Bolshevik party of about twenty, a thousand yards away, apparently examining the saddlebags. I asked the Persian N.C.O. to send a man down to them and to tell them that the bags only contained a lady's luggage and nothing of importance, but that we wanted them and would pay anything in reason for them. Through field glasses I watched the messenger ride down, cross the river and go up to the Bolsheviks. It was too far to see what happened, but after a few moments he started back, now at full gallop. When he was about half way back from the river a shot was fired by the Bolsheviks which passed over the village and almost like an echo; one was fired back by some Persian. That was all. The messenger arrived to say that the Bolsheviks would not give up the saddlebags and that they were very angry for one of them had been hit in the elbow and another, their chief, in the thigh. This was good shooting considering the few steady shots fired.

Later, the Khan, Ali Nagi Khan, and the commanding officer who was a relative of his, came and gave us a drink of some kind of spirit and invited us to a good dinner of which we stood in great need.

We learnt that Sarakhs was thirty-five versts distant. At the first shot of our skirmish the Persians had sent a mounted man to travel there as fast as possible to report that the Bolsheviks were attacking Naurozabad! The Persian Governor of Sarakhs acted with great promptness and immediately sent off a small party of twelve cavalry with three officers and gave orders for the infantry to start as soon as possible. After I had given a short explanation to the Persian officer at Naurozabad he sent off another messenger explaining exactly what had happened, and I also sent telegrams to be dispatched from the Sarakhs telegraph office, including several to the relatives of

Austrian prisoners of war to their new countries, Poland, Yugoslavia and Czechoslovakia.

I learnt that we had been fired on by a party of sixteen Baluchis in the pay of the Bolsheviks, under a robber chief, Abdul Kerim Khan. They were armed with old Russian Berdanker rifles. We ourselves had seven rifles of a better type, but only four of us fired and only two of us took aimed shots. The Bolshevik party also had the advantage of surprise and concealment in the long grass.

I heard later that the Bolsheviks in Tashkent, when they heard of this incident, reported that I had been killed but that they had had no real grudge against me and had given me a military funeral, paying me the honours due to a Russian officer! These details gave an air of truthfulness. The whole thing was done, I suppose, to distress my friends in Tashkent.

It snowed in the night and we left next morning accompanied by the cavalry escort sent so promptly from Sarakhs. Our road for most of the way lay along the bank of the Tejent River. We saw some flocks of duck and geese on the water. The road was cut out of the hillside in places, and it would have been easy for the party, with whom we had had our brush the day before, to lie in wait on the Russian side and to blot us all out on the narrow road at such a place. I must say that I feared this, but the Persians were quite light-hearted and free of this anxiety, and it turned out that they were right. We had a muddy journey largely in falling snow. We passed two villages and in the early afternoon of January 8th rode safely into Sarakhs.

CHAPTER XXV

SAFE IN MESHED

WE found Sarakhs to be a small town surrounded by a ruined wall and joined by a bridge over the river to the Russian town of the same name.

I was at once taken to the Governor and given a room in his house and later the rest of my party were sent to join me. That is, Manditch, his wife, and, after some difficulty, the three Russian officers. My servant, Haider, and my two Indian soldiers, were also entertained in the Governor's house. Azizov, the Turkoman officer, found friends here and the others were sent off somewhere else and came to me to complain of their treatment. I then learnt of the intense hatred of the Russians in this part of Persia.

I discovered that the Governor had wished the Persian Governor-General at Meshed to learn first of our arrival and so had held back my telegrams of the day before on the pretext that they could not understand them. I sent off some more myself. We found that the Russian money had very little value here. A one thousand rouble Kerensky note was only worth three tomans.

We woke the next morning, January 9th, all feeling very ill with the most fearful headaches. This was from burning a charcoal fire with all doors and windows shut, even the chimney stopped up, to keep the heat in. This the Russians always did but made some mistake in the arrangements on this occasion. I had visits from several Persian officers, some of whom spoke French. They were embarrassingly friendly and anxious to do all they could for me and for Manditch and his wife, once they knew they were not Russian.

It was only by insisting that the three Russian officers were my friends and that, if they were not allowed to stay with me,

I would leave the house and stay with them, that they were allowed into the Governor's house with me. One Persian officer actually with tears in his eyes, said: 'When the Russians were in Meshed they were always drunk in the streets and molested people; I could get over that. They also shelled the holy shrine of Imam Reza. That was a fearful sin for which they are paying now. But they also killed many people who could never be brought back to life and whose relations were still mourning for them, and I can never forgive that.'

I had wished to start for Meshed the next day but as the Governor had received no order from Meshed in reply to his report of our arrival, we could not go. Six Russians from Bolshevik Sarakhs visited the Governor in whose house we were staying. I thought that probably they had come in connection with our brush with their patrol at Naurozabad, but it turned out the only question was of the use of the water of the river for irrigation. I believe this was only an excuse, and the real object was to see us and find out more about us.

In the afternoon I received a telegram from General Malleson to say that our arrival had been reported to London, India and Teheran, and that orders had been wired to give me and the Russians with us every assistance. So the next morning, January 10th, we started off after thanking our kind Persian host for his hospitality. Our road led us past several villages and a tract of desert. We spent the night at a shepherd's camp at Shurok, where we were put up in one of their black tents, which also accommodated several sick sheep and goats. The tents are very like the tents of nomadic herdsmen of Tibet.

The next night was spent at the village of Ismailabad. The villages of this part of Persia are fortified against Turkoman raids. The houses are all exactly alike. The scarcity of wood causes a domed mud roof to be built, and this had led me to think at first that the village of Naurozabad, where we had crossed the frontier, was a graveyard.

We had been unable to get grain for our ponies at Ismailabad, so the next morning we stopped at a village, Gechidar, where the people were especially kind and hospitable, supplying us with all we required and preparing a warm room with a fire and a samovar for tea.

Arrangements had been made for us to stay at Langarak, but fearing we might have difficulty in getting my large party of Russians settled down, if we arrived late in the day at Meshed, I decided to push on ten versts to Kara Bulak, and so make an earlier arrival. That night we met a Persian customs officer who spoke French and who was very good to us, helping us in various ways and giving us information of the outside world.

On the 14th we reached Meshed. We got our first sight of the golden dome of the mosque of Imam Reza at eleven o'clock and reached the outskirts of the town just as they fired the midday gun.

My difficulties and dangers were over. It was pleasant to see the Union Jack waving over the barracks after such a long time under other colours. I rode up to the gate of the staff quarters and asked to see General Malleson. An Indian sentry stopped me and said that no Russians were allowed to enter. After crossing the frontier into Persia I had discarded my Turkoman clothes and was dressed in the only clothes I had. These were Russian, made in Tashkent, of a peculiar Soviet cut! I explained who I was and was welcomed in the staff mess for lunch. It was nice to be among my own kind again. One peculiarity I noticed and for a moment thought it might have been a post-war development. No officers wore medals. This I found was an idiosyncrasy of the General's!

My lunch seemed a banquet. It is true that I had had plenty of good Persian food for the last week, but I had not recovered from my diet of *sukhari* and ponies' grain washed down with a draught of Epsom Salts. This had pulled us all down in weight. On arrival in Meshed I weighed myself and found I was nine stone two pounds, nearly two-and-a-half stone less than normal.

I did what I could to help the Russians who had come with

me from Bokhara. It was not easy; they were fighting in a lost cause and the General in Meshed felt this and was not inclined to put himself out for these refugees, who were eventually sent to join the last remnants of anti-Bolshevik forces still holding out in Transcaspia. I tried to help them to sell their ponies. These ponies had just travelled six hundred miles in twenty-eight days, frequently doing over forty miles a day under hard conditions, carrying heavy loads, with little food and, above all, very little water. They were small, wiry animals quite unsuited to charge in line as cavalry but ideal for carrying an infantry-man and his weapons rapidly from one point to another. It seemed extraordinary that our remount authorities should have reported that *all* were unsound. No doubt they had technical unsoundnesses, but the facts had proved that these defects did not affect their usefulness.

In Meshed I met several Austrian prisoners, some of whom had escaped from Tashkent after I had done so myself. From one of these I learned that the Government had quickly realized that Manditch had deserted them; but at that time had no idea who his companion was.

During my long absence I had only three times received letters. In October and December 1918 and again in March 1919. These last had been sent from India via Kashgar in October 1918. Once my mail was intercepted by the Bol-sheviks who, presumably, had it read; another was burnt by my friends unread when they were in danger from a Cheka search.

Although there was this British Mission in Meshed I did not receive a single message from them. I had heard of one attempt as related in chapter seventeen.

I had sometimes felt my isolation a good deal and always felt that more might have been done to get into touch with me. Although my address was not exactly public property, up to June 1919 I was always in touch with the United States consul and even after his departure a message to his address would always have reached me. Of course I knew from my own experience how difficult and unreliable messengers were, but I always felt that greater efforts might have been made to send me advice, instructions (and possibly encouragement).

In Meshed I stayed with the late Sir Trenchard Fowle, our Consul-General, who was an old friend. A 'hotel' had just been opened in Meshed and in this I arranged accommodation for the Manditches. I thought they must be feeling strange and perhaps unable to speak to anyone, so I went over after lunch to see how they were. Here I was shown into a small bare room with very simple new furniture, but no carpets nor the finishing touches which make for comfort. Sitting at the table beside Manditch and his wife was a strange man wtih a large, fierce, black moustache, and a fair, good-looking young girl with a baby. These were introduced to me as Baltschisch and his wife.

The original arrangement had been that this Serbian Baltschisch, who was a friend of Manditch's, was to escape with us to Persia, but he had tried to go off on his own from Askhabad, had been caught by the Bolsheviks, and I had last heard of him firing his revolver into the ceiling of his room, saying he was not a Communist but an Anarchist! I was glad to see he had got away at last, and we all sat down round the samovar for tea.

The conversation was mostly in Serbian, but a good deal in Russian for my benefit. This conversation puzzled me. There seemed on the part of Baltschisch very little gratitude to the British for having accepted him and his family and for looking after them, feeding them and paying their hotel bill and all expenses. Criticism became more open and marked: The British were fools and idiots, and on this account would soon succumb to Bolshevik pressure. Had I understood all that was said properly, I might have said something to them. As it was, when I got outside with Manditch I asked him what was the meaning of this.

The explanation was peculiar. After his arrest and return to Askhabad, Baltschisch had made his peace with the Bol-

sheviks and continued his work as chief of the counter-
espionage bureau. He now planned a bold scheme — nothing
less than to come himself to Meshed and find out what the
British were up to there and what was the strength of their
forces.

So he 'escaped' again, but this time with the connivance of
the Bolsheviks, and reached Meshed as a refugee and was
staying as such as the guest of the British Government. Baltschisch had only known Manditch as an agent of the Bolsheviks and did not know me at all. On meeting Manditch in
Meshed he had jumped, perhaps naturally, to the conclusion
that Manditch and I were spying on the British in the same way!
Hence his contemptuous references to the British, who in their
stupidity were entertaining this quite considerable party of
Bolshevik secret service agents. What was the British secret
service up to? It was a most peculiar situation. I told Manditch that I would report the matter at once. He was terrified
that Baltschisch might be shot. I said he deserved it. Within a
quarter of an hour of my leaving the hotel Baltschisch was
safely locked up.

Baltschisch had planned to take the information he had
collected back to Tashkent in the following way:

All Russian refugees were being sent to India; they had to
travel on foot the long and tiring desert journey of over five hundred miles, to the railway at Duzdab, which would take weeks.
Owing to the presence of the baby, only a few months old,
Baltschisch had received special permission to travel to Baku,
whence he was supposed to go to Serbia, but actually intended
to return to Tashkent with his information. This plan was
confirmed by the fact that before our arrival he had actually
obtained permission from the British military authorities to
go to Baku instead of being sent to India.

I returned from my curious tea-party to the Consulate-
General. I was glad to see the last of my Soviet clothes when
Fowle fitted me out with some uniform. Later in the evening I
was told a lady wished to see me. I thought I knew no ladies in

Meshed. She was shown in and it turned out to be the infuriated Mrs. Baltschisch, carrying her baby. On seeing me in British uniform she was staggered, but pulled herself together sufficiently to give me some pretty efficient abuse. I told her that we had no quarrel with her and that I would do all I could to help her. Did she want any money; or perhaps Glaxo for the child? 'I will take nothing from you,' she shouted, and stormed out of the room.

The next morning she came again, this time calmer. 'I hate you for what you have done,' she said, 'but I must have money to live on.' I gave her something. She asked about her husband. I said I could say nothing about him; it was nothing to do with me. I could not help adding that perhaps the Russian secret service was not the most efficient in the world.

Baltschisch was not shot, a fate he richly deserved, and I heard that subsequently he was for several years employed by the Danube Steamship Company where, no doubt, he had excellent chances of acting as a means of communication between Vienna and the Russian ports on the Black Sea. Perhaps he has taken to a more regular mode of living. I never learnt his real name but I know that Baltschisch was a false one.

With the Manditches I left Meshed by car on January 27th. Travelling via Turbat-i-Haidri and Birjand, I reached Shush on the evening of the 31st. Here I met an old friend, Sir Basil Gould, our consul at Seistan. With him I went to Seistan and spent a few hours there and then rejoined the main road. The journey through this desert in January was very cold and snow was lying in many places. On February 3rd we reached Duzdab, the Indian frontier, and the terminus of the railway, and caught the train for Quetta and Sibi. I reached Delhi on February 9th, 1920.

My life in Soviet Turkestan was over. I saw no reason why any resentment should be felt especially after the lapse of years. I had made many friends in Tashkent, some of whom never had any idea who I really was; others did and helped me in spite of the great risks they ran. The most important of these who remained in Turkestan are now dead.

Ten years after these events I found myself in Peking where I met a well-known White Russian, General Horvath, who in July 1918 had been for a short time President of the Republic in Siberia. He had heard something of my doings in Turkestan and I asked him whether, in the event of some urgent matter calling me to England, it would be possible for me after this lapse of time to travel through Russia. He said that in his opinion I would be given a visa but would never reach my home!

Some years later I met the Russian Ambassador in London, M. Maisky. I told M. Maisky what General Horvath had said and asked his opinion. 'If you wish to return to Soviet Russia I will have your dossier looked up,' he replied. I assured him that the question was and had been purely academic!

APPENDIX

MR. AND MRS. MANDITCH were sent to their home in Serajevo. I have received several letters from them with pressing invitations to visit them.

Many of my friends from Tashkent eventually escaped and I was able to be of some help to them.

My great friend, Tredwell, the United States Consul-General, held various appointments, one of which was that of Inspecting Consul-General for Africa and Asia. In the course of these duties some years after I had parted from him at dusk in a Tashkent street he visited me in Sikkim on the Indian-Tibetan frontier. I again found him in Hongkong, was present at his wedding in Tokyo, and last saw him in New York in 1943.

Andreyev who had been, perhaps, my principal refuge in Tashkent escaped to Baghdad, where for a short time he worked as an engineer. Later he arrived in India and was given a subordinate post on the railways where he served for about ten years, receiving lucrative promotion. He visited me at our house in Sikkim with an Austrian lieutenant, a prisoner of war, who had helped me in Tashkent and who had married his sister, after farming for some time in France; he is now in England. Petrov worked in Bombay for some time and then decided to return to Turkestan, but was informed by the Soviet consul in Vienna that engineers trained in imperialistic traditions, and particularly those 'hardened' by prolonged stay in capitalistic countries, were not wanted in the U.S.S.R.! He then went to Chile and for some years I kept up a flagging correspondence with him. I was in Santiago in 1943 and did my best to find him. The only address I had was a post box number. This was insufficient and all traces of him were lost.

Miss Houston eventually made a very wonderful and courageous escape from the country. As private teaching was forbidden she had been forced to teach in a Soviet military school. In this way she became a Soviet worker and was able to get a transfer to a teaching post in Askhabad, on the Persian frontier. This was only the first step, as various papers beloved of Bolshevik officialdom, had to be obtained before the last document, the railway ticket or *mandat* for the train, could even be asked for. Eventually even this was obtained. She then had to wait ten days for her train. In our country a railway journey is a somewhat simple matter and this is one of the blessings of the comparative freedom from bureaucracy which we enjoy.

It was Miss Houston's intention to escape from Askhabad into Persia. Luckily for her she was warned by a friend that the Bolshevik authorities knew of her intention and had given orders that she was to be taken from the train as it passed Samarkand. She circumvented these orders by making arrangements with friends on the railway to let her travel a few days sooner on a special train by which some engineers were being sent to Askhabad. On arrival here she at once went into hiding and got into touch with a Persian who, for the large sum of two hundred and forty thousand roubles, agreed to send her with a guide through the mountains to Persia. With her guide and mounted on a small pony, minus a saddle, she travelled from Friday evening till Monday night through the mountains. She slept two nights in the open and after a third day's travel reached a smuggler's cave high up among the cliffs in the mountains. Here the guide, who had been exorbitantly paid for the job, deserted her, taking the pony and her knapsack which contained the few belongings she had been able to take out of Turkestan. The position looked terrible for her, left entirely alone in the heart of the mountains.

Luck was with her, however, for a party of fifteen cheerful smugglers turned up who eventually agreed, after putting her through a test of horsemanship, to take her on to Persia. The road was rough and things were not improved by a blizzard. At midday they halted to light a fire and melt themselves and she was given a dirty piece of bread which one of her rough friends produced from a knot in his not too clean sash. This with a sucked icicle was her meal.

The smugglers themselves could not eat as they were carrying out a Mohammedan fast. At last at dusk, on Monday, they saw the lights of the Persian customs post of Jiristan in the distance. 'There you are,' they said, 'there is the end of your journey.' She told them that one of them must come with her to get the promised reward. This was, to say the least of it, difficult and awkward, for in all countries the smuggler is the enemy of the customs official! However, she promised one of them a safe conduct and he trusted her word and influence and went with her. She was welcomed by the French-speaking Persian customs officer, but both he and his staff were horrified to see her accompanied by a noted smuggler whom they had been trying to catch for years. She smoothed things over and eventually her smuggler friend joined them at a meal and was given the promised reward and allowed to depart unscathed. The war between the smugglers and the customs was closed for those few hours to be reopened the next morning.

From Jiristan Miss Houston was able to get into communication with the British Mission at Meshed, where she eventually arrived.

There were many people with whom I had curious connections, but whom I never met. I often wonder what happened to them. Is Chuka, whose passport I used for some time, safely back in Rumania? Where is Kekeshi, the Hungarian cook, whose identity I used for a considerable time? What of Lazar, the Rumanian coachman?

A curious sequel to the incidents recounted above was the appearance in 1934 of a novel in Russian entitled *Chelovyek menyayet kojhu* ('The man changes his skin'), by Bruno Yasenski. The author was a Pole who was at one time editor of a Communist newspaper at Lwow. He worked for Communism in France, was expelled and, being refused asylum in Belgium and Germany, went to Russia. He visited Turkestan in 1930 where he got material for this novel.

The story was about an American engineer, Murray, who worked in Turkestan for the Soviet Government. He was found to have been an agent of the 'Imperialists' and had really been delaying and obstructing work instead of helping it on. In fact, he was a typical 'Imperialist sabotagist'. Murray's rooms were searched in his absence and here in the false bottom of his trunk was found an out-of-date map of Tashkent with crosses against certain places in Samarkandskaya and Moskowskaya streets. These were found to correspond with the positions of the Regina Hotel and Gelodo's house at 44 Moskowskaya, which a Colonel Bailey had occupied.

The author then inquired into the activities of Colonel Bailey and Major Blacker. He quotes from Colonel Etherton's book, *In the Heart of Asia*. Incidentally he states that when we left Kashgar for Tashkent, a worker in the Kashgar branch of the Russo-Asiatic Bank had written to warn the Bolshevik Government against us.

APPENDIX

We knew that this man had reported against certain Russians in Kashgar, but this is the first time we had heard that he was a Soviet agent reporting other news from Kashgar.

The author is astonished at the 'insolence' of my demand to be allowed to send telegrams in cipher at a time when our troops were in occupation of Archangel and Murmansk and were fighting in Transcaspia! This request, he said, was supported by the Commissariat for Foreign Affairs. The L.S.R.s were accused of desiring collaboration with the agents of 'English Imperialism', and later the same authorities were accused of releasing me after my arrest and thus allowing me to escape. So my friend, Damagatsky (an L.S.R.) was in trouble with his Bolshevik masters for the comparative mildness in his dealings with me.

The author evidently had access to the records of the various departments of the Government of that time and wove a few facts from the government archives in Tashkent into his story. Returning to his narrative he states that a photograph of Bailey found among the records in many respects resembled Murray. Further, Bailey was left-handed, a fact which he concealed but gave himself away in this respect when shaving! Again, an agent who had frequently observed Bailey in the street recollected that Bailey when walking with women did not 'like all men' walk on the lady's left, but always on the outside of the pavement. It was discovered that Murray also had both these peculiarities. What more natural than for the British secret service to send a man back who knew the country and was able to organize wrecking and sabotage for them.

The novel is followed by an open letter to 'Colonel F. M. Bailey' of a cynically complimentary nature.

The end of Bokhara was sad. The Young Bokhara Party had tried to seize power in the early days of the revolution but had moved too soon. They numbered only about three hundred.

In the spring of 1918 Kolesov, whom I had met as head of the Turkestan Republic, was in command of the army, moved on Bokhara to help the Young Bokhara Party. On March 1st he sent an ultimatum demanding that, within twenty-four hours, the programme of the Young Bokhara Party be acceded to and a constitution under the leadership of this party be granted. The Amir replied with an equivocal manifesto and Kolesov sent a commission to Bokhara to insist on full compliance. Fighting then broke out at

Kagan and rapidly spread to Bokhara city where Kolesov's delegates and almost the whole of the Young Bokhara Party were killed.

In the disturbances which occurred at this time the European Russians living in Bokhara territory, who were mostly connected with and lived near the railways, were massacred. The Bolshevik leader had received quite a wrong idea of the strength of the Young Bokhara Party, and he was eventually obliged to retire and to sign a treaty in March 1918. The Bolsheviks then left Bokhara alone for a couple of years.

The administration, as I had seen, was hopelessly out of date and the Bolsheviks were easily able to work up what we now call fifth column activities. Finally the Bolsheviks went to their rescue. With the aid of aeroplanes, armoured cars and armoured trains, the city was captured by a Bolshevik force under Comrade Frunze in September 1920. Three wagon loads of gold and precious stones were removed from the Treasury.

All western Bokhara, including Burdalik where I had crossed the Oxus, was occupied at this time, but the Amir kept up the unequal struggle for some months longer in the eastern districts of his country.

After the loss of Bokhara city the Amir retired to Guj-Duvan, forty versts to the north-east; he then travelled round to Karshi and Guzar where he was defeated in an encounter with the Bolsheviks, after which he continued his retirement to Baisun and Hissar. From Hissar the Amir sent letters to the Viceroy of India, but these letters never got through. His position here was very dangerous and so he moved south to Kurgan-Tyube.

At Kala-Wamar, on the Oxus, there was still a Bokharan Governor. The Amir wished to reach this place and thence make his way to Gilgit and India, but the Bolsheviks sent a force from the Pamirs to Kharogh (south of Kala-Wamar), to cut him off. Besides the Bolshevik force there was a great deal of snow which made the way almost impassable.

As he found himself cut off from Gilgit, he was obliged to move to Khanabad in Afghanistan, crossing the Oxus above the Serai ferry. In February 1921 the Amir left Khanabad for Kabul, where he arrived in May. The Afghans treated him as a prisoner and censored all his letters, but allowed him a sum each month for his expenses. The struggle was, however, carried on by the *Basmachi*, who were joined by the remnants of the Amir's forces.

Into this state of affairs appeared Enver Pasha with his Pan-Turanian dreams. The Turks came originally from Central Asia, and the Turki language, as spoken all over Central Asia, is very similar to Osmanli Turkish. But Osmanli Turkish had acquired a number of words from Persian, Arabic and other languages and the Pan-Turanians eliminated these words and replaced them by pure Turkish. This led to emphasis on the link so long severed between the Turks of Asia Minor and their cousins in Central Asia. This connection was strengthened by the fact that the Sultan of Turkey was generally accepted as the Khalif and head of the Mohammedan religion. Enver had married the Sultan's niece, but for political purposes described himself as son-in-law of the Khalif. Enver Pasha's object was to create a Turkish Empire in Central Asia which would later be united with the Turkish Empire in Anatolia and Europe. The *Basmachi* victories over the Bolsheviks seemed to give him a chance and formed a focal point for the carrying out of his ideas.

The movement inevitably became Pan-Islamic which led to dissensions and weakened it in some respects. It was suggested that Persia and Afghanistan should unite to resist this Pan-Turanianism.

The trouble was that no one really wanted Enver at this time. Everyone wanted to sit down and in their various ways recover from the war. Both the Russian Government at Moscow and the Turkish Government let him know that they wished to have nothing to do with him. He hoped to receive a warmer welcome in Afghanistan but on his way there, with seventy followers, he was captured by the Bokharan troops who had just taken the town of Doshamba. This town is now the capital of Tajikistan and its name has been changed to Stalinabad.

He was detained but given considerable local freedom and helped the Bokharan army with advice on strategy in the fighting against the Bolsheviks; he was, however, not entirely trusted by the Bokharans.

Enver had been in Turkestan just a year when on August 4th, 1922, he was surrounded and killed by Russian troops near Baljuan in eastern Bokhara. His mantle fell on Sami Bey, but the dream of founding a huge Turkish Empire in Central Asia melted away at his death and Sami Bey gave up in July 1923 and withdrew into Afghanistan.

The Bokharan army nominally consisted of fifty thousand men of whom half were *naukar*, a kind of militia, who were armed but lived in their own homes and could be called up in time of necessity. The other half were regular soldiers who lived in barracks and were always under arms. The best equipped and best trained of the Bokharan army was a detachment of about twenty thousand cavalry and infantry commanded by Turkish officers who had escaped from Russian internment camps in Siberia and Turkestan. Numbers of the rank and file were also Turkish ex-prisoners of war. They fought very bravely but were cut to pieces in the battles with the Bolsheviks in 1920.

After the Amir of Bokhara had fled, the Bolsheviks made a treaty with the new Bokharan Government, guaranteeing independence. They also signed a treaty with Afghanistan on February 28th, 1921, in Article VIII of which they guaranteed the independence of Bokhara and Khiva. In spite of this in 1923 they turned the Afghan Minister out of Bokhara thus abolishing its last shred of independence and it became a part of Soviet Russia.

In 1917, at the time of the Kerensky revolution, the Amir had withdrawn one hundred and fifty million roubles (about fifteen million pounds sterling) and sent it to different banks in London and Paris. I believe the securities in connection with this large sum fell into the hands of the Bolsheviks.

The Amir also had a large consignment of karakul skins to the value of about one hundred and twenty thousand pounds in Europe and America, but had difficulty in establishing the ownership. His agent double-crossed him and claimed that the skins were the property of the Bokharan Government and that it was his duty to take care of them, or the money they realized, until it was seen what sort of permanent government was established in Bokhara. In the end an unsatisfactory lawsuit ended in the Amir getting half the sum he claimed — the man who had double-crossed him getting the other half. Later a correspondent wrote to me that this man had been afraid to return to his home in Bokhara and had gone to Mecca 'to pray for his sins'.

In 1922, when I was political officer in Sikkim, the Amir of Bokhara sent my old friend and host, Haider Khoja, to see me. He was accompanied by one Haji Burhan, a typical narrow-minded Bokharan official. The population of Sikkim is entirely Hindu or Buddhist and the disgust of this hard-bitten, fanatical Mohammedan at the sight of so many 'idolaters' could not be concealed. I am sure that the whole scene, with its dripping bamboo forest, every tree festooned with fern, orchid and creeper, filled him with disgust — all so different from the deserts and oases of his lost Bokhara. He looked very out of place in his beautiful Bokharan clothes in these different surroundings. Haider Khoja had lived a good deal in Europe and wore European clothes, and was more broad-minded.

In August 1920 Haider Khoja and his son, Iskander, were obliged to fly from Bokhara to Afghanistan. They travelled with a party of refugees, including German and Austrian prisoners of war, and eventually reached Peshawar. When the party arrived in the Khyber, Haider Khoja presented a secret letter I had given him in case of need, to the political agent, Colonel (now Sir Francis) Humphrys, who welcomed him and helped him on the way.

Although he arrived penniless he claimed a third share in a consignment of karakul skins in Europe. He explained to me that of the other two part-owners, one had been shot by the Bolsheviks during the 'January Events' in Tashkent in 1919 and the other had 'disappeared' and might be presumed to have perished also. Haider Khoja Mirbadalev himself had no scrap of evidence but his bare word that he was entitled to a third share. The skins being perishable were sold by order of the courts in London and fetched about twelve thousand pounds. I arranged for Haider Khoja to come to London to put in his claim for his share of this. In this he failed.

In London Haider Khoja took me to an extraordinary place in the city. Here I found a portion of Bokhara where the merchants of karakul skins were doing their business dressed in their Bokharan clothes!

The one thing he did understand was karakul and he managed to start a very profitable agency in Peshawar for the purchase of these skins from Bokhara and their sale in Europe and America. This business, however, petered out and he died a few years ago, in straitened circumstances, in Meshed.

I learnt from him that my acquaintances in Bokhara Tisyachnikov Adamovitch and Galperan had been taken to Tashkent and shot.

In my various journeys in and out of Tashkent I never carried any papers that could identify me. I left such things behind and asked people who were beyond suspicion to keep them for me until I could take them again. In this way I lost several interesting records. In particular the notes from which this book is written were destroyed several times. First when I left them behind in Tashkent with friends on my departure from Tashkent in October 1918; again, when I left them with Edwards at Yusuf Khana in January 1919; again, for the third time, I destroyed everything myself when I left Ivan's house at Troitskoe, in February 1919; and at least once later. On each occasion, when I knew that my papers had been destroyed, I rewrote my notes from memory. No doubt sometimes my friends were unnecessarily cautious, but in those terrible times it was only the 'unnecessarily cautious' who survived. When searching a house the first thing the Cheka would do was to look into the stove. The presence of recently burnt paper was sufficient for a death sentence; so there was grave risk in holding incriminating papers until a search was in progress or imminent.

On leaving Bokhara, however, I carried everything with me in a small haversack. All names were carefully concealed, but still it was possible that these papers might give information to the Bolsheviks if found. My plan was that if we had to fight in the desert I should hide them in some place a few yards away so that if I should become a casualty there would be a chance that they would not be found. In crossing rivers I weighted the haversack with stones in case of an accident of any kind.

The names of people who helped me have been disguised. This was the wish of most of those whom I was able to ask. The names are taken at random from the Bible.

EPILOGUE

by Peter Hopkirk

BACK from the outer darkness of Bolshevism, if not quite from the dead, Bailey found himself an instant hero among his fellow-countrymen. *The Times* headlined his story: A CENTRAL ASIAN ROMANCE, while *The Daily Telegraph* headed its report: BRITISH OFFICER IN BOL-SHEVIK ASIA . . . AMAZING ADVENTURES. Even if these adventures had not achieved very much, no one cared, or even noticed. Given up for dead, he had suddenly and miraculously reappeared. Single-handed, and over many months, he had outwitted the Bolshevik secret police, even concealing himself within its ranks. He had pulled a fast one on Lenin and Trotsky and their bloodthirsty revolutionary mob, and finally escaped from their evil clutches through the legendary Silk Road cities of Samarkand and Bokhara. A more romantic tale could hardly be imagined—it was better even than Buchan—and just the tonic needed by a nation exhausted by four years of war.

No one was more relieved by news of his safe return than his widowed mother, who had received no word of him for months. Once or twice she had written to his chiefs inquiring anxiously after him. In one early letter, sent ten days after the signing of the Armistice, she had asked modestly: 'I know he has been sent on a special mission by the Government of India. I do not ask where he is, nor the nature of his mission, but I am naturally very anxious about him.' But there was little that they could then tell her to reassure her. Indeed, in Delhi and London it was feared that Bailey was almost certainly in a Bolshevik secret police cell, if not dead. At one time Delhi had considered obtaining Bolshevik hostages who, if necessary, could be traded for Bailey and other Britons believed or known to be in Bolshevik hands. In fact, they had tried to arrange the transfer to India of 26 Commissars from Baku who had been unfortunate enough to fall into the hands of their revolutionary rivals in Ashkhabad. However, before this could be achieved, the hapless captives had been brutally slaughtered to a man by their fellow-Russians.

EPILOGUE

After his escape from Bolshevik Russia, Bailey was granted home leave in Britain, where he married Irma Cozens-Hardy, the daughter of a Peer. They then returned to India where he resumed his career in the Indian political service, first serving in Sikkim, with responsibility for Tibet and Bhutan, then as Resident in Kashmir and finally as British Minister to Nepal. In 1938 he and his wife, who had no children, retired to Norfolk, where he devoted much time to his celebrated collection of butterflies, now in New York. Too old to serve in the war, Bailey helped form one of Churchill's guerrilla units intended to resist a Nazi occupation of Britain. After that he served as a King's Messenger, based in the United States, carrying secret dispatches between embassies in Central America and Washington. He also wrote two books on his pre-war Tibetan travels. He died in April 1967 at the age of 85, his lengthy obituary in *The Times* being headed: COLONEL F. M. BAILEY—EXPLORER AND SECRET AGENT.

Although a hero in British eyes, Bailey was an arch-villain in Moscow's. For some seventy years he has been portrayed by hard-line Soviet historians as a British super-spy sent to Tashkent to bring about the overthrow of the Bolshevik government there by supplying the counter-revolutionaries with funds, arms, advice, and encouragement. Every schoolchild in Soviet Central Asia was told about Bailey's nefarious activities on behalf of his imperialist masters. During the 1980s, at the height of the Cold War, I twice visited Tashkent, Samarkand, and Bokhara to gather material for my book *Setting the East Ablaze*. I took with me a copy of *Mission to Tashkent*, as I wished to retrace Bailey's footsteps, though naturally I did not advertise this fact.

My task was made more difficult by the fact that street names had been changed over the years, and buildings destroyed in the great Tashkent earthquake of 1966. This necessitated a visit to the local museum, where I was shown maps of the town at the time of the Revolution. It was then that one of the museum staff, discovering that I was British, mentioned the name of Colonel Bailey, adding that they were very anxious to obtain a copy of his book. Could this be obtained in Britain? Knowing that the book was banned in the Soviet Union, I asked the museum official whether they would be allowed to possess a copy, pointing out that it was very hostile towards the Bolsheviks. He assured me that, as professional historians, they would be allowed to have the book so that authorized scholars could study it.

At this point I decided to admit that I had a copy of the forbidden book with me (in fact, I had two, in case Customs officers came upon one of them), which I would be delighted to present to the Tashkent museum. Neither he nor his colleagues had ever seen a copy of *Mission to Tashkent*, and were overwhelmed at receiving it from out of the blue like this. As we talked about Bailey, I could tell that he was regarded by my Soviet friends with an uneasy mixture of awe and dread. It is not impossible, following the death of communism and the reappraisal of this period of Russia's history, that at some future date Bailey will be judged by post-Soviet historians, not to mention by local ethnic ones, to have been on the side of the angels all along.

MAP SHOWING AUTHOR'S ROUTES IN TURKESTAN FROM SRINAGAR TO MESHED

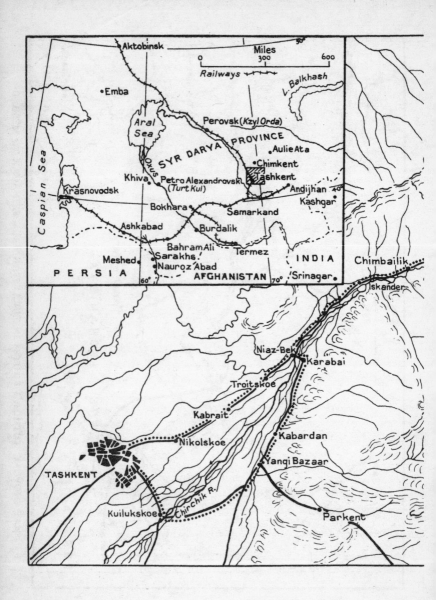

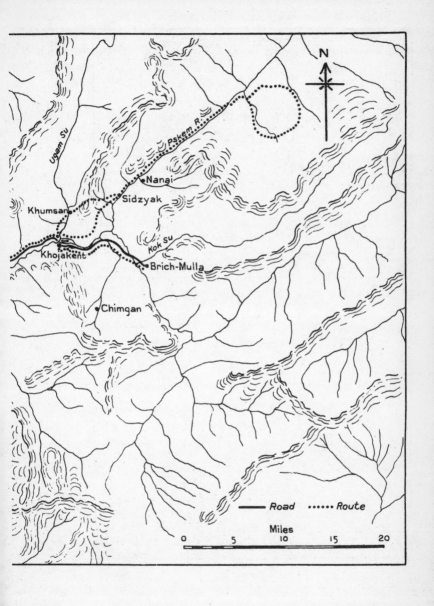

INDEX

INDEX

INDEX

INDEX